They wanted him to believe that . . .

Aliens have UNDERGROUND BASES in the desert.

Aliens are in cahoots with our government to exchange technology for ABDUCTION rights.

Aliens are farming human BODY PARTS for supper.

Aliens created humans and sent JESUS around after to keep us in line.

These stories would keep saucer fiends busy and TV producers wealthy for years. And it all started with just a few little, carefully chosen lies.

PROJECT BETA

They lied to Paul Bennewitz . . .
and things were never the same.

PROJECT BETA

The Story of Paul Bennewitz,
National Security,
and the Creation of
a Modern UFO Myth

GREG BISHOP

PARAVIEW POCKET BOOKS
New York London Toronto Sydney

PARAVIEW
191 Seventh Avenue, New York, NY 10011

POCKET BOOKS, a division of Simon & Schuster, Inc.
1230 Avenue of the Americas, New York, NY 10020

ISBN: 978-0-7434-7092-6

First Paraview Pocket Books trade paperback edition February 2005

10 9 8 7 6 5 4 3 2 1

POCKET and colophon are registered trademarks of
Simon & Schuster, Inc.

Manufactured in the United States of America

Designed by Jaime Putorti

For information regarding special discounts for bulk purchases,
please contact Simon & Schuster Special Sales at 1-800-456-6798 or
business@simonandschuster.com.

To Paul Bennewitz

In wartime, truth is so precious that she must always be accompanied by a bodyguard of lies.

—WINSTON CHURCHILL

CONTENTS

KIRTLAND

Very few venture outside at night during the New Mexico winter. The bone-chilling cold repels all but the hardiest or the inexperienced visitor. It was the way of this land even before 1630, when Alvaro Nuñez Cabeza de Vaca first stumbled onto the bewildered residents of an adobe pueblo hundreds of miles beyond the northernmost outpost of the Spanish empire. Cabeza de Vaca was greeted as a miracle worker, or some sort of god. It was not the first and certainly not the last time that the "Land of Enchantment" would befuddle its inhabitants.

Since World War II, this enchanted land has also been home to some of the most secret and sensitive projects that the military and its scientists have dreamed up and produced. The world's first atomic bomb was detonated here in

May of 1945, and like many choice areas of stark desolation throughout the Southwest, the test area is owned by the U.S. government and is still off-limits to the public.

It was in this setting that Paul Bennewitz, armed with a master's degree in physics, started a small company in 1969 to manufacture specialized temperature and humidity instruments for high-profile clients such as NASA and the U.S. Air Force. He was trying to earn his Ph.D. but his company, Thunder Scientific, became so successful that he had to devote all of his time to the business. The lab was located right on the border of Kirtland Air Force Base, which made his dealings with the military much easier. If he wanted, he could almost reach over his back wall and shake hands with a guard on base. By a strange coincidence, he could also walk across the road bordering his backyard and if there was a hole in the tall, barbed wire–topped fence, shake hands with another guard patrolling the perimeter. Whether he was at home or the office, the Air Force was always his neighbor.

With a devoted wife and two sons, Paul Bennewitz looked like he had achieved the dream. There was nowhere to go but up. He had joined the Coast Guard at seventeen during WWII, started Thunder Scientific, and was an accomplished aerobatics pilot and guitarist. The demands of his business now left little time for friends and socializing, but this did not bother him. Thunder Scientific and his family were all that he needed. What little time he had left was devoted to plowing through a small collection of Wild West novels, his only guilty pleasure. But he had a secret interest that would be kindled with a series of strange events that, in retrospect, almost seemed to have picked him out, rather than the other way around.

It was on a freezing, windswept night in the winter of

1979 that Bennewitz stepped out on his exposed second-story deck in the exclusive Four Hills neighborhood of Albuquerque for what was quickly becoming a nightly ritual. Ever since September, he and his wife Cindy were seeing multicolored lights floating and swooping about the small mountain range inside the base about a mile from his home. Through telephoto lenses so large that they dwarfed his cameras, Bennewitz compiled hundreds of photographs and shot thousands of feet of 8-millimeter film of these tantalizing objects. At times, the lights streaked away as quickly as a magician's sleight of hand, only to reappear seconds later, apparently miles from where they had just been. To Bennewitz, this was irrefutable proof that something unearthly was playing cat-and-mouse with the human race, daring us to react. In time, the fifty-two-year-old electronics expert would present this mass of data to the authorities, which he thought would waste no time in confronting the threat.

They would have no choice. The lights were flying around the Manzano Weapons Storage Complex, then the largest underground repository of nuclear weapons components in the Western world. The Manzano Mountains rise abruptly out of the sloping plateau on which the metropolis of Albuquerque lies, honeycombed with tunnels and shafts, which were crammed to their cavernous ceilings with nuclear weapons and replacement parts for all sorts of atomic devices. It was the most secretive and highly guarded area on the sprawling grounds of Kirtland. Summer storms often zap the peaks of the Manzanos with forks of lightning even when the area around it is clear, making it appear like some sort of mad scientist's aerie.

In 1939 a group of prominent Albuquerque residents suggested that the U.S. government would be welcome to use the area south of their growing town, and so the Kirtland Army Base was founded just before WWII as a training facility. Rusting, fifty-year-old tanks still stand sentinel in remote areas of the base as remnants from this period. After the war, abandoned homesteads and ranches on Kirtland's massive "south forty" were used as safe houses for German scientists "liberated" through the Office of Strategic Services' Operation Paperclip. After debriefing, they were shuttled to the White Sands missile range and the Los Alamos labs to put valuable Nazi know-how to use in the burgeoning Cold War. The remoteness of the place and the easy security it offered began to attract the notice of Pentagon intelligence types.

On the southeastern slopes of the Manzanos, concrete bunkers jut out from the mountainside—some near the bottom, others on seemingly impossible slopes farther uphill. These are the entrances to tunnels and underground rooms that are safe from all prying eyes and aircraft and spy satellites. Seen from the main road through the base, the bunkers seem isolated. The access roads are not visible—they are cut into the hill so as to be invisible from ground level. They are likewise camouflaged from above to foil observers in high-flying aircraft and from space. Satellite pictures of the area reveal no roads or structures. Are they just "painted" out, or are they hidden in some other way?

Viewed from a trail through the sage and scrub brush near the Bennewitz home, the mountains start to lose their innocent look. The 50,000-volt electric double fence that rings the entire base of the hills can be seen snaking over a distant rise. Over the years, Base Security has found a few people tangled in the fence or crumpled next to it, electrocuted to death. In some areas, visible only when the sun is at just the right place in the sky, the mountain is covered with what looks from a distance like pieces of broken plate glass mirrors littering the hillside; in all probability these are devices to foil satellite and aerial photography, and perhaps even ground-penetrating radar.

Some employees of private Air Force contractors Sandia National Laboratories and Phillips Laboratories (which share Kirtland real estate), as well as various Air Force personnel, have let slip that something else is, or was, stored in this impenetrable fortress. One former scientist who wishes to keep his anonymity recently said, "Some of the guys working on the base used to talk about other things that were in there." When pressed as to what this might be, his curt answer was "Flying saucers." There is really no way of knowing whether this was just a ploy or whether there really were captured UFOs sitting in the dark, tunneled recesses of the Manzano Mountains. Welcome to the first stop in the disinformation funhouse.

The area southeast of these mountains and out of sight from any civilian viewpoint is known as Coyote Canyon and is also home to some of Sandia National Laboratories' research and test areas. Sandia scientists were (and are) consistently at the cutting edge of defense research. The facility, formerly owned by AT&T, is now owned by the Martin Marietta Corporation and run by the U.S. Department of Energy. Technologies such as laser-guided missiles and electromagnetic pulse defense systems were pioneered here. Anything not under the Air Force or its contractors' strict control is regarded with immediate suspicion. The National Atomic Museum was moved off base sometime after the terrorist attacks of 2001, and large LED signs at all entrances warn visitors of the daily security alert status.

The security at Kirtland wasn't always so airtight. Sometime in the mid-1980s, an unidentified man pulled up to one of the entrances and announced, "Here's my ID" as he pulled a loaded pistol from his coat. He led the Kirtland security police on a wild chase and somehow managed to escape through a remote hole in the fence somewhere on the southern perimeter, although this may have been a sophisticated training exercise.

On a recent visit to the base I counted nearly as many security vehicles patrolling about as all other cars and trucks combined, and at least three or four no-nonsense, bullet-proof-vested-and-armed guards at every entrance. Hidden cameras and constant patrols are designed to keep the massive fenced perimeter secure. Anything or anyone that tries to fly in would likely be blasted out of the sky by hidden surface-to-air missiles. But if Bennewitz was correct, a few stealthy UFOs may have had better luck.

It would not be the first time. New Mexico has long been home to many strange objects that dart across the sky. From 1948 to 1950, under a spreading blanket of the emerging Cold War, the Air Force was alarmed by sightings of "green fireballs" that entered New Mexico airspace from extreme altitudes and streaked silently across the night sky for a few seconds, finally fading into the blackness. Most of the sightings described these phenomena traveling at great altitudes and along a generally level path, which led investigators to guess that commie saboteurs might have found a way to launch missiles (or something else) over our most sensitive installations. Some of the objects were observed over the sensitive nuclear storage areas of Kirtland Air Force Base and Los Alamos, even as expatriated German rocket scientists were test-firing captured V2s at the newly commissioned White Sands missile range some 200 miles to the south.

What if these strange green "comets" were being used to test the Russians' aim? If they could already hit targets in the continental United States while we were still tinkering with keeping our rockets from crashing on liftoff, how could we defend ourselves?

The Air Force inaugurated Project Twinkle to investigate these "green meteorites," but after three years of intense study, nothing was learned of their origin, composition, or purpose. Capt. Edward J. Ruppelt, director of Project Bluebook, the Air Force project investigating flying saucers, later heard that some Los Alamos scientists believed that the fireballs were something fired from outside the atmosphere by "extraterrestrial spacecraft." Los Alamos scientists were not on any government panels dealing with unexplained aerial phenomena, and it's not hard to see why.

Northern New Mexico was such a hotspot for UFO sightings in the early 1950s that the Air Force floated a proposal to set up "saucer spotting stations" across the countryside, outfitted with trained observers and sophisticated photographic equipment. The idea never made it past the suggestion stage.

The age of paranoia would soon be giving way to the Age of Aquarius, but the people whose job it was to stay paranoid began to look on this UFO thing as something that could be useful, not the constant public-relations headache it had been. Instead of trying to explain things away, official (and secret) policy at the CIA in the early 1950s dictated that flying saucers could be used as a cover for very terrestrial projects, such as the U2 spy plane. The Air Force cooperated and helped to drive attention away from actual sightings of experimental or classified aircraft. Since the CIA and USAF had spent so much time and effort ridiculing and downplaying the phenomenon, most educated people and those who prided themselves on a no-nonsense outlook now considered UFOs the products of delusions, hoaxes, and misidentifications. Anything unfamiliar in the sky (and maybe even on the ground) could be used to cover a multitude of shenanigans. The Air Force eventually realized that this could be taken a step further, and twenty years later, the perfect opportunity for this scenario would present itself, unsurprisingly enough in New Mexico.

Saucer-spotting stations and green fireballs were decades in the past when Bennewitz began to notice animated lights darting around the wilds of Kirtland Air Force Base, which covers almost as much real estate as the entire city. In time, he would become both annoyance and salvation to the Air Force Office of Special Investigations (AFOSI), the CIA, the National Security Agency, and the Defense Intelligence Agency. A whole pack of weirdness would become legendary in the history of UFO lore, and spawn a generation of stories and rumors that were believed as gospel, first by UFO researchers, then by the choir to whom they preached, and finally by consumers of TV, film, and late-night radio as the stories became part of the popular culture: Aliens have underground bases in the desert. Aliens are in cahoots with our government to exchange technology for abduction rights. Aliens are farming human body parts for supper. Aliens created humans and sent Jesus around later to keep us in line. These stories would keep saucer fiends busy and TV producers wealthy for years.

And it all started with just a few little, carefully chosen lies.

chapter 2

CLOSE ENCOUNTERS AND DEAD COWS

The New Mexico State Police office in Cimarron received a strange telephone call on May 6, 1980. The desk sergeant heard a frightened and confused voice on the receiver describing a weird experience the night before. All he could understand was something about incredibly bright lights and herds of cattle and the female caller's fear that she might have seen some strange "people." The officer asked her name for the report. "I'm Myrna Hansen," she replied. "Can you help me?" The woman had no idea at the time that her story would help Paul Bennewitz usher in a new and frightening age of alien interventions.

The cattle mutilation by aliens that Hansen would end up describing is a story that actually began years earlier with not a cow but a horse. In 1967, rancher Harry King of Amalosa,

Colorado, found his prized horse "Lady" missing. Saddling up another horse, he soon found Lady's carcass on a nearby mesa. The animal looked like it had been deliberately killed. The throat was cut and some of the hide on the head and neck was removed. The brain and stomach were missing as well. Circular "exhaust marks" around the body, as well as a substance that burned the skin when touched, only added to the mystery. In an effort to make sense of the senseless act, King connected Lady's disappearance and death with mysterious floating lights that were seen in the area. It was to be the beginning of an uneasy era.

As the phenomenon spread throughout the West in the early 1970s, the FBI became involved, even though the killing and mutilation of livestock was not specifically a federal crime. In Minnesota, Agent Don Flickinger of the Bureau of Alcohol, Tobacco, and Firearms investigated the possibility that satanic cults were involved. Even though he received anonymous threats and once found his front door daubed with blood, his agency never found the culprits. Hundreds and then thousands of reports continued to flood in from Colorado, Minnesota, Nebraska, Kansas, Oklahoma, Wyoming, South Dakota, Montana, Texas, and New Mexico. Some were misidentifications of natural deaths, but a core of cases convinced law enforcement that an organized and well-financed group was responsible. The mutilations were simply too difficult to perform in secret without access to surgical instruments and heavy equipment that could lift the carcasses and drop them in remote areas, leaving no footprints or other evidence on the ground.

Many had heard of the cattle mutilation phenomenon, and most UFOlogists had assumed for years that something from Out There was responsible. Bennewitz was keenly interested in the problem, and developed his own theories as to their origin. He was utterly convinced that the extraterrestrials were responsible, but he needed incontrovertible evidence. In May of 1980, Myrna Hansen's encounter delivered it literally to his doorstep, and the UFO abduction link to animal mutilations would be forged.

Ever since the summer of 1975, Gabriel Valdez, a highway patrol officer in the far northwestern corner of the state, had been investigating anomalous flying lights and the mysterious and grisly murders of cattle that had caused a growing unease to grip some of the remote ranching communities. Valdez was decorated with the Officer of the Year award and was regarded as a tenacious and expert member of the law enforcement community. He had a reputation for thoroughness and an outgoing personality.

In response to the growing panic among ranchers, former Apollo 17 astronaut (and then New Mexico senator) Harrison Schmitt had called a meeting with law enforcement, veterinary experts, and other interested parties to decide on a course of action. By early 1979, the trickle of panicked calls and letters to Senator Schmitt's office had become a torrent. Ranchers from all over the western United States were alarmed at the losses they were suffering. Like many others, Dulce, New Mexico cattleman Manuel Gomez was finding animals separated from the herd and left dead in his fields, in one case no more than a hundred yards from his home. The cattle often had their vital organs removed, and were almost completely drained of blood. Skeptics were quick to point out that internal organs were the first things predators would eat, and that the "surgical precision" of the cuts into the animals' hide only appeared that way to the untrained eye.

The ranchers and cops immediately disagreed with the

"experts." Predators would not drain the blood from dead cattle, nor would they attack livestock close to any human habitation, or try to drag them there. Officer Valdez and the ranchers had never found any canine or indeed human tracks around the mutilated carcasses. Occasionally the sort of marks that would be left by small Caterpillar-type tractors were found, as well as whitish powdered substances and even more strangely, in one case, torn and crumpled pieces of paper. Significantly, other more substantial objects like a gas mask, something that appeared to be some sort of measuring device, and a field covered with what turned out to be radar-reflecting chaff were also observed near the mutilations. (Some of the chaff was actually found stuffed in a dead cow's mouth.) Many of the cattle found on the Gomez and other ranches exhibited ligature marks on one hind leg, indicating that they had been lifted with a rope or cable and dropped where they were found. An abundance of broken bones buttressed this hypothesis. Predators refused to go near the carcasses, which were sometimes poisoned so badly that dead insects littered them. The area patrolled by Valdez had far more than its share of UFO sightings as well, lending another bizarre twist to this already weird scenario.

Valdez and three other law enforcement officers had actually cornered one of the furtive lights in a foggy pasture late one night. In an area about the size of a football field, the cops surrounded and then approached a glowing, hovering orange light. As they closed the distance between them, the light abruptly winked out. The moonless night concealed the object as it floated just over their heads with, as Valdez says, "a sound like a small lawnmower motor." This was not the typical behavior accompanied by the whining, whirring, or buzzing sounds usually associated with unidentified furtive flying lights or craft, unless the "aliens" around Dulce used gas-powered engines when shifting into low gear. Other sightings of UFOs in proximity to the strange animal deaths were not as easy to explain, but many of the crimes had the earmarks of having been engineered by a very Earthly power.

A retired scientist from Sandia Labs was keenly interested in the mutilations and devised a simple but brilliant experiment. On the night of July 5, 1975, Dr. Howard Burgess, along with Gabe Valdez and Manuel Gomez, ran about 100 head of cattle through a squeeze chute. They had rigged lights of differing wavelengths over the enclosure to see if specific animals had been marked or altered in any way that would show up under light outside of the visible spectrum. As some of the cattle passed an ultraviolet bulb, bluish-purple patches glittered on their backs and sides. "Those cattle were all from one breed and were all between one and three years old," remembers Valdez. The profile matched those of cattle who had been found dead on the Gomez ranch. Gomez immediately sold as many head of the "marked" group as he could. When analyzed, the glowing substance was found to contain high levels of potassium and magnesium, and was water-soluble. Something was silently flying over the herds at night, shining a UV beam (aka "black light," appropriately enough) and looking for the cows with the splotches on their backs to drag off and kill before dropping them back to the ground where it was certain that they would be found. If the bug-eyed baddies were picking up bovines for DNA research, they were certainly taking a low-tech approach to the project.

Senator Schmitt's mutilation conference was held in the Albuquerque Public Library on April 20, 1979 and was attended by veterinarians, cattle ranchers, the FBI and other law enforcement, as well as a mutilation researcher named Tom Adams and local politicos. An unnamed "director of research" from a local school in southern Colorado had been studying mutilations and mapping their locations for four years and wryly commented: "The only thing that makes sense about the mutilations is that they make no sense at all."

The public was invited to the Albuquerque mutilation conference and one of the many who showed up was Paul Bennewitz. He handed Gabe Valdez a Thunder Scientific Labs business card, asking him to keep in touch. Valdez would do just that a year later.

Meanwhile, the D.A.'s office in Santa Fe contracted one Kenneth Rommel Jr. to look into the problem. He was provided a substantial budget and given a year to look into the mystery. Valdez, the Gomez family, and others complained that the retired New York City FBI agent never talked to them or bothered to investigate any of the mutilations personally (at least not the most suspicious ones). Whoever was ripping the cattle late at night didn't give him much of a chance. During the Rommel study, the mutilations trickled off to nearly zero. It was as if someone had gotten word that an official investigation was in progress, and shut down any operations for the duration. Rommel's 297-page report, delivered in the spring of 1980, concluded that all of the mutilations had been misidentifications of natural cattle deaths, or were the result of hysteria among the backcountry folk. Details such as the precise cuts in selected areas, removal of eyes, tongues, and reproductive organs, and those ligature marks on the hindquarters—obvious evidence of creatures other than natural predators—were ignored. Ranchers and other locals in hard-hit areas were incensed. Valdez summed up the feelings of many: "The closest this guy had ever been to a cow before he came out here was on a dinner plate in a New York restaurant."

As the summer of 1980 began, the horrifying reports started up where they left off. Television documentary producer Linda Moulton Howe says that Rommel approached her in October of 1979 during her production of *A Strange Harvest* and "strongly asserted" that the subject of her documentary was nothing but the result of hide-gnawing coyotes. The more paranoid or suspicious sensed an agenda behind Rommel's report.

But before all of this madness, a whole lot of people had been dealing with anomalous experiences of another sort, which they had never asked for, at least consciously, and the UFO research community would soon witness an explosion of "abduction" cases, ignited in part by the experience of the twenty-seven-year-old bank teller named Myrna Hansen.

The Cimarron officer who had taken the call from Hansen knew Valdez as the "cattle mutilation guy," and called the Dulce office to ask him what to do. When Valdez heard Myrna Hansen's story, he immediately got his new friend, Paul Bennewitz, on the line. Yes, Bennewitz could get a sympathetic party who knew about UFO entity encounters, and was a professional psychologist to boot, but the witness had to come out to Albuquerque for the procedure. With a few phone calls, Valdez arranged for one of the Cimarron officers to drive Hansen and her son the 200 miles to the Bennewitz home.

Bennewitz's early and abiding interest in things otherworldly had brought him into contact with the Aerial Phenomena Research Organization (APRO), a civilian UFO study group, in Tucson, Arizona. He was a card-carrying member, and occasionally did scientific consulting work for the group. Hansen had an unbelievable story to tell, but Bennewitz was used to unbelievable stories. Their imminent meeting would spawn many way-out tales.

Hansen told Bennewitz that she had been driving in northeastern New Mexico late on the evening of May 5 when she and her young son saw two huge, silent objects hovering over a mountain meadow. She described one of them as "big as two Goodyear blimps"; the other was triangular and somewhat smaller. The abduction itself and the frightening bit about the cattle would emerge later, under hypnosis.

Before the UFO abduction "craze" hit in the 1980s, there was little to go on for the still-in-its-infancy science of abduction studies. Confronted with a strange sighting and the incongruity of arriving home over two hours late worried the witness, and piqued the interest of Bennewitz. At this point, the "abduction database" was not as polluted with accounts that would provide a template for the experience and botched hypnotic regressions by eager researchers, and this may have made recall difficult, but paradoxically more accurate. Amateur hypnotists asking leading questions is one of the most frequent areas that skeptics use to assault UFO investigators, and in many cases they have a valid point.

UFO abductions are a vast and controversial subject. Much of what is seen in the movies and on TV is based in part on a few solid cases, but they only tell part of the story.

chapter 3

BLUE LIGHT

On May 7, 1980, a mere two days after her jarring encounter, Myrna Hansen arrived in Albuquerque. The single mother brought along her eight-year-old son. They were given a room in the spacious Bennewitz home, and Paul Bennewitz began to delve into her encounter.

Even after intense questioning, Hansen couldn't seem to get past certain points in her story. Bennewitz thought that a trained mental health professional might be able to dig deeper and release whatever she was covering with what appeared to be many layers of fear. APRO director James Lorenzen suggested a call to Leo Sprinkle, a psychologist and tenured professor at the University of Wyoming who had been investigating UFO contact cases for over ten years.

Sprinkle seemed the best bet in the APRO arsenal for getting to the bottom of the story.

Sprinkle flew to Albuquerque from his Wyoming home on May 11 on Bennewitz's nickel. When Sprinkle arrived, the three spoke informally about the case for a while, then Sprinkle put Hansen under hypnosis to access any details that she couldn't recall consciously. Bennewitz and Hansen both wanted to do the hypnotic regression in Bennewitz's Lincoln Town Car, parked in the family garage—the windows sealed with thick aluminum foil. Both were under the impression that the aliens were beaming some sort of "rays" at her and controlling her unconscious mind. It was obvious that Bennewitz had been planting dangerous ideas in her mind, made more receptive by her fear and confusion. Sprinkle was flabbergasted about doing the hypnotic regression in the car, but said, "It seemed to make them both feel better, so I went along with it." She lay down in the back seat, allowed herself to relax into a hypnotic trance, and began almost without prompting:

> I'm driving. My son's right there in my ear, talking to me. I'm half tuning him out. The light is so bright. I feel like it's coming in on me. I stop the car and we get out. This isn't real. It can't be happening. What is it? There's another one. The bright is confusing. I want to leave, but I want to see what it is. My son wants to leave, but I've got to know what's going on. So much commotion. They're landing. Oh, God! Cattle are screaming! But I've got to know who it is . . . The light is so bright. It's orange. I want to see them; I want to go to them. I'm out of the car. Screaming of the cattle;

*it's horrible, it's horrible! Incredible pain! I still want
to go to them, but . . . But they're mad.*

Hansen was driving home to New Mexico from a trip to
Oklahoma on the evening of May 5 with her son and expected to arrive home in the small town of Eagle's Nest at
about 9:00 P.M. It was almost 1:00 A.M. when they pulled into
their driveway tired, confused, and wondering about what
they had seen in the sky on the way there. As she went
deeper into the trance, she recalled being undressed, a physical examination, and just before she entered one of the craft,
that she had also seen a struggling cow sucked up into its underside in some sort of "tractor beam." At the time, Sprinkle
had been involved with just one other case of "cattle mutilation" in connection with a UFO encounter, and it had only
been two months since he had spoken with that witness,
even though the incident had happened in 1973.

The main participant in that case was named Judy Doraty,
and she had been driving back from a bingo game on May 23
of that year outside of Houston, Texas, with her daughter,
mother, sister, and brother-in-law. Suddenly, everyone in the
car noticed a bright light in the sky that was pacing them.
When they arrived home, it moved in closer and the passengers and a group who came running out of the Doraty house
saw a huge disc with rows of windows float silently over the
house and an adjacent field. It soon shot off straight up into
the sky, going from "very, very big to very, very little in a matter of seconds," Doraty recalled. She had been having night-
mares and unrelenting stress since the experience,
something that no one else in her family seemed to be suffering. The other passengers remembered that she had

stopped the car and gotten out to look at the enigmatic light as it approached them. On March 13, 1980, Sprinkle put Doraty in a relaxed state and brought her back to the point where she was standing next to her vehicle.

> [There's] like a spotlight shining down on the back of my car. And it's like it had substance to it. I can see an animal being taken up in this. I can see it's squirming and trying to get free. And it's like it's being sucked up. I can't tell what the animal is. It's a small animal.

Doraty remembered that she was not taken on the craft she observed, but said that when she was outside, she experienced some sort of bilocation and was present on the craft and standing by the car at the same time. The "small animal" turned out to be a very young calf, which was dissected on the craft with quick precision. The carcass was dropped back on the ground. With some difficulty, she also recalled seeing her daughter being examined. She got back into her car and drove home, the craft now a distant blob of light following them at a distance all the way home, where it then swooped down not fifty feet from the ground while the amazed Doraty family watched. After zipping away, it hung in the sky like a bright star long enough for everyone to go inside and return several times to see if it was still there.

This case was on Sprinkle's mind as he questioned Hansen and her son, but the boy couldn't recall much else besides the actual sighting and the panic of the bellowing cattle. Over the course of two long sessions that day, his mother described her recollections in a detailed, if disjointed way. She had been taken to an underground "base," had seen body parts floating in vats, received what she thought was an explanation from her captors as to what they were doing with her and what their presence on Earth meant, and finally, felt that some sort of device had been implanted in her body so that the aliens could monitor and control her thoughts. Sprinkle was both startled and excited by the case, but his professional demeanor kept his emotions in check.

These and more details of the hypnosis contained many of the stories that would later make the UFOlogical rounds and would be bandied about for the next twenty years. Other abduction researchers would confirm some of these elements, while others simply became grist for the sensationalized rumor mill. Goaded by outside forces, these rumors would become the legendary bedrock of the more way-out personalities and groups on the UFO circuit, most of whom would never realize that Paul Bennewitz and Leo Sprinkle were possibly the first to bring them to light.

Many of these details were to be repeated in the future by other "abductees" who had never heard of Sprinkle, Bennewitz, or UFO abductions. Barring extensive suggestions from the hypnotists or even something as exotic as psychic cueing, the experiences must be real, or there is a control force that very much wants us to believe these scenarios. By the late 1990s, some of the accounts had actually evolved into encounters with reptiloid-looking entities abducting and raping women, although "serious" researchers tended to consciously ignore such accounts, just as many initially rejected elements of Hansen's story.

It should be noted that there was at least one other witness to the Cimarron event, however. Recently one of the retired Cimarron officers confided to Valdez that it was his wife. She had seen the flying objects, bellowing cattle, and something horrible happen to one of the calves, but wouldn't say any more about it. They didn't want to get involved because of her husband's position in the department. He also figured that one UFO expert in the New Mexico State Police was probably enough.

At the end of the abduction, the entities brought Hansen and her son back to the pickup point—car and all—and gingerly put them down on the road.

> *They lowered the ship, I got in the car. My son is in it and I don't know how they did it. Just [bump] on the ground—not heavy, not hard. Lots of blue light all around.*

In the middle of this recall, she blurted out:
Where's Roswell, New Mexico?
No one had mentioned Roswell, and there wasn't even a book on the purported 1947 saucer crash out at the time. Both Sprinkle and Bennewitz ignored this curious detail. It would have been an easy target after *The Roswell Incident* was released that August, but Bennewitz never made a connection. If he hadn't been so focused on his other conclusions, it might have been a factor in the plus column of his building "übertheory."

"Paul was really interested in what was coming out in the hypnosis sessions, because he thought that this would prove his theories," Sprinkle recalls. "He was intrigued because of the cattle mutilation aspect, the number of UFOs, the onboard experience, and what really excited him was that the ship went underground. He associated that with an underground cavern he had been thinking about. He thought the case was going to break the UFO mystery wide open." Bennewitz urged Sprinkle not to divulge any of the information they had discovered that day. The psychologist asked if he could at least share it with Jim Lorenzen and his wife, Coral, down at APRO. Despite his strong reservations, Bennewitz finally relented.

It had been an exhausting day. It was well past sunset by the time Myrna Hansen was finally brought out of her final trance. She was allowed to rest.

Out on his upper deck, with a commanding view of Kirtland Air Force Base and the blazing lights of the city spread out before them, Bennewitz discussed his theories with Sprinkle while they waited for a cab. Earlier in the day, Bennewitz had shown him some of the films that he had taken of the strange lights near the Manzano storage facility, and apparently, video as well. "Paul asked me if I saw the small, grayish streaks that appeared in the picture once in a while," recalls Sprinkle. "He said that they were alien ships moving too quickly for the eye to see, but would show up on video and film. I didn't really see anything, but I knew he had very good eyesight, because when we were standing outside, he pointed out distant landmarks that I couldn't see at all." It seems strange that an electrical physicist would not be able to recognize videotape dropouts, which is the most obvious explanation for short grayish streaks, but the multicolored, shooting lights were not as easy to dismiss as technical anomalies.

The Hansen regressions had gone so well that Bennewitz asked Sprinkle to come back again as soon as he could to see if there was any way to fill in the missing sections in her recall. He promised to buy another round-trip ticket for Sprinkle. But when Sprinkle returned, things would be drastically different.

chapter 4

THE IMPLANT

O n June 3, 1980, Leo Sprinkle rang the doorbell and after a long pause, Bennewitz appeared toting a pistol on his hip, and a rifle in his right hand. "He told me that the aliens could come swarming over the walls at any minute." He needed to protect himself, his family, and Hansen—the aliens' prized possession. Because of the tension and increased paranoia, a strained hypnosis session followed. Bennewitz wanted to cut the session short, but it continued until Sprinkle thought that they had uncovered everything that Hansen could reveal without completely falling apart.

Sprinkle was aghast at the startling transformation in Bennewitz: "Between May and June, his demeanor, his reaction to me, and his attitude and take on the whole situation was much different. His attitude toward me as a colleague had changed. Now they were threatening him and might be in his house at any minute. I tried to discuss it with him, but it wasn't discussable. The stuff that came out during the second session was scary enough that not only Bennewitz thought that the aliens were a threat, but Hansen felt that way too. When I suggested they go public with this information, they looked at me like I was not only weird, but immensely wrong. It was a short session, then a quick good-bye." Without fond farewells or long discussions at the door, Bennewitz called a taxi and watched Sprinkle disappear into the night. He hopped right back on a plane and was home in Wyoming within a couple of hours. He hadn't even been gone a day.

Bennewitz was more convinced than ever that some kind of malevolent force was afoot, controlling and monitoring Myrna Hansen's every move. The unidentified signals he had detected had to be part of the equation, he reasoned, since they seemed to coincide with her ever-growing fear and difficulty in recalling more details. Hansen had become dependent on her host to make sense of the smallest details, but this dependence was paradoxically pushing her ever deeper into a vast conspiratorial maze where alien life forms dictated her every move and thought. Bennewitz convinced her that salvation lay in proving his theories and developing a way to fight the malevolent influence.

Bennewitz set to work and looked for a more sympathetic abduction researcher and hypnotist. University of California at Berkeley engineering professor James Harder seemed like a perfect match to help figure out what the pesky aliens were doing. In 1975, Harder had been one of the first on the scene to hypnotize UFO abductee Travis Walton in what became the "case of the decade."

Walton had disappeared after he and his companions were clearing brush in the Apache-Sitgreaves National Forest in eastern Arizona and sighted a UFO hovering over a break in the trees. Walton and his workmates claimed that he was zapped by a beam from the craft, and then disappeared for almost a week. Harder was a strong believer in the so-called "extraterrestrial hypothesis" of UFOs and not unexpectedly found that after the blue beam had hit Walton, he had been taken on board and met several different types of alien beings before he was unceremoniously dropped by a highway five days later. Many questions remain about the ultimate reality of this case, but even some skeptics have concluded the Walton may have been telling the truth as he saw it, even if it may have been unconsciously embellished after the fact. Walton still travels and lectures about his experience, and seems primarily concerned with critics who doubt his truthfulness and even his sanity. In contrast to many other UFO abductees, the experience was never repeated.

Harder and Bennewitz began moving Hansen around, trying to find any location that would block the "rays" that were affecting her mind and the hypnosis sessions. Bennewitz didn't appear to consider that Hansen might be delusional or confabulating at least part of her story to make her therapists (and possibly herself) better accept the experience, whatever it was. Everything in this area of UFO inquiry was so unique at the time that Harder and Bennewitz were convinced that they were blazing a new trail in abduction studies. For better or worse, they were. Bennewitz set to work devising ways to block the evil radio signals.

There is a device called a Faraday Cage that effectively protects anything inside it from most radio waves and magnetic fields, but their nonexistent budget wouldn't allow the desperate researchers the use of such a sophisticated piece of equipment. The methods they used would be almost laughable if not for the fact that Hansen was subjected to them all. They tried hypnosis in cars, hotel rooms, and basements, and ended up just short of the ubiquitous aluminum foil hat: They reportedly lined the underside of an umbrella with foil and held this over Hansen during some of the sessions. The jerry-rigged contraptions seem beneath the scientific and technical capabilities of Bennewitz, but at long last, they finally believed that the technique was perfected, and described this in a letter to APRO director Jim Lorenzen on August 28, 1980 (underlining in original):

> *[Hansen] is being badly beaten on by the alien with their beams—24 hours a day. These beams have been measured and we are now getting a handle as to what they may be . . .*
>
> *If you could possibly observe the following precautions in any of your present and future [UFO abduction] regressions your data will be more accurate.*
>
> *1) Use as many different expert psychologists as possible.*
>
> *2) Do not regress unless:*
>
> *A) There is an unbiased witness acquainted with the process—[sic] present taking verbatim notes if possible.*
>
> *B) The regression must be done in a shielded enclosure. The best options I am aware of are:*
>
> *1A) An automobile in a garage—use 3 layers of heavy aluminum (barbeque type) foil to cover all windows—grounded to the chrome trim*

> *around the windows* <u>*thoroughly.*</u> *Masking tape can be used to hold it in place.*
> *Precaution:* <u>*Do not*</u> *ground the auto . . .*
> 2A) *The very best option is to use an X-ray room. It is lead-shielded; A two story or larger building where the room is totally shielded.* <u>*Not*</u> *a one story building because generally the ceiling will not be shielded. Inspect and make sure the room is* <u>*shielded.*</u>

Although this may be a limitation of his typewriter, the message was printed in capital letters, lending a sort of manic urgency to it all.

A curious postscript to the letter advises abduction researchers to "place an EKG electrode . . . on the right inside middle forearm . . . our most recent regression tapes indicate no alien interference when using this method in a hotel room. Use a banana plug [electrical contact clip] and heavy wire to ground to room outlet hotel ground system." This presents a pretty crazy picture of Bennewitz and Harder schlepping poor Hansen to remote hotel rooms and hooking her arm up to the ground plug in an electrical outlet while holding up an aluminum foil-covered umbrella, then putting her under hypnosis to elicit more tales of cattle mutilation and journeys through underground tunnels. The combined effect of all these things happening to Hansen may have made her desperate to say almost anything, extrapolating her ever farther from the original experience, however weird it was to begin with, but Bennewitz was not to be deterred. As James Lorenzen later put it, "He was prone to make great leaps of logic based on incomplete data," and he was taking Harder and Hansen with him.

Harder recalls little from the hypnosis sessions or time he spent with Bennewitz. Perhaps it was a period he would care to forget.

Bennewitz and his research partners were basically working from scratch, even though Sprinkle had been regressing suspected UFO abductees for over a decade by the time he arrived in Albuquerque. There were precious few other UFO abduction–type reports to compare with in 1980, and Budd Hopkins's seminal book on the subject, *Missing Time,* wouldn't be published until the following year. And it took almost another decade for the UFO community to accept that abductees might be "implanted" with some strange kind of device. When the phenomenon was popularized by Hopkins and later others like Whitley Streiber in his trio of abduction books (*Communion, Transformation,* and *Breakthrough),* the "implant" theory was a common feature. Were these later and wildly popular accounts influenced by Bennewitz's original studies? Much has been written on the distinct possibility of "cueing" of victims when in a highly suggestible, hypnotic state, and critics have attributed much of the abduction phenomenon to "expectations bias." Bennewitz may have created his own bias, keeping his expectations frustratingly ahead of each new twist in the unfolding story.

While looking for confirmation of his suspicions about underground bases, Bennewitz stumbled into the "control implant" phenomenon purely by accident, and soon became obsessed with this aspect of the case. While later researchers seemed comfortable with the "tagged animal" model, Bennewitz quickly elaborated an alien conspiracy theory, dropped his fear of publicity, and within a year wrote another long and detailed letter to Jim Lorenzen (underlining again in original):

Apparently based on my two year study and find-ings here in New Mexico, all encounter victims who have encountered and <u>been</u> <u>picked</u> <u>up</u> have come back with implants or metal links both in the back of their necks and also in the end of each radial nerve atop the skull – deliberately inserted by the alien for partial or complete programming and image control. Obviously this is now appearing useful to the alien for direct con-trol of the story reported and told by the victim while under regression. During regression, this part is espe-cially noticeable, if alien control is getting through in an unshielded environment as the patient will "stall out" in certain portions of the regression as they at-tempt to tell some part of the encounter that is not al-lowed by the alien and is unpleasant.

Depending on the willingness of the victim to spread their [alien] story of benevolence and their confor-mance to program—the alien can control all major physical responses—sound, sight, pain—nerve or deep pain—create headaches, sinus, etc. High fre-quency buzzing or singing and loud cracks or sounds in the head when the control beam is abruptly pulled off. In other words if the alien desires, they can punish the altered encounter victim severely . . .

The implants are inserted at the time of contact, tak-ing apparently, at most, approximately fifteen (15) minutes to complete. They use special surgical tools, one described as looking like a thin shiny alloy tube with a blade along one side, the tube possibly magnify-ing, allowing optical access to the nerve site . . . It is possible that it [the implant] ties into the Media Lem-niscus by feedback which branches up into the thala-

mus and thalamic nuclei, the integrator for all normal
sensory functions of the mind and body and suspected
to be controlled by the alien . . .

Those having the implants will initially return from
the encounter complaining of extreme headaches . . .
they will also generally claim and begin to exhibit ap-
parent psychic powers. Though the normal possibility
of normal [sic] psychic ability is not questioned nor is
issue being taken here, those who are encounter vic-
tims for all intents and purposes have become walking
optical and audio detectors for the alien and may ap-
pear to have alien input . . .

No one but Paul Bennewitz (and possibly James Harder)
knew how he came to these conclusions. A researcher who
befriended Bennewitz during this period said that his ideas
began to mimic plotlines and story elements from 1950s science-fiction movies such as *Invaders From Mars* and *Invasion of the Body Snatchers.* He may very well have been
unconsciously influenced by pop culture, but there were no
movies about cattle mutilations yet, and that problem had
been growing like a cancer since the early 1970s.

More dead and mutilated animals were being found almost weekly on Gabe Valdez's patrol, which centered on the
small town of Dulce, New Mexico. Dulce is basically a
crossroads on a minor state highway with a general store and
a gas station, and sits on the edge of the Jicarilla Apache Indian Reservation, surrounded by thousands of square miles
of high-altitude mountainous scrub and forest. Paul Bennewitz would soon begin a process that would help trans-
form this unprepossessing speck on the map into a nexus for
UFO fanatics for the next fifteen or twenty years, annoying

the local population and keeping the tribal and state police quite busy.

By degrees, Bennewitz began to suspect that this area was the site of an underground alien base and that the extraterrestrials who occupied it were slowly taking over the power structure of the U.S. military, the American government, and ultimately, the world. He became convinced that the cavelike facility that Myrna Hansen had described was located here, and that the alien beings were using it as a central location from which to conduct reconnaissance, abduct and implant human victims, and perform cattle mutilations. It was the most paranoid scenario that one could imagine, and in time, it would become even more intricate, containing just enough truth to convince the choir to which Bennewitz was preaching unwittingly, and many outside the saucer sanctuary as well.

Elsewhere in the Southwest, the sinister wheels of fate would soon begin to turn.

chapter 5

PICTURES OF PICTURES

ennewitz was getting increasingly worried. Acquaintances at Kirtland said that they had no idea what he was talking about when he tried to broach the subject of the shooting, hovering things he was seeing near his home. Even when he told them about the impossible speeds and pulsing lights, they told him that he was probably watching helicopters doing maneuvers and practice missions. Faced with this apparent stonewalling, he decided it was time to go over their heads.

Base Security commander Col. Ernest Edwards was sitting in his office one afternoon when the base operator patched through a call from someone claiming to know about a "serious security problem." Before he could decide whether his secretary had let through some sort of crank call,

Paul Bennewitz was on the line, and introduced himself as the president of Thunder Scientific Labs. Edwards listened with some interest, but decided to pass him off to someone whom he had once introduced to a visiting National Security Agency representative as his "drug man," Air Force Office of Special Investigations (AFOSI) Special Agent Richard Doty. This duty simply involved checking for allegations of illegal drug use on the base, but it was only one of Agent Doty's minor assignments. The AFOSI has jurisdiction over all criminal and security investigations at Air Force facilities. Most AFOSI agents must carry a high security clearance. Agents need to know what they are protecting so that security threats can be recognized quickly.

Bennewitz carefully described to Doty what he had seen and recorded, all the while trying to keep what he really thought was going on to himself for the moment. Bennewitz then asked Doty if he could come to the base and discuss his research. Even though the claims were a bit extreme, Doty and AFOSI were always alert to anything that could potentially hurt or even help their security work. Perhaps Bennewitz had stumbled onto something important, and if not, the security issue could be stopped before it became a problem. Besides, Bennewitz was a trained scientist and contractor who did regular business with NASA and the Navy, as well as the Air Force. He was a also a scientific professional who had proved more than competent in his electronics work, so his opinion carried some weight.

Instead of a visit to Kirtland, Doty suggested that he should first come and visit Bennewitz at work, and requested a small tour. At this point, Doty didn't know anything about the physicist, and an innocuous visit might give him some idea of what he was dealing with.

Doty was greeted at the front door of Thunder Scientific and after looking over the products and projects that were spread throughout the lab, he asked what Bennewitz had discovered that warranted Air Force attention. Bennewitz described the strange signals that he was picking up, and the lights he was filming over the base. Doty knew nothing about the lights, but he was mildly alarmed about the radio signals. When he returned to the AFOSI office, Doty wrote up a report recommending that a meeting be scheduled with base security officers, scientists, and other command-level personnel.

The National Security Agency (who maintained a considerable presence at the base) as well as a mysterious and special investigative detachment of the AFOSI called the "PJ" branch asked Doty to make another trip before the meeting, this time to the Bennewitz home to see his operation first-hand. Bennewitz was delighted at the interest and readily agreed to another visit. The Air Force was now calling *him*, so he had to be onto something with potential. It was to be the first in a series of tragic disconnects by Bennewitz.

Doty was also asked to take a partner along, someone who was in a position to evaluate anything that could be of interest.

Physicist Lew Miles was known around the Kirtland base as someone who had a deep and long-term interest in the subject of UFOs. During his childhood in Oregon, Idaho, and California, his mother had premonitions that had awakened his interest in the paranormal. Miles had joined the Air Force at the age of eighteen and had been assigned to a base in Japan during the occupation. He'd seen only one thing in the sky that he ever believed was "unidentified," but was convinced that behind the UFO subject was an objective reality that could be discovered and studied. His access to classified information was a tool in the quest. Ultimately, after almost three decades of access to some of the U.S. government's most closely held secrets on UFOs, he believed he had come no nearer to the truth than he was allowed. Like many high-level players in the game, he was never given all of the keys, and the tantalizing, unqualified "answer" remained elusive.

As chief scientist and director of the Kirtland Test and Evaluation Center, he also knew about most of the research projects, which included some of the most sensitive defense studies in the country. He had been involved with Project Bluebook as an occasional consultant when he was assigned to the Foreign Technology Division at Wright-Patterson AFB in the 1960s. J. Allen Hynek was an acquaintance, and Miles had worked with the Project Bluebook astronomer more than once. The 1981 Defense Intelligence Agency list of projects and personnel lists Miles as director of the Weapons and Systems Division in the "Directorate for Scientific and Technical Intelligence" in charge of "Ballistic Missile, Aerodynamic, Naval, and Ground Systems"—an impressive resume to be sure. Miles readily agreed to go along to check out Bennewitz's setup. His personal interest in UFOs and long involvement with the subject was considered a plus, and he certainly relished the opportunity to perhaps see something spectacular firsthand.

On October 26, 1980, Doty and Miles arrived in the Four Hills neighborhood and were greeted at the door by Bennewitz and his wife. After a few preliminaries, the duo was guided to the inner sanctum: the home lab. The two visitors' eyes widened. This man was serious—or crazy. In the cramped room, transformers hummed, a reel-to-reel tape recorder whirred, and between banks of oscilloscopes and meters, tinny speakers played a constant symphony of static punctuated by bursts of electronic data.

Surprised by the instant attention, Bennewitz nevertheless realized that the Air Force was actually taking him seriously and pulled out all the stops. The electrical physicist laid out glossy 8x10 prints on the table and gave Doty and Miles a tour of his homemade radio receivers, the array of antennas pointed at the base, and his analyzing equipment. He played recordings of the best sections of the signals he had received. He showed them film and video of the lights. He took them out on the deck and presented his view of the Manzano range and the base. He also brought out pictures he and others had taken of unidentified lights in the vicinity of the Dulce area, and made a case for his suspicion of an underground facility there.

Miles noticed that Doty was occasionally hanging back and letting him talk privately with Bennewitz. He appreciated this courtesy, but Doty had not suddenly taken a page from Emily Post. He had brought along a small, easily concealed camera and was busily and surreptitiously snapping pictures of the photos, the equipment, and even the interior of the Bennewitz home. He was doing this at the express request of the NSA. The pictures would spark even more interest from intelligence and security organizations that were already (or soon would be) monitoring his movements and phone calls to try to determine who Bennewitz was working for. Perhaps he was an unwitting dupe, innocently carrying out his work while envious eyes watched, eager ears listened, and friendly acquaintances or "UFO researchers" asked certain probing questions.

An "Internal OSI Form," written and signed by the base

security investigations commander, Thomas Cseh, details the Doty/Miles visit to the Bennewitz home, but for some reason fails to mention the concealed camera caper. Perhaps this fell under the jurisdiction of the NSA and the agents were not required to report this activity to AFOSI headquarters. When multiple security agencies have overlapping jurisdictions, AFOSI agents will often take "taskings" from them in addition to their Air Force duties. Later, NSA-affiliated agents would flash AFOSI identification badges when they called on Bennewitz.

It has become fashionable since at least the 1960s to automatically assign evil and misguided motivations to spies and other government employees. Many of the gaffes and pathologically and political- and power-driven actions of our government are often undertaken with little or no oversight. There are certainly many other actions and projects that have never come to light that would have brought scandal and deserved prosecution to the people and organizations involved. Secrecy and power have always been a breeding ground for misguided shenanigans or worse. Most of the people serving in intelligence and counterintelligence sincerely believe that they are protecting their country and that the most important part of their job is keeping the United States out of war by stopping things before they can happen. The fact that this state of affairs (especially in the climate of the Reagan years) was primarily supported and encouraged by defense contractors and political demagogues feeding off one another's needs and public fear is for the most part not a topic of concern to intelligence agencies, and the situation has changed little since the early 1980s. In fact, it appears to be getting worse.

The U.S. intelligence community exists in principle to

protect the country from enemy (and occasionally friendly) intelligence organizations, and to keep things that are developed with U.S.-sponsored brains and money from becoming an enemy or potential enemy's latest breakthrough. These men and women are also tasked to keep an eye on what the other guys are developing before they become political or military problems. It is a waste of time and money to crank out a defense system if someone steals it out from under you. Conversely, effort is saved if you can commandeer the other guy's latest toy, or figure a way to defend against it before he even gets it off the ground, or out of the laboratory. Such is the way of the wicked world of international spying and maintaining the balance of power. The Bennewitz affair was just a small example of hundreds of similar situations in a variety of guises that are occurring all the time, and the vast majority of these little shows never leave the files or mouths of their puppet masters.

Richard Doty and Lew Miles returned to Kirtland. Doty wrote his report and Miles offered his opinion that although there might have been something unidentified in the photos and videotape they had been shown, they didn't show enough detail to be worth anything to the Air Force. This may be misleading, as it appears that someone at the 7602nd Air Intelligence Group at Fort Belvoir in Virginia was *very* interested in the Bennewitz material, but this was not revealed publicly until over a year later when a document describing a detailed analysis of some of Bennewitz's pictures was released to a UFO researcher and eventually Bennewitz himself. No one but Doty and Miles know what they thought of the recordings of coded radio transmissions, but this aspect of Bennewitz's project kept at least a few intelligence organizations interested enough to keep a close eye on his friends, movements, and phone calls for the next few years.

The players assigned to watch Bennewitz ultimately did not care about his theories on alien invasions or underground bases. Their sole interest was keeping the queen bee at the center protected, and as long as anyone with whatever interest came anywhere near anything sensitive, they would direct him down any other tunnel than the ones which led to the queen's chamber.

Colonel Edwards was very likely the one who called Bennewitz to tell him that he was requested to give a briefing at Kirtland Base in mid-November 1980. No record exists of this call, but Bennewitz could scarcely believe it: The Air Force was actually taking the alien invasion seriously.

chapter 6

THE MEETING

We have to consider the possibility that these signals may be of extraterrestrial origin.

—Anonymous Kirtland AFB colonel after first hearing about signals picked up by Bennewitz

Fifteen days later, early on the morning of November 10, 1980, Bennewitz drove onto the grounds of Kirtland with his photos, films, and recordings in hand, ready to make his best presentation to the Air Force brass. As Bennewitz stepped into the meeting room, he was introduced to base commander Brig. Gen. William Brooksher, four colonels, two AFOSI men (including base AFOSI head Maj. Thomas Cseh), and a couple of scientists from the Air Force (Phillips) Weapons Lab, which is still headquartered at Kirtland. Major Cseh signed the FOIA-released pages that document this meeting.

Apparently, Richard Doty was not there—at least he isn't listed on the roll call. Perhaps he didn't need to be, or didn't have the "need to know." The "Multipurpose Internal OSI

Form" lists a "Dr." in front of Bennewitz's name throughout. Paul Bennewitz did not have a doctorate in anything. He did possess a master's degree in electronics. How Cseh came to assume this remains a mystery. It would not be like Bennewitz to inflate his credentials. He hadn't done it before, and apparently never did to anyone who met him afterward. For some weird reason, Cseh may have done this to induce an element of plausible deniability if the accuracy of the released document ever became an issue. A slight, but intentional slip can also spell disinfo, or at least someone covering his tracks.

Former NSA employee Thomas Deuley, who was assigned to check information security at the base on a couple of occasions in 1980, was told by one of the men who were there that as Bennewitz made his presentation and slowly started mentioning UFOs, aliens, invasions, and his work with Myrna Hansen, the officers started to leave "so that at the end there were only a couple of them left." Deuley did not know their names, but the FOIA document reveals that at least Weapons Lab director Dr. Lehman was present at the end when Paul asked for financial assistance from the Air Force to help him continue his UFO research. The mass exodus from the meeting wasn't because the officers didn't take the information seriously; they simply had too much to worry about and as soon as they figured out that Bennewitz's reports had nothing to do with their areas of responsibility, they quickly lost interest.

Richard Doty was later told that some of the officers were "very interested" in the pictures and recordings before the meeting, and that afterward, a few of them decided to continue a "scientific investigation" of Bennewitz and analyze the signals for any evidence that he was eavesdropping on something that he shouldn't have been. Significantly, the interested parties tended to be associated with NSA operations on the base.

An educated guess as to who else stayed to the end might include Major Cseh, since security leaks were his beat (and the obvious fact that he was there to report on the entire meeting). Dr. Lehman was there to decide if there was any indication that Bennewitz was tapping into any of Sandia or Phillips labs' research. If an ordinary citizen could see lasers blasting through two-foot-thick concrete walls or shooting supersonic targets out of the sky, or even hazard a guess somewhere near these scenarios, security would be compromised and the time and money spent plugging the leaks could be anything from merely annoying to hopelessly crippling, and as we shall see later, might have cost countless hours of training, preparation, and even lives.

Sometime after the meeting, the decision was made from somewhere in the AFOSI or DIA that Bennewitz would not be asked to "cease and desist." The photographs, and in particular the radio signals, were too important to let go. The AFOSI wanted to find out exactly how he had found and recorded them. This is one of the prime rules of counterintelligence: As long as nothing important is given away, let the target continue his modus operandi—continue to allow the possible breach in security long enough to trace the sources of the leak, and find out where the information is going. Cseh, Doty, and the rest wanted to maintain the illusion that they were just as concerned as Bennewitz until they found out what his motivations were, who may have been listening to him, and exactly how his operation worked. The NSA hadn't yet told the Air Force what they were doing and interagency confusion would reign as long as the NSA deemed it necessary to keep their coded transmission project under wraps.

In a seemingly innocuous detail mentioned at the end of the meeting report, Major Cseh wrote: "At the conclusion of the presentation, Dr. BENNEWITZ expressed an interest in obtaining financial assistance from the USAF in furthering his investigation regarding these objects. Dr. LEHMAN advised Dr. BENNEWITZ to request a USAF grant for research. Dr. LEHMAN advised Dr. BENNEWITZ he would assist him in filling out the proper documents." If Bennewitz appeared to be the half-cocked crank that many have assumed he was, this gesture was designed to keep him calm and massage his ego with delusions of official Air Force sanction. But things were not that simple. If Bennewitz did apply for and receive this grant, he never talked about it. Later though, another intelligence organization with a heavy presence on the base—and there are many indications that this was the NSA—reportedly granted Bennewitz $75,000 for a research and development study. This was directly related to his discovery of the strange signals emanating from the base, but more needs to be explained before this little tributary is followed upstream. Paul Bennewitz had ingratiated himself with the right people, but they kept his interest for reasons that would turn out to be wrong for his well-being.

chapter 7

DISINFORMATION 101

All warfare is based on deception.

> —SUN TZU, *THE ART OF WAR* (CA. 500 B.C.)

"Disinformation" is not lying. The Reagan administration adopted the term "misinformation" in the early 1980s to soften the blow when they were caught fibbing about matters of record or abuses of trust or the Constitution. The term "disinformation" was coined by German intelligence in WWI to give a name to their techniques of deliberately leaking real-appearing secrets about troop movements, weapons strength and capabilities, and the like. The KGB (in all likelihood stealing the term from captured German agents) adopted the term *dezinformatsiya* to describe some of the methods they used to effectively dupe NATO and the United States throughout the Cold War. According to their own definition from a KGB manual, "Strategic information assists in the execution of state tasks and is

45

directed at misleading the enemy concerning questions of state policy." When asked by his first intelligence chief, Felix Dzerzhinsky, what disinformation should be directed at the West, Vladimir Lenin replied, "Tell them what they want to hear."

To disinform is to give your mark just enough good stuff in a story that a cursory investigation will bolster the whole caboodle. If it is also what he wants and/or expects to hear, then so much the better. Finally, if the target believes the story enough to act on it, your job is considered a success. For example, if a certain intelligence agency is worried about civilians (and by extension, foreign governments) who are asking too many questions about the newest secret weapons research, they could carefully announce to a selected few press outlets that A) They are testing something out in the desert at a certain location; B) It does involve aircraft; C) The aircraft does not take off from a runway; and D) The testing does not involve offensive weapons. That is all, they say, they can reveal. If we go out to this remote desert site and park off the highway we might see lights floating up into the night sky from time to time. Carefully placed foreign agents would be looking into the skies around this area to try to determine what this super new aircraft is capable of doing. The catch is that "B" and "C" are not true. The project might in actuality be a ground-based system that is able to reflect radar waves off the ionosphere to catch incoming aircraft and missiles before they are visible over the horizon or curvature of the Earth. Maybe.

This sort of scenario has been used for centuries to keep people who don't "need to know" out of the way, and it still works beautifully. In fact, many disinformation schemes have been shut down at the last minute because the "giveaway factor" is too great to have even part of it revealed in order to mislead an enemy. Sun Tzu, the ancient Chinese general, described this in detail in his classic treatise on warfare.

If you still think that the Soviet Union wasn't clever enough to fool the combined resources of the United States and NATO throughout the Cold War, consider this: During the mid-1960s, the KGB repeatedly misled the CIA to convey an impression of weakness in their missile arsenal by deliberately skewing guidance communications during live-fire tests. The ruse worked, mainly because the Russians leaked to the CIA exactly what they were expecting (which of course was the prime directive in Soviet disinfo).

Russian intel operatives worked with rocket scientists to develop guidance telemetry that deliberately sent inaccurate data to U.S. intelligence—who were listening in from stations in Iran and Pakistan. CIA analysts had a preconception that U.S. rocketry was superior (hadn't we stolen the best scientists and technicians from the Germans?) and the biased data reinforced what they "knew" already—the Communists were failing miserably. Later, U2 and satellite photographs of the craters left after the missiles hit the ground gave the lie to Soviet electronic disinfo, and the Americans had to play "catch-up" after embarrassing proclamations of U.S. superiority were announced by Secretary of Defense Robert Mc-Namara. Gen. Jan Sejna, a member of the Czechoslovakian Central Committee, defected in 1968 and during debriefing revealed that the Soviet Politburo approved long-term global plans for disinfo at least fifteen years in advance. Lies told over many years are easier to believe and cover up—just like much of the UFO lore that has entered our collective unconscious.

By the late 1960s, U.S. intelligence had learned their

lessons well and began to use the disinfo tool not just on enemies foreign, but domestic "subversives" as well. The history
of the CIA's Operation Garden Plot reveals that undercover
agents had infiltrated almost every radical faction in the
United States by the late 1960s—including UFO researchers.

It is a documented fact that UFO groups, from the serious to the silly, have always been watched and infiltrated by
secret agent men. It is easy to figure why this went on from
the 1950s to the 1970s: Some of the more way-out groups es-
poused dangerously communistic ideas and spouted one-
world-government rhetoric. The G-men were also worried
about any Soviet bloc infiltration and the slim chance that
valuable UFO sighting information would fall into the wrong
hands. This all seems pretty silly now, but at the time loyal
citizens lost their careers and maybe even their lives in the
fury of finger-pointing and pervasive paranoia. Anything off-
track raised hackles in the establishment, and though no one
in the UFO arena was ever sent to jail for studying saucers or
claiming to have spoken with the disc jockeys, the potential
for poisoning patriotic minds kept the FBI and CIA busy for
many years.

Considering the fact that disinfo programs may be
planned decades in advance, we may well wonder on what
base much of the modern UFO lore rests. Bill Moore, a researcher and writer specializing in the anomalous, had been
ruminating on these very ideas for almost a decade when in
the late summer of 1980, he was suddenly drawn to the very
center of what would become known as the Bennewitz affair.

chapter 8

THE MAVERICK

Williams Leonard Moore rides a 1000cc Honda motor-cycle, can fix just about anything on wheels, and these days, prefers not to talk to any UFO researchers. He still maintains the P.O. box that was the mailing address for the Fair Witness Project, a research organization he formed with a small group of like-minded compatriots in the early 1980s. Although he is now in his late fifties, he still maintains the barrel-chested build author Howard Blum described in his 1990 book *Out There.* Moore now prefers T-shirts and leather jackets to stuffed-shirt suits, since he has no need for the appearance of respectability he cultivated when he was chasing down witness reports and government leads on UFO cases.

Bill Moore locks on to you with his eyes and probing conversation, and with a few well-placed queries quickly determines if a new visitor is sincere or simply interested in proving their own agenda. He has no time or patience for the latter type, and will let you know this in no uncertain terms. He considers most UFO researchers bumbling, ego-driven showmen, and their catcalls and condemnations purely the product of envy. Moore had never really had any patience with most of them. He left the crowd and was content to stand on his own. History teaches that the loner has a rough road to travel, and Bill Moore figures he was cut in the mold.

He had certainly been around. After graduating with a B.A. from Thiel College in Greenville, Pennsylvania in 1965, he went on to do graduate work at Duquesne University and Moorhead State University—both also in his native Pennsylvania. Later, he taught English, French, and humanities courses in junior and senior high schools in Minnesota, then became a labor-relations expert, before he decided to make writing his vocation. For someone who had always been averse to authority and especially its abuses, the UFO phenomenon offered a unique way to combine the two interests, since the saucers had always befuddled the authorities by pitting them against something over which they had no control. Moore moved his family to Prescott, Arizona in 1979 to pursue writing full-time, and to be closer to the Aerial Phenomena Research Organization in Tucson, where he had accepted a position on its board of directors.

His first book, coauthored with *Bermuda Triangle* author Charles Berlitz, was *The Philadelphia Experiment,* published in 1979. In the course of research for the book, he had met and befriended a strange character named Carl Allen. Allen, who also used the alias "Carlos Allende," had been peppering

UFO researchers with strange letters and tall tales for over a decade. He had marked up a copy of M. K. Jessup's 1956 book *The Case for the UFO* with comments from three "gypsies" and sent it to the Office of Naval Research. The hoax was so convincing that a few of the junior naval officers contracted the Varo Electronics Company in Texas to produce a limited facsimile print run of the defaced book. The edition, printed in color to distinguish the three colors of ink that were scrawled throughout, included an introduction by two of the naval personnel. In it, they stated, "Because of the importance which we attach to the possibility of discovering clues to the nature of gravity, no possible item, no matter how disreputable from the point of view of classical science, should be overlooked." Although (or perhaps because) the deception was discovered years ago, the book has achieved mythical status, and surviving copies routinely sell for hundreds of dollars. Author Jessup, for his part, came to attach much significance to the "Varo Edition," and asked zoologist and anomalies researcher Ivan Sanderson to keep it safe in case anything should happen to him. Six months later, on April 20, 1959, Jessup was found dead in his car, a tube running up from the exhaust to one of the windows.

Another of Allen's "stretchers" involved the U.S. Navy's supposed use of Einstein's proposed unified field theory in a 1943 experiment to render a destroyer invisible. Allen alleged that the run-through went awry and caused crew members on the ship to become invisible, go insane, and even cause a few deaths. After some dedicated digging, Moore found that the experiment was conducted to see if the Navy could make its ships invisible to radar or possibly simply to degauss the ship so that mines would not be attracted to the hull. The crewmembers' sickness and need for a subsequent cover-up were caused by the high voltage/low frequency electromagnetic fields created around the thick cables strung throughout the destroyer's innards to make the degaussing operation possible. Although Allen had a great story to tell, he was basically a low-level con artist, and Moore followed the story to its more mundane conclusion. The more gullible or conspiratorially-minded came to their own conclusions and a minor industry grew up around the story, which continues to this day.

To put it mildly, a major industry centers around a story that Moore and longtime UFO researcher Stanton Friedman happened to stumble upon while Moore was still publicizing *The Philadelphia Experiment*. On a visit to Baton Rouge, Louisiana on February 20, 1978, Friedman was waiting for an interview with a local reporter about his UFO research. The appointment was late, so Friedman got to jawing with the station manager. The man happened to know about a retired local Air Force Intelligence officer who claimed to have handled the wreckage of a flying saucer in July of 1947. He urged Friedman to look up a man named Jesse Marcel, who had retired to the Cajun country of Louisiana where he had been born and raised. Friedman found him in the phone book and paid a visit.

Marcel stated that in early July of 1947, as the ranking intelligence officer of the Army Air Force stationed at Roswell, he had been called out to investigate what looked like an airplane crash a number of miles northwest of the town. The story, which he had kept to himself and family members up to that time, would revitalize the sagging UFO research field (at least in the public eye) and give Roswell a most unique place in the history of small-town festival themes. In 1997, at a celebration for the 50th anniversary of the event, the town's population swelled from about 20,000 to nearly 400,000 inhabitants, and included everything from a golf tournament to a "crash and burn"-themed UFO parade down the main street.

Eventually, Moore and Friedman would interview almost 100 witnesses, most of whom had not talked about, or even thought of, the event for over thirty years. Despite numerous attempts by everyone from groups of scientific skeptics to the Air Force itself to explain it all away as everything from high-altitude radar reflectors to crash-test dummies and Japanese secret weapons, the core of initial witnesses formed the basis of a mystery which has yet to be entirely solved, even if one even partially suspends belief or disbelief.

In 1985, the Roswell book came back to bite Moore in the behind. He was contacted by a lawyer representing Edwin A. "Buzz" Aldrin and told that he was the target of a lawsuit because of something that was apparently thrown into the book at the last minute by Berlitz. The offending passage had to do with Aldrin's supposed sighting of a UFO while puttering about on the moon. Moore had done most of the research and Berlitz had been the chief writer, but both were named in the lawsuit. Moore recalls Berlitz saying that he would "take care of it," but due to cold feet or the advice of his lawyer, he eventually hung Moore out to dry and face his part of the suit on his own. Berlitz was independently wealthy from a large inheritance as well as his successful language schools business and he had author's insurance. With little money to hire a lawyer, Moore fought on, finally forcing Aldrin to withdraw his suit "with prejudice" and was left with $30,000 in legal fees. The episode wrecked his finances and contributed to the breakup of his marriage. Relations between Moore and Berlitz cooled significantly as a result of

these events, and eventually Moore broke completely with
him over Berlitz's stated belief that his main purpose in writing books was to make money and that truth necessarily took
a backseat in that process. "Tell your readers what they want
to hear," Berlitz once said to Moore over a drink at the Yale
Club in New York, "and they will not only love you for it, but
they will pay you for it. People want entertainment," he said,
"and I write my books to fill their need."

If that wasn't enough to sour Moore on the UFO subject,
what happened in the meantime surely would. It turns out
that one of the first baited hooks the AFOSI threw into the
UFO community was to become the first snare directed at
Moore. When caught, he would be reeled in slowly.

In July of 1980, a letter with no return address arrived at
APRO headquarters. Jim Lorenzen read it with some interest, and passed it on to APRO administrator Bill English to
send to Moore in Prescott for his reaction. Hundreds of letters from anonymous sources arrived every year, and most
were easily discarded into the kook file or the wastebasket.
Other than the identity of the sender, which was not mentioned, this one included names and locations that could be
easily checked. It described the experience of Craig Weitzel,
an eighteen-year-old who was then a member of the Civil Air
Patrol, a program for Air Force cadets-in-training. The incident had taken place about twenty miles east of the state
capital in the Santa Fe National Forest near the town of
Pecos.

The two-page letter stated that the writer had to remain
anonymous for his own protection, and told of a spectacular
UFO sighting that had occurred on July 16, 1980. Weitzel
and "ten other individuals" were on a midmorning training
exercise when to their surprise they saw a UFO . . .

> . . . *land in a clearing approximately 250 yards NNW of the training area. Weitzel observed an individual dressed in a metallic suit depart the craft and walk a few feet away. The individual was outside the craft for just a few minutes. When the individual returned, the craft took off toward the SW.*

The mystery writer also mentioned that Weitzel had taken pictures of the thing.

When the training group returned to Kirtland, Base Security officers debriefed them. The next day, "a man in a dark suit with black hair and sunglasses," who said he was from Sandia Labs, visited Weitzel. He said his name was "Mr. Huck." Weitzel was told to turn over his photographs, but informed the stranger that he had already given them to the Air Force. This dark and menacing figure fitted the classic "Man in Black" profile to a T. Jumbo-budget movies notwithstanding, the figure of the man in black visiting witnesses with threats of dire consequences if they talked has been a mainstay of UFO mythology ever since the 1956 publication of Albert K. Bender's *Flying Saucers and the Three Men,* which spun tales of strange men in trenchcoats harassing UFO witnesses.

With the tone of an implied threat, and true to form, Mr. Huck told Weitzel not to mention the sighting or pictures to anyone. The writer concluded his letter by saying that he knew that the Air Force was keeping the remains of a crashed UFO in the Manzano storage complex.

Leonard Stringfield, who specialized in researching stories and reports of crashed UFOs, once called his work "a search for truth in a hall of mirrors." Rumors, secondhand stories, and lies confronted him constantly, yet he was convinced that the government had indeed retrieved a few downed flying saucers. He was well aware that this may have been just the impression that his contacts in the intelligence world wanted him to have, but the stories were so consistent across a wide range of places and history that he could come to no better conclusion. The Weitzel letter contained all the classic earmarks of a good story that had actually happened, with a wealth of spurious details thrown in that made its funhouse reflection distort in just such a way that the curious would come running.

When Lorenzen sent the "Weitzel letter" to Bill Moore, he was almost convinced that the story was hogwash, but since there were names, places, and dates that could be checked out, he urged Moore to look into it. Moore located Weitzel, and talked to him briefly by phone. The young cadet confirmed that he had indeed sighted a strange, silvery object in the skies, but denied ever having taken any pictures, much less received a menacing visit from someone who told him to shut up about it. He also said that the incident had happened on a military range in the Southeast, not in New Mexico. The "Weitzel letter" was a load of manure with a rhinestone thrown in, and became one of the first lessons in the UFO disinformation game. Moore did not take the bait this time.

A few more details emerged years later when Computer UFO Network contributor Chris Lambright contacted Weitzel, and was told that he and his companions had been waiting for a helicopter to come pick them up at the end of a search and rescue exercise when they spotted an "unusual silvery object hovering high in the sky which left the area," to use his words, "exponentially." He reiterated that he had not written the letter.

The mysterious writer said that Weitzel had reported the Man in Black incident to a "Mr. Dody" who was apparently a Kirtland Air Base security officer. Whoever had written the letter had the wherewithal to know details of the incident and use them to titillate someone at APRO. The idea, as it turns out, was to put out feelers to see who could be used by the AFOSI as an "insider asset." At this point, Moore had no idea that he was on the wish list. And Moore's involvement with Bennewitz was still in the future.

An Air Force physicist who met with Bennewitz on a few occasions expressed impatience with his fellow scientists when confronted with anomalous data. "If you find one white crow, it means that all crows are not black. A lot of scientists intentionally ignore this." In the rush to certitude, the white crow in the midst of a murder of his black fellows is routinely ignored. What would you do if a skyful of white crows was scolding and pecking at you? Paul Bennewitz had to decide, and perhaps his quixotic adventure may be considered in this way. The problem was that most of the crows were only dipped in white paint.

Moore could see some of the painted crows, but he would also come to believe that his cooperation with those who were doing the painting might give him an advantage.

chapter 9

SILVER SKIES

B y late 1979, Moore and Berlitz had finished the manuscript for *The Roswell Incident* and mailed it off to the
publisher. The Moore family began their move to Arizona and Moore waited for word to start a promotional tour.
He had been in contact with APRO while he was working on
the Roswell book, and Jim and Coral Lorenzen were so impressed with his work that they asked if he was interested in
joining the board of directors. Moore quickly accepted.

The book arrived in stores in September of 1980. That
same month, it happened that a debate on the UFO subject
was scheduled by the Smithsonian Institution, so Moore set
off from Arizona and conducted his own promotional tour
along the way. After a radio interview (at station WOW, no
less) in Omaha, Nebraska, a secretary stopped him in the

lobby and said that there was a call for him. The voice on the other end identified himself as a colonel at nearby Orfutt Air Force Base and then said, "We think you're the only one we've heard that seems to know what he's talking about." The colonel asked if Moore could meet for coffee and a chat. Since he was leaving for the next stop on the book tour in less than an hour, Moore took his number and said he would get back to him.

On the return trip, after another interview at Albu-querque's KOB radio, Moore was again requested at the switchboard. He picked up the phone and identified himself. "We think you're the only one we've heard that seems to know what he's talking about." This got Moore's attention, and this time he had a couple of days open. A meeting was set up at a local restaurant. The enigmatic voice refused to identify itself, melodramatically instructing that he should look for a man who would be wearing a red tie.

Moore arrived about fifteen minutes before the appoint-ment and parked across the street to keep an eye on things. He scoped out the area to see if the situation was some sort of trap. Just as he had satisfied himself that everything was kosher, a commanding tap came from the passenger window. All Moore could see from the driver's seat was a bright red tie set against a crisp white shirt. Not knowing what to expect next, he carefully got out and faced his visitor, who smiled and in a voice tinged with the hint of an Eastern European accent said, "Don't we have an appointment?" Moore fol-lowed the gaunt, besuited man inside. They took a booth in a quiet corner. (The isolated restaurant booth seems to be a fa-vorite meeting place among spooks.)

"What makes you people think that I 'know what I'm talk-ing about'?" Moore asked. The rest of the conversation was primarily a monologue in which his new acquaintance told Moore that he represented a group of intelligence agents in the U.S. government who were tired of the secrecy surrounding the UFO subject and were eager to release more accurate information to the public. They wanted to do this through a reputable researcher. He would be given small bites of the story over time, and could do with it as he wished. Would Moore be interested in participating in such a program?

There was a catch. "Good deals" always have a catch, especially in the espionage world. To get at the UFO info, he would have to agree to give the government people something in return. The legal tender of intelligence and counterintelligence is information, and Moore would have to provide the kind that they couldn't get on their own. He was not immediately told exactly what this involved, but after years of probing and guessing at what the U.S. government knew about UFOs, he knew at least this much: He was being offered a researcher's dream—a pass through the closely guarded gate of intrigue and programmed confusion that had dogged the best minds on the subject since retired Marine Corps major Donald Keyhoe and his civilian UFO group, the National Investigations Committee on Aerial Phenomena, had raised the UFO secrecy banner in the 1950s. With nary a qualm, or much time to think it over, Moore agreed to the Faustian bargain.

As he sized up this figure with the piercing eyes and began to absorb what was being offered, Moore was thinking (as he would later explain, repeatedly) that he would play the disinformation game and get his hands dirty just enough to lead those directing the process into believing that he was doing exactly what they wanted him to do. All the while he would continue to burrow his way into the defense and intelligence matrix to learn who was directing it and why. By the time the game was over, Moore would need more than a hand-washing to clear himself of vicious charges from other researchers and the conflicting and often false evidence that was passed to him over the next decade.

The two shook on the deal. Moore was told that he would be asked to appear at another clandestine meeting soon. Just before they parted company, a manila envelope was pushed across the stained red tablecloth at Moore, with the understated remark, "Here's something you might be interested in." As soon as he was safely outside, Moore carefully opened the envelope. A single sheet of paper fell into his hands. It described a project called "Silver Sky," which appeared to have something to do with Air Force UFO investigations and reports back to the Pentagon regarding sightings and encounters.

The partially redacted report named names, dates, and places associated with a spectacular UFO landing in southern New Mexico that had occurred in 1969. Headed by the ubiquitous "FOR OFFICIAL USE ONLY," "RESTRICTED," and punctuated with "SECRET" caveats, the meat of the message said:

COLLECTION REQUIREMENTS FOR PROJECT "SILVER SKY"

1. (S) OL1702A IS TASKED WITH CR FOR SILVER SKY. ALL REPORTING UNITS WILL PROVIDE OL1702A WITH DATA THAT WILL BE INCORPORATED INTO CR REPORT 19-107 DUE BY 31 DEC 69 THIS HQ'S.

2. (S) 1703 WILL CONDUCT 168 INTERVIEWS OF FOLLOWING PEOPLE PER MSG 012700Z

SEP 69. A) MICHAEL STEVERS, ROSWELL NM B) DOROTHY ADAMS, SUNSET NM, C) EVELYN FUHRER, SOCORRO NM, D) MER-RITT WINSLOW, HONDO NM. IT IS EX-TREMELY IMPORTANT TO OBTAIN PRECISE DETAILS AS TO THE OBJECT THESE PEO-PLE ALLEGEDLY SIGHTED. ALSO PER-SUADE THESE PEOPLE TO SIGN SECURITY PLEDGE (DD FORM 1420) IAW NATIONAL SECURITY ACT OF 1950.

3. (S) FOR DET 1700: YOUR QUESTIONS RE-GARDING RECOVERED SPIKE CRAFT CAN-NOT BE ANSWERED BY THIS HQ'S DUE TO SECURITY RESTRICTIONS. QUESTIONS HAVE BEEN ADDRESSED TO CIA/INO. DO NOT PROCEED WITH ANY OTHER SECU-RITY PROGRAM PROCEDURES UNTIL YOU HAVE RECEIVED FURTHER GUIDANCE FROM THIS HQ'S.

4. (S) 1158 TECH OPS SQ HOLLOMAN AFB NM WILL BE USED TO REPORT ALL DATA TO THIS HQ. DO NOT, REPEAT, DO NOT UTI-LIZE BASE COMM CENTER TO TRANSMIT SILVER SKY INFORMATION.

5. (S) CAPT. WRIGHT IS PROJECT OFFICER, PLEASE DIRECT ALL FURTHER INQUIRIES TO HIM.

The witnesses named in the document all lived within fifty miles of Roswell, in towns with names like Hondo, Socorro (famous for a 1964 UFO landing), and Sunset. ("168 INTERVIEWS" referred to the type of interrogation, not the amount.) Perhaps this man and his intel colleagues thought of this exercise as some kind of inside joke, or they wanted to start their new recruit in an area that he knew fairly well. Moore has never found out what the precise reasons were, but within a month he paid a visit to these bumps on the road map to try to put faces to the names in the report. He stopped in at rural post offices and started to reel off his list of witnesses. Not one name matched the residents on file, or anyone that the postal employees knew of. They either didn't exist, or had moved away or died since the Air Force had talked to them. (Moore eventually found out that the Air Force had spoken to the witnesses, but in connection with other sightings.) The Silver Sky document was a fake. Project Silver Sky itself may have never existed either. Moore was surprised and not a little annoyed that he had traveled the 500 miles or so from Prescott to a dead end, which had been deliberate from the get-go.

It was with a mix of confusion and anger that Moore arrived for his next encounter with the mysterious counterintelligence man in late October of 1980. In yet another Albuquerque eatery, they sat down with an AFOSI agent whom Moore had not seen before. The man was introduced as Special Agent Richard Doty from Kirtland AFB. After a few preliminaries, the questions started. "Well, what did you discover?"

Moore threw the paper down on the table and, trying to sound less annoyed than he actually was, replied: "This whole mess is a lie. None of these people exist."

The agent and Doty looked at each other and smiled.

"What's going on?" asked Moore.

"You passed the test," said the man whom he would eventually refer to with the code name "Falcon." Within a few years, Moore and his colleagues would begin to assign code names to their growing coterie of contacts so that they could talk freely about developments without fear of identification if they were overheard. All were given the names of birds, and were collectively referred to as the "Aviary."

Many investigators would have immediately trumpeted their new find on an obscure but dramatic UFO landing case, but Moore had been careful. "We wanted to know that we could trust you," said Falcon, "and you did exactly what we wanted you to do." The intelligence people had even checked with the Hondo post office to see if Moore had shown up. The "spooks" knew that if they were going to recruit someone to cooperate with their schemes, they needed someone on the "inside" of the UFO community who would not only follow instructions, but could be trusted to keep things to himself while doing it.

The meat of the deal was finally laid on the table: Moore would keep an eye on selected UFO researchers and report on their opinions and feelings about rumors and cases making the rounds in their small community. The Falcon also revealed that he held a high position in the Defense Intelligence Agency, which is basically the military's very own CIA. Elaborating on the offer from the previous meeting, he said that he represented a group of highly placed people who were unhappy with the secrecy surrounding the UFO subject, and wanted someone they could trust in order to release information to the public in a controlled way.

Falcon told Moore that Richard Doty would be his main counterintel contact. Moore remembered the Weitzel letter reference to a "Mr. Dody," and things started to fall into place. The letter had contained not only references to an internal Air Force matter, but the misspelled name of the man on the inside who was going to be working with Moore to find out what was going through the minds of prominent UFO researchers. Many months later, Moore was talking to Doty in one of their many informal conversations and found out that "Huck" was one of the many aliases used by Kirtland AFOSI agents. (For his part, Moore says that one of the secretaries in the AFOSI office was named Mrs. Huck.) Doty told Moore that he had composed the Weitzel letter on orders, "as bait." Years later, in the course of an interagency investigation, he maintained under questioning that Craig Weitzel had written the letter under orders, but had "kind of screwed it up." The multiple stories were vintage Doty.

Falcon was a bird of a different feather. His misdirections always served a purpose and seemed to closely follow a master script. He would become Moore's mentor of sorts over the next decade, providing information (or disinformation as he saw fit) and guiding Moore and his partners through the maze of U.S. government and UFO knowledge. They would be led down many passageways that came to dead ends or turned away from the secrets at the center, but as Moore began to negotiate the twists and turns, perhaps he could begin to map the territory and follow things as close to the center as he could. Falcon and his colleagues were happy to let out bits and pieces of the UFO puzzle (at least as they knew it) so long as sensitive defense projects like the ones going on at Kirtland were kept out of sight and mind of the public, and any other uncomfortably interested parties. At the same time, they could see what Moore did with the information, and how it flowed through the tributaries of the UFO rumor river. Moore was well aware that much of the material he would be seeing and hearing about would consist of lies upon lies, covering a smidgen of truth. He hoped that he would be able to "separate the shit from the candy," as he put it.

"Falcon was truly an enigmatic person," Moore recalled. "He hardly smiled, didn't tell jokes, and there was no small talk. For instance, if you asked about his family, he would give a blank stare, and quickly move on to the subject at hand." For the Falcon, time and words were valuable commodities, and neither were wasted. Moore was an asset, and nothing more. He was just another game piece on Falcon's board.

If spies have a dictionary, the Falcon probably wrote the entry on "spooks," and his backlit profile is next to it.

chapter 10

TRUE ADVENTURE

How can anyone believe that Bill Moore wasn't actually on the take for a simple golden handshake or two? He repeatedly denied that he was paid in any way for his cooperation. No matter how much we try to cover up shady activity with high-sounding rhetoric, one of the basic elements of human nature is a "childlike" desire for discovery. As Maxwell Maltz, the 1950s pop psychologist and author of *Psycho Cybernetics*, put it, "Man is essentially a goal-seeking creature." Most of us pay for this right, taking adventure vacations and indulging in hobbies that satisfy this urge, since the task of simply having enough cash to survive takes up most of our time and energy, and our society is set up for most of us to be the grease, not the wheels.

But what if you don't care about money so much? What if

the goal is to look back on an interesting life? This concept may be alien to most—something we see in the movies or hear as stories when we are children, but Moore actually believes in this "childish" concept. It contributed to the breakup of his marriage and the loss of many potential friends and allies in the UFO field, who couldn't understand the concept of knowledge as its own reward, and a careful, methodical and, yes, selfish desire to learn as much of the truth as he could. He would have to do things that would appall his compatriots, partly because it involved deceiving a few of them, but mostly because they weren't the ones who had been contacted. They would loudly condemn him in one breath, but quietly ask what he had learned in the next.

The spooks had chosen well in recruiting Bill Moore. If he wasn't let into the castle of secrets, he had at least been in the courtyard while most never make it past the moat, and he didn't even have to enlist. He would be led down many paths that are invisible to most, and his cooperation with the men who had the keys would open many doors, if just a crack. What Moore would see, hear, experience, and write about over the next ten years would change the way the world looked at the UFO subject, and the way Bill Moore looked at himself and his chosen mission. It was a breathtaking turning point.

In turn, Doty (and others in the intelligence world) would have a contact on the "outside." Moore also mentioned another factor: "I think they were in it for their egos as well." For those in the intelligence biz, the satisfaction of a job well done lies in effectiveness and anonymity. The man in the next cubicle down at the AFOSI cannot be truly impressed when an operation goes off without a hitch, but a cleared civilian can be both confidant and confessor. Moore could also act as a go-between when agents wanted or needed to pass information between themselves, or because of his contacts, find out something that they had not been able to access.

Moore would later perform many other services for the AFOSI which were completely unrelated to the UFO subject. These activities kept him interested in the intelligence game, and allowed his "handlers" to keep their hooks in.

One day Falcon and Doty pulled up at a predetermined spot in Albuquerque and asked Moore to get in. Private cars were one of the Falcon's favorite meeting places since he could control the environment by making sure that there were no "bugs" planted, with the added plus that it is virtually impossible to eavesdrop on a conversation in a moving vehicle. The trio drove out to a lonely spot in an empty park and stopped the car. While they were discussing matters at hand, Moore noticed that men would occasionally appear out of the brush and trees and try to peer in the windows. This happened with uncomfortable regularity, but Moore kept quiet about it, somewhat secure that he was reasonably safe as long as he stayed inside. Many of these fellows were dressed in uncomfortably tight pants. Some hurried by tottering on high heels in unflattering minidresses. Falcon acted as if nothing was amiss, and Doty occasionally smiled and stifled a laugh. Moore wondered what sort of test this was supposed to be, but kept his cool.

A few weeks later, he was handed a dossier on someone who was on the AFOSI's (and most likely others') most-wanted lists for passing unauthorized information, dipping into the petty cash, or perhaps something more serious. The package contained pictures of the suspect, lists of his friends and contacts, and likely hangout spots. Moore was told to concentrate on the bars along the Santa Monica Boulevard "strip" in Los Angeles. The purpose of the earlier episode in

Albuquerque was now obvious. "Rick and the Falcon had a good laugh over that one," says Moore. With the homophobic question out of the way, they directed Moore to start asking around for their quarry in the gay bars of West Hollywood. "I never found the man, but I talked to a few people who knew him," Moore recalls. He passed on what he had found to the AFOSI, who soon tracked him down.

Because of his fluency in written and conversational Russian, Moore also became involved with certain assets stationed deep within the USSR. "What they would do," says Moore, "is send all these postcards to UFO researchers. Most of them were innocuous requests for information, but a few, like the ones I sometimes got, contained encoded bits of information on facilities, weapons systems and defense, and other things." The texts of the handwritten messages were innocuous requests for UFO-related information, but sometimes contained keywords and phrases. When he received the cards, Moore would call (or receive a call from) an unlisted number in an untraceable government exchange and read what was written on the card. "Thank you" was all that the Voice would say at the end of each call before abruptly hanging up. Each recipient received only part of the message, which was collated by the anonymous caller, who presumably passed it up the chain of command. The cards themselves were then sent on to a P.O. box in Washington, D.C., and Moore never had the slightest idea what was being passed though his hands, which was, of course, according to plan. Some of this information was likely related to one or more of the secret projects at Kirtland Air Force Base.

Soon after the Silver Sky adventure, Moore was told that he would be receiving his first package of "real stuff" soon.

Moore had left the UFO carnival midway and entered the first room in the hall of mirrors. He was told to go back to Arizona, continue as normal, and await the next call. He went home to Prescott and continued to serve on the APRO board while he fielded calls, looked over old cases for any new insights, and occasionally interviewed witnesses. His "bosses," Coral and Jim Lorenzen, had always known that they and their group were being watched, but had long ago learned to live in an uneasy truce with this uncomfortable situation. It is possible to live an almost normal existence while immersed in a state of constant paranoia. For those who deal in secret information, it's a given. For the rest of us, it takes getting used to.

In the mid 1960s, Paul Krassner, the counterculture icon, Youth International Party (YIPPIE) member, and publisher of the satirical broadside *The Realist*, began to notice that he was being followed and that his phones were tapped when he started to publish reports critical of the Warren Commission. At the height of his paranoia, he was walking though Golden Gate Park in San Francisco. Krassner had just been given a joint of the best pot he had seen in weeks. Just as he was savoring the thought of a triumphant return to his apartment and an afternoon of bliss, he espied a San Francisco Police Department cruiser on the other side of the park. The car made an abrupt U-turn and Krassner panicked. He hid the joint in a hollow tree and whistled his way around the corner. When he was sure the cops had left, he went back to find that someone had stolen his prize. Krassner then realized that fear was ruling his life and he had to let it go. The solution was simple: "It got old after a while," he said.

From the beginnings of their activity in the UFO arena,

the Lorenzens had faced a choice that many dissidents like Krassner had to make. They could quit, or assume that they had nothing to hide and continue with their work. With Moore's agreement to cooperate with an unknown cornucopia of intelligence agencies, that decision had entered its most intimate phase. Without revealing any specifics, in time he would let on to Jim Lorenzen that he was involved with certain people in the government. Lorenzen urged him to continue, "but keep APRO out of it."

"He thought that they were going to be set up to look bad or take some sort of fall," said Moore, "and he wanted no part of it. It was all right with him if I continued on my own." The Lorenzens had been targets of surveillance in the past, and they had no illusions about government interest in their activities. "Coral [Lorenzen] was occasionally upset about it, but Jim kind of accepted it," he says. Doty claims that APRO was "full of people" on the Air Force payroll (or at least with kindred interests like Moore) who would investigate specific cases and determine if there were any security issues before passing the information on to AFOSI and "sanitizing" their reports to APRO.

Assured that they had their man, the spooks moved ahead with their plan. They would no longer look at the UFO research field as an annoyance. The political stakes were too high to overlook anything that was even remotely promising as an avenue to fool enemies, causing them to waste valuable time, money, and manpower. Counterintelligence knew that the Russians and other adversaries constantly monitored the UFO grapevine for snippets of useful information on secret hardware and black budget projects. According to Moore, "two or three" other researchers had agreed (or later agreed) to the same deal he had been offered. He still refuses to divulge their identities, because "It is up to them to decide if they want to reveal themselves."

Ever since the 1950s, enthusiasts had suspected a high-level cover-up of the UFO subject. In the 1960s, they had become sure of it. Now UFOlogy was slowly losing its innocence for possibly the second time in its short history.

chapter II

MYSTERY MAN

I worked for almost ten months trying to get an interview with the enigmatic Richard Doty. After an abortive series of email questions that were either partially answered or completely ignored, there was little hope that this man, whose former job with the AFOSI had been to pepper inquisitive UFO researchers with routine misdirections and half-truths, was ever going to give me a straight answer about anything. Because of this history, he had been slowly easing himself out of the quagmire he had dug for himself, and was loath to go near it again.

A sort of dubious karmic justice had been visited upon Doty as a steady torrent of accusations was thrown in his direction for years after he retired from the AFOSI. The inconsistencies in the disinformation he and his superiors had generated for years were pounced on by angry UFOlogists, and for some reason, Doty felt he had to answer the charges in heated letter exchanges and later, through Internet flame wars. "It was really none of their business," he stated later, "and I disinformed those people to get them off my back." He enjoys playing the mystery man.

After repeated assurances that I was not a wide-eyed alien chaser or invested in any specific agenda, Doty finally agreed to meet up if I made the trek out to New Mexico. He gave directions to a lonely Denny's restaurant off I-40 about fifty miles east of Albuquerque. Like all good spooks, he arrived at the exact minute of the hour we had agreed upon. Perhaps he had been watching me from the parking lot all along. The man was not what I expected, but that, somewhat paradoxically, did not surprise me either.

Richard Charles Doty greets you with a warm handshake and an easy grin. After only a few minutes of conversation, I sense that he is holding back more than the average Joe, and Doty cultivates this persona. There are the stories of family history (he says there are five people in the Doty clan all named Richard), AFOSI and spook lore, his adventures in the Air Force, and the strange and fascinating people he has met and worked with. Once these niceties are concluded, and he has you in his conversational grasp, weirder tales begin to emerge.

"Yeah, UFOs are a real thing, and there are aliens visiting Earth," he says.

How does he know?

"I have seen and heard things that most people will never be exposed to. They don't have the clearances and need to know. I did."

Does this bother him?

"No."

And so the conversation went, Doty baiting and reeling with tidbits of information, while I tried to get the sense of what is real and what is not. I finally figured that "the truth is out there," somewhere in between the extremes of tight-assed skepticism and wide-eyed-idiot belief. Doty is keenly aware of the dynamic, and how to pull most people toward one or the other. To get to the bottom of the Bennewitz era, Doty's recollections of events have to be checked as they intersect with other sources and known facts. Doty is definitely not boring, but unlike Paul Bennewitz, most of us would not stake much of our worldview on information from this former AFOSI Special Agent, no matter how compelling the stories. Admittedly, Bennewitz and others didn't have the benefit of 20/20 hindsight.

Doty was tested and tracked throughout his career to become first a base security guard and eventually a Special Agent in the AFOSI, which was his official title while at Kirtland. It became his passion as well. It was only later that he realized his progress had probably been monitored from somewhere in the higher echelons of the Defense Department, and that he was destined for a very special assignment, which would eventually take most of his time.

In the tradition of military families, Doty's father (and to some extent his uncle Edward) had been his childhood mentors, and had originally suggested that he might want to consider a life in the Air Force. Uncle Edward had been a career officer and since his master's degree from UCLA was in meteorology, he had served throughout WWII as a weather specialist. His military record notes that he was assigned as chief of the Air Force Weather Research Station at his alma mater at the end of August 1947. He was only twenty-seven years old at the time. Interestingly, the record also states that his duty at the time was "directing work in the Air Force Atmospheric Divergence Project." The dry language of bureaucratese reveals nothing about the nature of this study. Perhaps this had something to do with weather control, or maybe it was something more prosaic. Richard Doty recalls the project as an attempt to "change or neutralize gravity in the area around a rocket to increase the efficiency of space travel." Another ploy?

In 1948, Edward Doty was tapped to head Project Twinkle, the official Air Force inquiry into the "green fireball" phenomenon perplexing residents of southern New Mexico, and giving the Defense Department an opening salvo of Cold War jitters. He had certainly encountered the UFO phenomenon in his work, and passed this interest on to his young nephew.

Young Richard entered the Air Force in 1968 as a combat security policeman. Sometime after basic training, he said that he was taken to a room and shown films of UFOs. Close-up films. The airmen in this select group were at first incredulous and wondered if the whole thing was some sort of test, which of course it was. The confused men were told that the reality of what they had seen would need to sink in over the next few months. Doty and others who could handle it were then shown and told other things about the military and government history of UFO involvement.

Soon after this episode, Doty says he was assigned to a guard unit at Nevada's notorious Area 51. In 1969, no one save the local residents (some of whom had been forcibly removed from their land and homesteads) knew about the weird goings-on some 200 miles northwest of Las Vegas. The U2 had been developed and tested here in the 1950s, and before the base of operations was moved elsewhere, Lockheed's F117 Stealth Fighter flew test missions from the 30,000-foot runway. Doty was assigned to guard duty outside of a medium-sized hangar.

One evening, while Doty stood at ease surveying the desolation of the Emigrant Valley spread out before him, he watched as an aircraft mounted on a trailer was rolled out onto the tarmac. As he turned to get a better look, he realized that the thing had no wings or tail or indeed any control surfaces that would identify it as a conventional aircraft. The huge dull-black disc was wheeled out on an equally huge trailer towed behind a large truck. It was moved out a distance from the building and then "started up." It made no sound, but emitted a blue electric-coronal discharge from the bottom. As it lifted off, the trailer was moved away. The craft went up about 200 feet or so, and moved around the area in small circles. One night later in the testing, Doty overheard one of the technicians say, "I think we can get this thing out of the atmosphere." Doty was later assigned to stand near one of the test equipment areas and was required to wear protective goggles like the other guards and scientists in the area.

Doty was stunned, but kept up a stoic demeanor. At one point during this assignment, the commanding officer called Doty aside and asked him if he had seen the black craft. He stammered out an affirmative, but otherwise kept quiet.

"Airman Doty, do you know what that craft was?" asked the officer.

"No sir."

"That was what is generally known as a UFO, and it's not one of ours. It's 'on loan.'"

"Yes sir."

"Someday, if you play your cards right, you will know a lot more, but for now, you are to tell no one about this, and you are not to discuss it with anyone. Is that clear?"

Doty never talked about it again. If true, the Area 51 testing exercise may have been a complete farce with the only purpose being to gauge the reactions of certain personnel. The infamous Robert Lazar/Area 51 case of the early 1990s has many of the earmarks of this sort of theatrical operation. A physicist, Lazar claimed to have worked on captured UFOs for the Defense Department. If Lazar was not supposed to talk about his knowledge of flying saucers, strange security procedures, and odd stories about things like "element 115," no one would have ever heard of him. As it is, the episode entered the lore and lexicon of the modern UFO age, and ended up as a mainstay of popular culture, just as many aspects of the Bennewitz case had a decade before. This is just what the counterintelligence people assigned to protect the secrets of Area 51 wanted.

The fact that Doty remained close-mouthed about the episode was duly noted by the higher-ups, and probably led to his later assignment at Ellsworth Air Force Base in South Dakota, where by a strange coincidence the dramatic UFO landing and encounter described in a "leaked" letter to a tabloid had supposedly taken place.

In 1978, a little-known government document claimed that a UFO had landed at Ellsworth Air Force Base in South Dakota and one of its metallic green-suited occupants had not only melted an M16 right out of a sentry's hands, but had left a nuclear missile inoperative while still in its silo. Bob Pratt, a reporter for the *National Enquirer* tabloid, was assigned to look into the episode when the magazine received the supposedly secret document describing the incident. He found that some of the principal witnesses mentioned in the text either didn't exist, or in one case, was out sick on the night in question. The *Enquirer* declared the document a hoax. But this made little difference to Paul Bennewitz, who knew that the story contained a grain or two of truth. The fact that the tabloid hacks had rejected this intelligence leak just made it more important. Details of figures in metallic suits and *War of the Worlds*–type disintegration rays could not hide the essential message: Extraterrestrials were interested in our military establishments and more specifically, in disarming or crippling our weapons of mass destruction.

Doty claims to have actually seen a bright light over a disused corner of Ellsworth Air Force Base while out on patrol, but apart from a couple of frightened guards under his command who had gotten close to the thing, no weapons were melted and no beings were seen.

Doty later insisted that he had nothing to do with the letter to the *Enquirer,* but considering his later activities at Kirtland AFB and with Bennewitz, perhaps his UFO sighting was used and elaborated on for dramatic effect, and he may have been shown this technique as a sort of counterintelligence training. He (or someone in the AFOSI) would later use the actual experience of another group of Air Force personnel as the basis for the Weitzel letter. But in 1980, Doty was trying to figure out just what Paul Bennewitz was trying to warn him about, and determine if he was a danger to the security of Kirtland Air Force Base and its tenants.

As Doty began to immerse himself in the lore of UFO research, his assignment was to keep his ears open for anything useful to the AFOSI, NSA, and DIA in their campaign to confuse the UFO community so that curious eyes could only focus on the distorted reflection of anything that might compromise secret (or perhaps embarrassing) projects and hardware. His training in disinfo had focused on classic cases and techniques developed by the Germans, Soviets, and curiously enough, the South African intelligence services—since expert disinformationalists often thrive in an atmosphere of limited resources and funding. Good counterintelligence operatives (and wise military leaders) will drop their prejudices and learn from the enemy and any others of divergent ideologies.

One morning when Moore was visiting the AFOSI offices, Doty asked him about a then little-known UFO crash story that had hung around the fringes of the grapevine since its revelation in Frank Scully's 1955 book *Behind the Flying Saucers*. One of the ubiquitous flying discs had supposedly streaked down in a fiery fury a few miles northeast of Aztec, New Mexico in the late 1940s. Moore had looked into it as the possible basis for a book. Even though he had eventually determined that the story was a hoax perpetrated by a well-known confidence trickster named Silas Mason Newton, Doty grilled him on the details. In later disinfo releases to eager UFO researchers, Doty and his superiors repeated the story, knowing that a cursory look at history would confirm the rumors they wanted to spread. UFO hounds eager to put two and two together (not caring that it added up to five) would assume that Air Force insiders were carefully leaking evidence of an actual event. It was an elementary act of disinformation.

Doty fondly remembers Seely Howard, one of his instructors in the arcane art of disinformation. Air Force Intelligence had hired Howard away from his former employer after discovering that his skills were badly needed in spy work. Predictably enough, Howard had worked for the Prudential Insurance Company. The man was a master in the fine American art of convincing customers to plunk down cash for things that they didn't need. The master salesman had sagely advised, "There are three sorts of people you will be dealing with: The first are the ones who will believe anything you say. The second are those who will (at least at first) refuse to believe you. The last is the group who won't believe you at first, but might be willing to be convinced." He quickly taught Doty and the others how to sell an idea or situation to the fence-sitters, and then concentrate on the skeptics. The ones who could be brought over into friendly territory, after being convinced that they had come to conclusions based on their own research (but fed a steady diet of truth mixed with falsehood), would in many cases turn out to be the most rabid supporters of the engineered point of view. The fury of the truly converted is a powerful thing.

Seasoned AFOSI agents are usually told what to do only in broad outline, and as long as their mission is accomplished, most are given a good deal of latitude in how to go about it. Richard Doty relished the chance to play a cat-and-mouse power game with gullible UFO students and researchers. He has pointedly mentioned that some of his orders were "personally distasteful," but he carried them out as a good soldier. By his own admission, he met with Paul Bennewitz "many times" after his first visit to the Bennewitz home with Lew Miles. In time, Bennewitz came to consider Doty a friend and confidant. "I genuinely liked Paul, and we became good friends," Doty says. His feelings may have partially stemmed from a sense of pity and even guilt over the things Doty had to do to Bennewitz in order to keep him off-track regarding projects at Kirtland.

Years after his AFOSI involvement with saucer researchers, Doty's career reached an apotheosis of sorts when he was actually invited to become a consultant for *The X-Files*, a position he says he held from 1994 to 1996. In time, he also wrote the screenplay for an episode, "The Blessing Way," which aired on September 22, 1995, although producer Chris Carter received writing credit. Doty also appeared as an extra in two episodes: "Anasazi," which aired on May 19, 1995, and "Paper Clip," shown on September 29 of the same year. He tried to write another, but says that it was "killed" by a government agency that he was required to run everything past before turning any of it in for production. After the final season of the show, *X-Files* producer Chris Carter was reportedly spotted at the Los Angeles FBI shooting range, which makes one wonder who was courting whom.

"The way I see it, there are two levels to the UFO subject," Doty says. "The lower level is what the public and UFO research groups know, and the other is the one that only a few people know about—the real history of mankind's interaction with them." When pressed as to what this might be, he will only comment that he knows what is involved at that higher level, and that it is unlikely that anyone outside that circle will ever find out what it is. He insists that he was in position to know this history because he was assigned to reveal only what was needed to cover up sensitive projects, and that he was ushered into this cabal since he needed to convince others of a distorted version of events.

But how could he know that what he was told was the "real" story? Perhaps his view of the subject was controlled as well. Yet Doty says he saw enough to convince him of an ongoing contact between Earthlings (at least those in need-to-know positions) and whatever is in control of the UFOs. The rest of us will likely never know the whole story.

Many other retired military personnel have echoed these sentiments, and after hearing a few of these accounts, it is hard to resist the possibility that someone, somewhere, indeed knows of a real, ongoing contact between the human race and something that is not. Variously identified by such names as "The Advanced Theoretical Physics Working Group" and "The UFO Working Group," private associations of retired officers and intelligence types have been quietly looking into the matter for years. Many of these men are now working under the banner of the National Institute for Discovery Science (NIDS), a group that is extraordinarily well funded by tea bag and real estate magnate Robert Bigelow.

It begins to look like there may be a third level of understanding beyond the two in which Richard Doty believes.

chapter 12

RIDERS OF THE RADIOACTIVE SAGE

The problem with keeping things like this secret is that they are removed from the free market of ideas, and understanding proceeds at a much slower pace.

—WHITLEY STRIEBER, *MAJESTIC*

Meanwhile, back at the base, the AFOSI had its own problems. Out on a routine patrol near the Manzano complex just after midnight on August 9, 1980, three guards saw a bright light descend to the ground in Coyote Canyon in an area that is not visible to anyone outside the complex. The guards contacted Sandia Labs' security control, which sent one of their patrols out to the site. As one of the guards approached a security-alarmed nuclear storage bunker, he noticed a very bright light hovering motionless near the ground behind a building that was part of the facility. Taking a shotgun, the guard got out of his vehicle and walked toward the light source. He thought he was looking at a landed helicopter, and tried to radio back for help and advice, but found that his walkie-talkie had stopped working.

He crept closer to confront the intruder and realized that the light was actually a round, disc-shaped object hovering motionless just a few feet off the ground. Just as he was about to shout out a warning, the object shot straight up and was lost to view in seconds.

This was not the first or the last time that furtive lights were seen zipping about secure areas of Kirtland. Other documents from the Defense Intelligence Agency passed on to Moore in a ubiquitous manila envelope in February of 1982 and later released to other researchers under the Freedom of Information Act in 1983 described multiple events that also baffled Air Force investigators.

Now known collectively as the "Kirtland Documents," the pages consist in part of "Complaint Forms" filled out by Doty and his AFOSI superior, Maj. Thomas Cseh. They describe the aforementioned event and include a report from another security guard about an episode that had happened just a month after the first incident. On September 2, 1980 at about 11:30 P.M., three Air Force security policemen saw a bright light swoop overhead at high speed and stop suddenly over Coyote Canyon. It is difficult to convey the strangeness of this sort of movement, but it is often described by witnesses as appearing like the UFO is at the end of an invisible flashlight beam that is swept across a wide sweep of sky. The thing appeared to land and stayed on the ground for some time before leaving by (again) shooting straight up, just like the "disc" that had been seen in August. The documents refer to the bunkers in the area as storage for "HQ CR 44 material." "Headquarters Collection Requirement 44" refers (or referred) to nuclear weapons and their security.

Were these lights flying around the Manzano Weapons

Storage Complex on the nights that Paul Bennewitz had his 8-millimeter film and 35-millimeter cameras whirring and clicking away? He had told a few people that he had seen what looked like security patrols making their rounds while he was filming the lights and their dramatic nighttime dances. The guards seemed not to notice, almost as if they had expected to see these displays, or perhaps the lights were invisible to them from their vantage point far inside the base. He didn't know. Bennewitz's lights had been appearing since late 1979; the Coyote Canyon sightings (at least those that have come to public awareness) were confined to August and September of 1980.

Many years later, Gabe Valdez guessed (perhaps with hints from some of the right places) that many if not all of the UFOs Bennewitz had seen were likely unmanned surveillance platforms undergoing testing on the Kirtland property. Doty intimated that Valdez was on the right track, but claimed ignorance about the details. He also said that the lights were part of an NSA program for which he lacked the proper clearance.

But why fly such advanced and secret devices in the open where they could be seen by the greater portion of metropolitan Albuquerque? Perhaps this was part of the testing as well: Find out what people could see and what they said about it. If they were going to be flying over hostile towns and cities taking pictures, it was to the Air Force's (or perhaps the NSA's) advantage to see how the locals would react. If the whole thing could be swept under the rug as "UFOs," so much the better. Other residents saw the lights as well, but either reported them to the authorities, who were assured that the Air Force would look into it, or wrote it off as an exciting (if distant) UFO sighting. Confusion and ridicule is a valuable tool in the right hands (or wrong ones, depending on point of view).

Bennewitz had been filming the lights for over a year by that time, and anything that didn't move like a plane may have been seen as an alien craft. Many in the UFO community and others outside of it dismissed his claims when it seemed that Bennewitz was seeing things that weren't there, or had grossly exaggerated what his eyes told him. But for at least three nights, the Air Force had seen mysterious flying lights too, and they didn't know what to think this time.

The National Security Agency and the AFOSI didn't either, but they did know that the security of sensitive projects might have been breached, and sent out NSA and Special Investigation teams to conduct their own investigations. The AFOSI detachment was dispatched from the special, secretive PJ squad. The "PJ boys" were sent out when matters particular to the most sensitive installations and projects were concerned. Three agents from each organization showed up at Kirtland and stayed for a month, investigating and questioning the witnesses, taking measurements, and very possibly staking out the area for a few weeks to see if anything else would land when trained security agents were ready to meet them. Then, after filing their reports, they quietly left for whatever was next on their duty lists. Kirtland security heads later tried to find out what was in those reports, but they had disappeared as quickly and anonymously as the people who had written them. No more sightings on Kirtland real estate ever came to light, or at least there was no official acknowledgment of them. Is this because the investigation had somehow stopped the visits or their cause? No one has talked.

To add to the Air Force's headaches, there was another unexplained event they (and most likely the NSA/DIA as well) had to confront. On August 13, four days after the first Kirtland UFO sighting, every radar facility in the Albuquerque area had completely shut down at the same time, from 4:30 in the afternoon until 10:15 that night. Military, civilian—every single radar tower in the area was down, and the backup systems didn't kick in like they were supposed to. Like the old horror story of the babysitter getting threatening calls from inside the house, the Defense Nuclear Agency (who had jurisdiction of security over the area because of the nuclear materials stored there) called in to tell Kirtland that they had triangulated the signal, and the "hostile jamming" was actually coming from somewhere inside the base, near the Coyote Canyon area. Base police were sent out to search the remote canyons and arroyos, but found nothing. At 10:16 P.M., all radar suddenly went back to normal. Albuquerque Civilian Approach and Control independently verified this event from their logs about a month after it occurred.

In an Air Force "Complaint Form" later released under the Freedom of Information Act, an anonymous communication officer evaluated the jamming incident. Although no names show up on the released form, Richard Doty possibly reported it, as the typeface is consistent with other reports from Doty's typewriter. It concluded, in part:

> *The presence of hostile intelligence jamming cannot be ruled out. Although no evidence would suggest this, the method has been used in the past. Communication maintenance specialists could not explain how such interference could cause the radar equipment to become totally inoperative. Neither could they suggest the type or range of the interference signal. DNA [Defense Nuclear Agency] monitors reported the interference beam*

was widespread and a type unknown to their electron-ical [sic] equipment.

Sandia Labs said it wasn't anything they were testing, even though the center of the jamming signal was less than a mile from one of their groups of buildings, tucked safely in a small valley nearby. Much like the Manzano bunkers and roads, this facility doesn't show up well, or at all, on any aerial or satellite pictures. In fact, due to some sort of sophisticated and advanced optical camouflaging, the Coyote Canyon complex doesn't even show up in pictures taken from the road leading up to it. One black-and-white photograph of the lab buildings taken in the mid-1980s shows a large white blotch with a few major features visible where they should be. Aerial photos show an indistinct group of buildings that have either been deliberately painted out in released images or to which the same principle of photographic camouflage has been applied (see the photo insert).

The UFOs seemed to lose interest in the base at the end of the summer of 1980 and the mysterious radar jamming apparently never happened again. Paul Bennewitz didn't learn of these security breaches until years later. It was too little, and way too late.

chapter 13

THE SAUCERS SPEAK

eginning in early 1980, Bennewitz had become increasingly alarmed with what he was seeing, learning, and thinking, and had written hundreds of pages on the matter in letters to Jim Lorenzen at APRO. He urged Lorenzen to release his findings on the alien invasion "to all available investigators and other UFO organizations and News Services." He was now certain that the alien abductors were recruiting an army of totally mind-controlled humans, who were unwittingly gathering intelligence and waiting for the signal to lay down the red carpet for their masters.

I was unable to locate any replies from Lorenzen during my research, and Bennewitz apparently never shared them with anyone. (Or perhaps they are still locked away in a storage space in Tucson, jealously guarded for some strange rea-

son by a couple who had worked for APRO for a period near
the organization's demise.) Associates at the time recall that
Lorenzen's interest was piqued because he knew that Bennewitz was a trained scientist, and seemed to be zeroing in
on some sort of phenomenon that was making appearances
on a regular schedule, even if he didn't believe that Bennewitz had interpreted his sightings, pictures, and other data
quite objectively. As far as Lorenzen could tell, the signal was
almost lost amid the paranoid noise.

Even before the Hansen abduction, Bennewitz had described his research, which had been going on for eight
months, in a letter to Lorenzen dated April 8, 1980. He was
writing a book, and boasted that he was "beginning negotia-
tions as a start with Doubleday" to publish his story. He
promised to donate 5 percent of the proceeds (he did not say
whether it was net or gross) to APRO because he believed
that Lorenzen was "a prime instigator" in his investigations.
Any encouragement was probably a godsend to Bennewitz,
since most people wouldn't even listen to him past the first
few sentences, and he was learning about things that no one
else had ever heard about, much less guessed at. How can
you explain a thousand-mile journey to someone who hasn't
taken the first step?

The custom-built listening station now took up all of Bennewitz's home office and was starting to spill into the master
bedroom upstairs. He had been steadily modifying the
equipment to zero in on what he thought were the low-
frequency signatures of alien-piloted flying discs. The signals
were recorded twenty-four hours a day on a huge reel-to-reel
recorder. Bennewitz would zip through them looking for
messages, which he would inevitably begin to find.

His efforts were not without precedent in the history of

attempted communication with alien races. Nikola Tesla, the much-maligned genius and inventor who had immigrated to the United States near the turn of the twentieth century from his native Czechoslovakia, claimed that he had picked up communications from space while tinkering with his wireless setup. Tesla had demonstrated a radio-controlled boat in a pond in New York's Central Park in 1895 while the Italian Guglielmo Marconi was still struggling to send tinkerings across his laboratory. Tesla later went on to invent the alternating current (AC) system of power transmission, after demonstrating its superiority over Thomas Edison's system, and proving it to the satisfaction of pioneering power magnate George Westinghouse.

In 1956, UFO contactee George Hunt Williamson released *The Saucers Speak!*, a book that described what he said were successful efforts to communicate with the Space Brothers "by means of radio telegraphy." While he was living in Prescott, Arizona for about a year in the early fifties, Williamson had recruited railroad radio worker Lyman Streeter to receive and decode messages such as "HELLO RADIOMAN. ARE YOU SURPRISED MY BROTHER?" The historic communications were apparently accomplished through a modified system of Morse code.

Bennewitz was compiling thousands of pages of data, but it was electronic gobbledygook as far as he could tell. There were patterns trying to make themselves known, but they were all out of focus. His effective, homemade antenna array, listening in to the nightly stream of signals, was pointed right where he could see all those weird lights, dancing so maddeningly nearby. If he could make the connection between these two phenomena, those in the need-to-know loop would have to take notice, and more importantly, act on his findings. He wouldn't just be another babbling dork sending desperate letters to the president. Perhaps the deluge of data could be handled better by a computer.

In the early eighties, random access memory was measured in kilobytes and processor speed squeaked by in the double- or even single-digit hertz range. Bennewitz built many of his own computers and wrote the software as his needs changed. Now, instead of calculating circuit resistance or budget estimates for Thunder Scientific, he needed to figure out something that had never been seen by civilian eyes. He set himself to the task, and in a few months, he had the beginnings of a pattern. Like the British agents who cracked the German Enigma code in WWII, Bennewitz focused in on commonly repeated phrases and oft-used words like "and" and "the." Unlike the theoretical mathematicians commandeered by the Brits, Bennewitz would plug in other words like "UFO," "alien," "spaceship," and "abduction," and not so miraculously find a perfect fit. He later wrote that he had "established direct contact with the Alien using a computer and a form of Hex Decimal Code with Graphics and printout." Before long, he might even be talking to the UFOnauts themselves.

The expected alien progress reports on soil samples and the curious habits of Earthlings was not what came chattering from his dot-matrix printer. It read more like some science-fiction nightmare, and confirmed his worst fears, because it eerily echoed the abduction stories that had come tumbling out of Myrna Hansen when Len Stringfield had put her under hypnosis a few months earlier. He showed the results to Cseh and Doty. The AFOSI men realized that even this could be used to their advantage.

Astronomer J. Allen Hynek had been working for the U.S.

Air Force as a scientific consultant since the mid-1950s. After the close of Project Bluebook in 1969, he had reportedly continued to receive about $5000 a year to do little more than basically sit on his hands. Hynek was one of thousands of academics the government keeps on the payroll in case they might be needed—sort of like egghead sleeper agents. In the meantime, Hynek had founded the Center for UFO Studies (CUFOS)—one of the most respected organizations in the world for the scientific study of UFOs—and he steadily campaigned for its respectable status in the eyes of his peers. In the meantime, there are indications that he figured prominently in Paul Bennewitz's growing suspicions about the aliens.

The sole source for the following information is Bill Moore. Hynek died in 1986, and his associates either do not know about these allegations, or refuse to talk. All deny the story is true, or at least seriously doubt it. Moore claims that he met with Hynek at the 1982 Mutual UFO Network convention. Moore was there to answer an outreach request from MUFON to merge with APRO and form one organization. James and Coral Lorenzen were dead set against this, and Moore was serving as their proxy. During a particularly uninteresting presentation, Hynek suggested they take a walk to a bar down the street. On the way, Moore dropped off a roll of pictures that he had taken almost a year before in New Mexico. As they sat down, Moore brought up the subject of Bennewitz. They had a couple of beers, talked about it for a while, and then Hynek dropped the bomb: Sometime in the midsummer of 1981, he had delivered the computer program (and apparently a whole new computer) to Bennewitz at the request of the Air Force, but did not tell Bennewitz this when he delivered the setup. Since he still received a small stipend every year to do minor consulting work—as he had done in his Bluebook days—this was one of the last tasks he was asked to do. Moore was surprised, but not enough to have his world turned upside down.

The incident that threw him occurred the following day. As he walked into his hotel room, the phone rang: "So, how did the pictures turn out?" Moore thought that someone at the convention was playing a practical joke, but as far as he knew, he and Hynek were the only ones who had left to take a walk. After a few seconds, he realized that the voice at the other end of the line was Falcon, and he wanted to let Moore know that he was being watched—not every minute, but often enough so that if he was thinking of getting away with something (such as any sort of interaction with "unauthorized" people), he would need to think again. There was also the possibility that Hynek had been asked about their activities the day before, and had filed some kind of report. Or perhaps Hynek was simply told to tell the software delivery story to Moore and gauge his reaction.

Moore said that Bennewitz had told him the program had "been modified by the aliens themselves" to facilitate better communication with him. Did Hynek tell him this, or did the AFOSI suggest it? No one is willing to say. Perhaps the "aliens" (or whatever was on the other end of the signals) themselves helped to refine the communications while subtly steering Bennewitz just where they wanted him to go.

Curiously, in one of many letters to Jim Lorenzen, Bennewitz remarked: "A personal opinion—either Dr. Hynek is very blasé and likes walking into a 'fan' or he has been set up to do exactly what he is doing; having previously been set up with Gov't projects." He went on to say that poor Hynek was just another victim of the U.S. government, which "has also done precisely what the Alien wishes to be done." If Hynek did deliver the alien "decoding" program to Bennewitz, perhaps he accepted it warts and all because he thought that if the UFO pilots were willing to make a stab at communications through Hynek and the Air Force, it was at least worth a try.

With the assistance of one of his Thunder Scientific employees, Bennewitz had come up with the original program, but the delivery of the new system allowed him to start delving into the nitty-gritty of alien philosophy. For some reason he apparently never guessed that the program was devised solely for his use and his prejudices about what he was hearing and recording. If the old program produced a smattering of vague references to abductions and the like, a sample of the text coming out of the "AFOSI program" was downright crazy:

GROUND GROUND WOMEN OF EARTH ARE NEEDED FLEXIBLE THE NEXT DISCHARGES OUR SHIP ALL OY [sic] WOMEN DO NOT COMMAND THE NORTH AMONG US YOU HAVE MANY FRIENDS WATER VERY SHORT RESIST ALL ATTEMPTS AT ALTERATION LISTEN ORANGE MAKE PEACE

VICTORY OUR BASES OBTAIN SUPPLIES FROM THE STARSHIP METAL TIME IS YANKED TIME IS YANKED MESSAGE HIT STAR USING REJUVENATION METHODS GOT US IN TROUBLE SIX SKY WE REALIZE TELLING YOU ALL MIGHT HELP YOU

OUR BASES OBTAIN SUPPLIES FROM THE STARSHIP MILITARY OF U.S. DELIVERED EM-

BRYOS BY US USE GRAVITY CELL IN GOOD
WAY TO TRAVEL UNIVERSE NINE OUR COM-
MAND THE NORTH VICTOR GROW WOMEN
ARE NOT NEEDED IN OUR SOCIETY WE ARE
NOT UNITY—WE ARE SEPARATE

WE WOMEN DO NOT MARRY REALIZE WE
ARE NOT UNITY—WE ARE SEPARATE VIC-
TORY GROW WE HAVE NO OBLIGATION TO
KEEP SECRET NOW OXYGEN UJUMP [sic]
HAVE MANY ON OUR SIDE UNIVERSE WILL
CONTACT YOU IN UNIQUE WAY WATER IN-
TAKE WE WILL TELL YOU NOW LISTEN NINE
MANY HATE YOU BECAUSE YOU KNOW DIS-
TANCE IN KM IS WE CANNOT TELL MILITARY
OF THE U.S. MAKING HUMANOIDS REASON
FOR HATE IS YOU ARE GOOD—WE TRUST
YOU   TAKE   VAST   PORTION   UNIVERSE
AGAINST OUR AGGRESSION THE NUMBER OF
OUR CRASHED SAUCERS IS EIGHT NERVE
YOU WE REALIZE TELL THE TRUTH

JUMP JUMP OPPOSITE ALIEN FORCES
MEAN NO HELP TO YOU TMETAL [sic] WE
COME INVISIBLE KEEPING CHANGE WE
WILL NOT JOIN SIDES WITH ANYONE OUGHT
OUR RACE IS DYING ON THE HOME PLANET
MESSAGE

. . . and so on.

It appears that the program assigned words or phrases to
the pulses that Bennewitz was picking up and spit out something that had enough syntax to make a sort of sense if the
reader gives in to the human need to find patterns, meaning,

and order, and meaning is just what Paul Bennewitz wanted. Moore later said that the program "assigned entire words, sentence fragments, or sometimes even entire sentences themselves to the various individual pulses of energy within these transmissions." Paul Bennewitz came to rely heavily on this program to make sense of his data and the things he heard from his abduction regressions with Myrna Hansen. Unfortunately, almost all of the words spilling out of the computer were part of a quickly growing pile of pure, unadulterated dung.

chapter 14

THE SHADOW BASE

Public Affairs is the liaison between the military and the general public, ensuring that information concerning the base is available to internal and external audiences as deemed appropriate.

—**KIRTLAND AFB PUBLIC AFFAIRS OFFICE**

The low-frequency electromagnetic pulses being picked up and recorded by the antenna array and reel-to-reel machines at the Bennewitz home had always been of particular concern to the powers at Kirtland. One source of the transmissions, even though they could not be used for any sort of communication, might have been the huge electromagnetic pulse testing platform that was built to test aircraft vulnerability to EM pulses, such as those that would be encountered in enemy territory or during a nuclear blast, and there was such a device on the base. Due to its massive size, it was in plain view of the public.

When discussing the "Trestle," as it was called, "huge" is an understatement. It was and remains the largest wooden structure in the world. A C5A transport, which is considerably larger than a Boeing 747 passenger jet, can be rolled out onto the Trestle's platform. The fact that it holds this distinction is one of the reasons it is still standing, years after it was mothballed. Another cause of its staying power may be that it would just be too expensive to dismantle. Its silent hulk is located at the northern end of one of the Kirtland runways, and passenger jets on final approach to Albuquerque International fly about 300 feet right over it. Passengers sitting on the left side of the plane can see the Trestle in all its gargantuan glory. Engineers from Sandia used to have foot-thick solid wooden bolts and nuts from the structure in their offices as souvenirs. Metal parts of any kind would not only deflect the electromagnetic pulses, but might actually come loose and shoot out of the wood during tests, weakening the structure and endangering personnel and equipment. Everything from jet fighters to the largest transport planes were tested on it. One former Air Force physicist commented that the Trestle was basically useless because it couldn't generate even half of the electromagnetic energy expended in even a small nuclear detonation, but it still stands in the midst of other EMP testing facilities, surrounded by warning signs and lighted alarm towers. It is easily visible from a couple of miles away in the Four Hills neighborhood and from the porch of the Bennewitz home. Newer facilities used for EMP testing of airframes and other hardware apparently lie below the tangle of transmitters and antennas that dot the area underground and away from eyes and cameras.

The low-frequency pulses were ultimately not a topic of concern to the AFOSI—the Trestle was impossible to hide, and the Soviets knew what it was. If Bennewitz was picking up the tests on his equipment, there was nothing in the EMP pulses that would have concerned him either.

Kirtland Air Force Base actually consists of four facilities: Sandia and Phillips labs, the Manzano storage complex (run by the Atomic Energy Commission), and the base itself. Sandia and Phillips conduct weapons and defense research, Manzano stores (or once stored) nuclear weapons and components, and the base is currently home to the 377th Air Base Wing. During the mid-1980s, more than 160 different government agencies had active "addresses" at Kirkland, including a branch of the Office of Naval Intelligence—more than 500 miles from the nearest ocean. Paul Bennewitz lived less than a mile from the Manzano Mountains perimeter fence, and it was over this sensitive installation and others located behind it that he had trained his cameras.

From the west, the view presented to the public, the Manzano Mountains are scrub-covered hills topped by a few small radio towers. But in 1947, the Air Force and the newly created Atomic Energy Commission decided to take advantage of the mountains' location on the base property and initiated one of the most extensive underground building projects in history. On August 24 of that year, the *Denver Post* reported that "[The Army and Navy are jointly] building what people here believe to be the world's first underground atomic shelter and experimental laboratory in a nearby mountain range." The next day, the Portland *Oregonian* headline shouted "Mountain Caverns Dug For 'Super Defenses.'" The FBI was checking backgrounds and clearing new employees as fast as they could so that the workers needed for the massive digging operation could be shuttled out to the Manzano site. "Nine thousand workers on the job by October 15" was the figure being thrown around. But people cannot always be counted on to keep things quiet, and the open secret making rounds in beauty parlors and taverns around Albuquerque described a "large opening in the mountain rumored to be for housing of long-distance atom-bearing bombers." When the excavation was in full swing, the Manzanos "resembled an overgrown anthill" to commercial airline passengers landing at the municipal airport.

By October 21, Secretary of Defense James Forrestal sent a memo to the Chiefs of Staff for the Army, Navy, and Air Force, establishing the Armed Forces Special Weapons Project (AFSWP) to continue the work of the Manhattan Project. The *Oregonian* article named "Sandia Base" as the "principal field installation of the AFSWP." The operation was headed up by Gen. Leslie Groves, the man who had been in charge of the Manhattan Project, which had started with a huge and successfully secret project at Los Alamos, and ended with the dropping of two atomic bombs on Japan.

Underground bases have been the subject of rumor and speculation ever since 1947. The DOD and the private companies it contracts have learned their lesson in matters of secrecy during the construction phase, and other underground facilities have almost certainly been constructed throughout the continental United States since the late 1940s, though precious little has been seen or learned about them. In the meantime, tunneling and digging technology has continued to advance. Manzano was essentially hollowed out with shovels and dynamite, but the newest facilities may have been literally melted out of the Earth's crust with atomic-driven heating elements attached to thirty-foot diameter boring machines, for which patents exist dating from the mid-1970s. The rock left behind forms a vitreous-surfaced (glassy and smooth) tunnel, and the molten rock forced aside in the operation fills in any cracks or fissures that develop. This eliminates the need for conventional buttressing, and the tunnel is ready for a roadbed or rails, as well as lights, air circulation, and other necessities.

Manzano's reputation as a nuclear weapons storage facility, and possibly even a manufacturing center, raises red flags with regard to possible radiation problems in the air, ground, and water near Albuquerque. The Environmental Protection Agency maintains an ongoing project to test milk from dairy farms around the Nevada Test Site area for radiation. An EPA employee also routinely travels in these same areas to purchase livestock that are slaughtered and tested as well. In addition, the members of about forty families from this area of the country are brought in about twice a year to be examined.

Curiously, one released picture of the scanning device used on area residents looks suspiciously similar to some of the "alien" devices described by UFO abductees. The subject lies on a large, steeply reclining chair during the EPA procedure. Researcher Richard Sauder stated in his 1995 book *Underground Bases and Tunnels* that he had called the EPA office in Las Vegas and was told that there also "may have been" some monitoring of livestock that were possibly exposed to residual radiation from testing at Los Alamos National Laboratories northwest of Albuquerque. He was also told that this monitoring was conducted by the Lovelace Medical Center, which actually operated an animal research facility on the grounds of Kirtland Air Force Base, in addition to its existence as a legitimate hospital and medical research center. In the early 1980s, Lovelace also maintained a human medical facility a mile or so south of the nuclear storage area, where it conducted tests on terminally ill patients who had consented to experimental techniques.

Myrna Hansen was taken here for questioning at least three times after Bennewitz had told the Air Force of her plight. At Bennewitz's request, Doty arranged for Hansen to be X-rayed at the Lovelace center to locate the implant that Bennewitz was sure was embedded near the base of her skull along the spinal cord. The object did in fact show up on the ultrasensitive X-ray exposure, but Air Force doctors were satisfied that it was a natural growth and pursued it no further. During his meetings with Base Security and other intelligence personnel, Bennewitz told of the underground rooms and tunnels that Myrna Hansen visited during her abduction. Doty recalls that while under hypnosis with an Air Force psychologist, she described and drew one of the facilities at Manzano in great detail. "She even knew what the elevator looked like," he says. How she was able to do this was a priority concern to the intelligence detachments charged with security of this area.

There have been conspiracy discussions on the UFO grapevine and in books about the subject of "military abductions" for almost a decade, and the possibility that Hansen was inadvertently involved in some sort of experiment gone awry is remote but certainly not impossible. According to Ann Druffel, a longtime California researcher, many UFO abductions occur in an altered state of consciousness, and Hansen may have accidentally seen things as she "traveled" in this state. The fact that the Army's "remote viewing" program of psychic spying was in full swing at the time could have opened up this possibility to various need-to-know officers. The intelligence community knew that the Soviets had been deep into paranormal research for many years, and there was talk of a "psychic gap" in the United States. If anyone with the talent can look into your most sensitive installations seemingly at will, the purpose and effort expended in hiding these areas is for naught.

Over the last century, and especially from the 1960s onward, paranormal researchers have discovered that psychic sensitives are able in some way to bypass restraints of time and space that hinder most of us. The Army remote viewing program, which operated under such names as "Grill Flame" and "Stargate," lasted from the mid-1970s to the early '90s and fielded armed forces personnel and others who were put under contract to find lost planes, look into enemy installations, and locate captured personnel, among other tasks. Skeptics point out that the program was closed down after a study concluded that the psychic spies had found nothing of intelligence value. Why the Army wasted time and money for almost twenty years with something that didn't work is not addressed by this study or those who insist "It can't be, so it isn't." The fact is that a few of the psychics who worked in this program were able to successfully describe objects and facilities that were later confirmed through conventional intelligence channels.

Furthermore, anything with personal meaning for the psychic tends to be more accurate. For instance, one of the protocols developed by Drs. Russell Targ and Hal Puthoff in the early 1970s emphasized the importance of feedback to the experimental subject with regard to the information that they had "viewed." If a sensitive was provided with information on their accuracy after the fact, it tended to "close the loop." This is the way remote viewers transcended the normal flow of time. Training whatever sense was involved would often improve it for the subject of the experiment, sort of like exercising a muscle. In other words, "past" and more significantly, "future," became irrelevant. All information was more easily accessible to the viewer when some sort of information or event provided confirmation later. Myrna Hansen could have been an "accidental remote viewer" when in an altered state induced by her experience, whether by aliens or through other means more close to home. Unhooked from normal consciousness, she "knew" that she would later be questioned by the Air Force, and the fact that she was near such a secret installation could have caused her to lock on to it. Admittedly, this scenario is far-fetched, but Doty and his AFOSI associates couldn't come up with anything better. Eventually, they were satisfied that this was a one-time event, and that she hadn't been able to see or sense anything else of concern.

Part of the (dis)information leaked to Bennewitz, and later to other researchers, described a project to destroy alien underground bases with atomic weapons and penetrating "bunker buster"–type bombs. A statement sent out to UFO researchers in 1988 from William Cooper (who became one of the most notorious propagandists on the scene in the early 1990s with his "limo driver did it" theory of the JFK assassination) states that Project Excalibur was:

> *Established to develop a weapon which would destroy the alien underground base and any future underground bases which the aliens might construct. It is to be a missile capable of penetrating 1000 meters of tufa/hard packed soil such as that found in New Mexico with no operational damage. Missile apogee not to exceed 30,000 feet . . . Device will carry 1 megaton nuclear warhead. This project is ongoing at WX division, Los Alamos National Laboratory, New Mexico, and is still in development.*

There are presently hundreds of citations of this "anti-alien base" project available on the Internet. With a little extra information and perseverance, narrowing the search to "Excalibur X-ray laser nuclear" brings up a few references to something else. In the late 1970s and early '80s, before more extensive test ban treaties were in effect, Excalibur was the code name of a Dr. Edward Teller–initiated project to explode low-yield nuclear devices in hollowed-out underground cavities at the Nevada atomic test site. The huge release of energy in the X-ray spectrum was then directed along specially designed and excavated tunnels, which channeled the pulse to a device that produced an "X-ray laser" beam. X-ray lasers were being developed as a possible "directed energy" weapon under the Strategic Defense Initiative. After nuclear test bans took effect, scientists at Sandia and Lawrence Livermore labs discovered ways to increase the energy yield of lasers without having to rely on a nuclear explosion to start the reaction, and the original project died a quiet death. It was replaced by the "Brilliant Pebbles" program, which relied on a huge armada of small satellites that would wait around in orbit until an attack was launched and then go into action to actually ram incoming ballistic missiles at high velocity and presumably destroy them, or at least knock them off of their programmed kilter. The problem of radioactivity that might then rain down on the Earth and slowly poison all life was apparently preferable to ground or low-atmosphere detonation. Perhaps Brilliant Pebbles was an Ed "Dr. Strangelove" Teller idea as well.

In a letter dated December 13, 1987, John Lear, one of the speakers at the "alternate" 1989 Las Vegas MUFON convention (and then a compatriot of Cooper's), urgently warned of a project at the Nevada Test Site connected to the "alien war." Lear wrote that a UFO "control group" called MJ-12 (more about which later) had recently come to the conclusion that "there was no use in exciting the public with the 'horrible truth' [about the alien invasion] and the best plan was to continue the development of a weapon that could be used against the EBEs [Extraterrestrial Biological Entities] under the guise of 'SDI' . . . "which Lear believed had nothing whatever to do with a defense from Russian nuclear missiles. Lear continued, "As these words are being written, Dr. Teller . . . is in the tunnels of the Nevada Test Site driving his workers and associates in the words of one, 'like a man possessed.'"

A former Defense Department physicist stated that Teller may have been one of Bill Moore's "aviary" collection of contacts. "It would be just like Teller to tell those kind of wild stories," he said. "He really liked to lay it on thick sometimes."

Lear had been interviewing Bennewitz extensively for at least a year. Under later questioning on the "UFO Updates" Internet discussion group, he listed many of his sources as "C.I." or "Covert Intelligence." Were these the same spooks that had been whispering in Bennewitz's ear? Lear repeatedly refused comment on the exact origin of his government sources. "C.I." also works as an acronym for "CounterIntelligence," an allusion Lear could not escape. Lear claimed to be a former pilot with the CIA's notorious "Air America," which flew covert operations in Vietnam. Lear was certainly one of the most expert pilots around, and he had maintained contacts in the intelligence world, but his spook buddies may have had their own agendas, and Lear never seemed to consider this before making his announcements. He later appeared at UFO conventions with a hired cordon of burly bodyguards to emphasize that what he was revealing could get him killed. Many witnesses agreed that this was more comical than intimidating, but Lear seemed sincere in his fears.

The Excalibur ruse is one of the best examples of the kind of disinformation that was tested on Paul Bennewitz. To the surprise and most likely the delight of the originators, it eventually grew to mythical status in the UFO community. Since Excalibur was associated with missile and space defense, it was logical to hide it under the "Alien War" banner. A remark Falcon made about "bringing a few moles out of their holes" alluded to the fact that the Soviets and others knew full well that the UFO subject was used as a cover for defense projects, and KGB assets and agents in the United States clustered around these sorts of rumors. It has been intimated that another of the UFO researchers whom Moore named as being in contact with the intelligence world had also worked on the Excalibur project, possibly as a photographic consultant.

Curiously, in a lower corner of a 1972 map of Kirtland Air Force Base there is a lone track leading out to the southwest from the Manzano complex. It was christened with the name "Shock Tube Road." Perhaps this refers to a sort of pipe that is used to trigger a blast for mining, but in light of the Excalibur revelations, perhaps it is something more. Or not.

In the mid-1980s, Moore and his research associate Jaime Shandera asked one of their Air Force contacts if things could be hidden underground off the base, yet still be usable and accessible from entrances on Kirtland real estate. "Sure, it's possible," he said. "What you do is take the Tramway exit off the I-40 and follow it until it reaches the foothills of the Sandia Mountains. Take a left at the tramway turnoff. Go to the first right turn off the road. You follow that up the hill

until it dead ends and look for one of those temporary buildings like you find at a construction site. Take a look around
there . . . Oh yeah, there is a private plane parked nearby at
the Coronado airport. That's right near the Bien Mur Indian
Center, and there's a building behind there that's an entrance
to the same facility."

They followed the instructions, driving through a residen-
tial neighborhood until the private homes faded back into
the ubiquitous chaparral and they ended up at an artificially
leveled-off hillock tucked away in a small valley near the border of the Sandia National Forest. The temporary office
building was there, but the blinds were drawn and the doors
were locked. No signs on the property or lettering on the
trailer "office" identified the site in any way. The porch of
what appeared to be the lodge at a local country club could
be seen at the top of the next hill, so maybe someone had at
least seen some construction activity. Next to the trailer were
two huge concrete slabs that rose a few inches above the
level of the gravel. The slabs looked as if they had only recently been poured and smoothed over. Jutting out from
near the center of each were large steel or tin pipes with covers over them to keep the rain and snow out. Moore and his
friend felt a slight but steady stream of air escaping from
both of them. Something was down there. Something that
needed fresh air and wanted desperately to be anonymous as
possible. Extensive underground facilities are not only prob-
able, but highly likely, as we have seen. Was it connected to
Kirtland's complex under Manzano Mountain, or possibly to
the headquarters of Sandia Labs, about fifteen miles away?

Maybe it was nothing and they were being played with
just like Paul Bennewitz.

chapter 15

FLUSHING MOLES

Never attempt to win by force what [you] might otherwise
win by fraud.

—Niccolò Machiavelli, *The Prince*

The events and organizations that were called like moths
to the flame that Paul Bennewitz had lit were there to
make sure that whatever they were trying to protect
would never see the light of public truth. National security
was on the line, and all is fair in love and spooking. The people and situations that were starting to swirl around the
owner and founder of Thunder Scientific Labs were invisible
to him, and that's the way the NSA, DIA, and AFOSI liked it.
The men and women whose job it was to keep things buried
did not want the graves disturbed, or the underground tunnels leading to them breached.

During WWII, as in all wars, the Allies were desperate to
exploit anything that would slow down their enemies, costing
them money, time, and manpower. The British intelligence

service, with the assistance of the U.S. Office of Strategic Services (OSS—the precursor to the CIA), devised a plan to confuse the Germans in occupied Holland. They built and only partially completed a few copies of an intricate device that appeared to be a coding machine. The guts of the things had gears, springs, and analog readouts and did nothing except look important. They then had covert operatives plant these devices in places where the Nazis might find them. Legend has it that they never found out what had happened to the nonsensical gizmos, but if luck was with Allied intelligence, the Nazis would have wasted a good deal of time and effort poring over them, taking their attention away from more useful matters.

One of the intents of art is to communicate to others on a subconscious level. Many examples of spycraft sound like elaborate art projects, which on many levels they really are. One devious and masterful Cold War example unfolded in the 1970s: A certain Soviet KGB commissar was causing problems for the CIA, since he was just too good at his job. He had foiled all attempts to infiltrate his cell. He had ratted out moles, and ran a tight ship. From the standpoint of Western intelligence, he was untouchable. The chink in his armor therefore lay not with him, but with the concentric circles of agents and bureaucrats that surrounded his position. U.S. agents arranged to have a message delivered to him through a convoluted series of channels. The note was purposely passed through as many hands as possible to allow any number of suspicious paranoids to see what was contained in it. It never reached its intended target, since the anonymous communication contained a seemingly innocuous message that went something like, "The present is ready to be delivered. Meet at the candy store." When called before the committee, the commissar had no idea what was going on but could not defend himself against the suspicions aroused by the anonymous note. He was quickly replaced with someone more to the CIA's liking (i.e., dumber).

Exposés and spy novels are full of such episodes. Most UFO researchers never read these books, and like most of us, they will take anything on face value if it comes from someone in a position of authority, or even someone who claims to be.

Paul Bennewitz would come to trust at least some of the words of Richard Doty and other Air Force people who passed along important information vital to his research. He made the mistake of thinking that any of them would give up more than they were allowed. His Achilles' heel was his credulity, as long as whatever he was told or saw seemed to square up with what his theories and hunches were telling him. To be sure, he was an intelligent, even brilliant man, and usually knew when he was being misled, but his single-minded quest revealed a blind spot. As long as his questions kept him away from sensitive projects at Kirtland, or sent him on wild goose chases, the agencies that were monitoring his activities felt that their job protecting national security was well done.

If the Air Force, Sandia Labs and Phillips Labs, the Defense Intelligence Agency, and the National Security Agency didn't want any attention drawn to the base and their activities, then why were they encouraging Bennewitz to keep looking and make more noise? Wouldn't that draw more attention to the very things they were trying to hide? Moore asked Falcon these same questions. The magic trick involved misdirection of attention and more. Moore was told that the main objective was to draw curious eyes away from the center of activity while, as the Falcon put it, "bringing a few moles out of their holes." If Bennewitz and others shouted long and loud enough, the ones who the spooks were truly worried about would come calling, pretending to be innocently interested in UFOs while actually trying to gather as much information as they could on anything that was being developed at Kirtland and other bases around the country. Meanwhile, the UFO fanatics could be counted on to look for spacemen in flying saucers. The game had obviously ratcheted up a few notches since the 1950s.

When visitors came out to the Nevada test range to look for UFOs in the late 1980s and through the '90s, Naval Intelligence, base security, and the private guards hired from Wackenhut Corporation were not particularly worried about right-wingers and curious UFO-spotters. What they were assigned to look for were the thrill-seeking tourists who sat on a mountain overlooking Area 51 and had their cameras pointed at the facilities on the ground, instead of the things in the air, and seemed to have much more expensive equipment than the average foreign tourist generally carried around. This scenario has been repeated many times near other facilities where UFOs have a habit of appearing. The saga that unfolded in the late 1980s near Gulf Breeze, Florida, where civilians saw lights zipping about at night, just happened to be located near an air base. Rumors flew and pictures, some of which were almost certainly faked, were taken and published, first in the local paper, then as images for the UFO believers to drool over, and finally as a book published (with a hefty advance for the authors) by Avon Books. If the objects in Gulf Breeze remained unidentified by the military as well, then they were probably at least as worried as the Kirtland gang had been in 1980, although the objects seen may have been classified aerial tests, just like the ones out west.

Former Special Agent Walter Bosley was assigned to counterintelligence duties with two detachments of the AFOSI from 1994 to 1999. He says his office was proudest of the fact that for years, UFO stories (among others) were part of a program to keep various stealth technology projects under wraps, and usher any meddling inquiries behind the laughter curtain. Bosley's duties once required a visit to the joint McDonnell-Douglas/Air Force "Plant 19" in the Palmdale area north of Los Angeles to check into "physical security issues." One night, he happened to see a radar/visual test of an unusual airframe. From his point of view the thing, mounted on a huge pylon, didn't look anything like a traditional aircraft, and was actually hard to see at all. As Bosley put it, "It was similar to other airframes in that the radar return showed up as something about the size of a bird." From just a few hundred feet, the aircraft would have been completely invisible to radar, which is designed to pick up objects from hundreds of miles away.

Reports of strange lights, huge black triangular-shaped aircraft, and even the classic flying saucer have trickled out of this area of Southern California for years. As long as the UFO-watchers sat waiting for aliens, the Air Force and McDonnell-Douglas, Lockheed Martin, and other defense contractors in the area were happy. The AFOSI did everything they could to encourage this impression. Bosley also took a hard look at the UFO community: "I also initiated an investigation to look at hostile intelligence services and their use of unwitting U.S. citizens to collect info on defense technology. We went to a few UFO events around Southern California to check this kind of thing out." Bosley and his unit continued an AFOSI tradition that stretched back to the early 1950s.

Unidentified objects in the skies certainly show up with uncomfortable regularity near military installations, and as long as it's not "one of ours," the personnel who work at these facilities are very likely just as confused about them as anyone else. Intelligence and security jocks only seem concerned if the objects pose a threat to the operation of the base or any secret projects that are conducted therein. If not, they remain legitimate unidentifieds and are probably filed as a simple curiosity. No one outside of the inner loop at Kirtland or in the higher echelons of the National Security State in 1980 knew if the vertically shooting lights were ever really a threat to operations or secrecy, but Paul Bennewitz was starting to poke his antennas and cameras where they didn't belong. The need-to-know cabal had to stop him or steer him away from the test range, or the strange honey he thought he was making might attract the wrong kind of bees.

chapter 16

THE AGE OF AQUARIUS

By late 1980, communications from Paul Bennewitz were arriving almost weekly at the office of the private UFO research group, APRO. His theories were becoming more fantastic with each letter and phone call. Jim Lorenzen asked Moore if he could pay a visit to Bennewitz on his next trip to Albuquerque to try to determine what was worthy of interest. Lorenzen knew that Moore was talking to Defense Department insiders, and the subtext was that he might be able to figure out what was valuable to UFO research, and whether or not his organization was being set up to take an embarrassing fall. Falcon had also asked him to see Bennewitz as well, but for different reasons of course.

After a couple of meetings with Falcon and Richard Doty, Moore was actually invited onto the grounds of Kirtland AFB and into the offices of AFOSI on orders from Maj. Thomas Cseh. The AFOSI wanted to know what Moore knew about the UFO subject, so that they could begin using the information to misdirect other researchers—although Moore did not know this at the time.

On November 17, 1980, Moore drove onto the base and to the nondescript AFOSI office to meet with Richard Doty. The interview was finished and the two were shooting the bull about various other subjects when Doty called Moore over to a video screen, which displayed classified AFOSI communications before they were printed on the teletype. "Take a look at this," he said. Boldly headed with the word "SECRET," the message originated from AFOSI headquarters at Bolling Air Force Base in Washington, D.C. (although Doty recalls that the originating agency was the NSA). Moore did a double take at the contents. Even though the Air Force position was that it was still officially "out of the UFO investigation business," the glowing, flickering text described a detailed photo analysis of three still pictures and two short pieces of 8mm film. The photos and filmstrips were apparently obtained from Paul Bennewitz when Doty and Lew Miles had paid him a visit in late October. In one of his many letters written to other UFO researchers, Bennewitz said that some of the film he had sent in for professional processing had disappeared for a time, and that perhaps this was the film referred to in the report Moore saw. Near the end of the text was a reference to something called "Project Aquarius."

The teletype referenced itself as an answer to "REQUEST FOR PHOTO IMAGERY INTERPRETATION YOUR MSG 292030Z OCT 1980," meaning that on October 29, 1980 at 8:30 P.M., someone had received the photos and film Doty had picked up from Bennewitz. Someone at Kirtland had requested an analysis of the images. A detailed look at the document unravels some of the events that were swarming around the major players in the story.

The document in its pristine condition was only seen by Bill Moore in the offices of AFOSI, and once again in February of 1981, when he was handed a heavily edited and rewritten version of the message, and told that he was to give this copy to Paul Bennewitz. When he asked why the new version was riddled with changes, Falcon replied that it had to be "sanitized" to protect sensitive projects. It was the first time that he had been asked to lie to a fellow researcher. This sort of commitment to the deception bothered Moore, and he sat on the document for a few months, until he was gently warned that all operations were off unless he followed through.

Moore explained, "My understanding, although I never knew for sure, was that Bennewitz was expected to wave it to the press and others as proof of what he was saying about an alien invasion, at which point the document would be denounced as counterfeit and Bennewitz would be further discredited." He called Bennewitz and arranged to visit him at work sometime late in the summer of 1981.

"I went to his office at Thunder Scientific and told Paul that we needed to talk somewhere where we couldn't be overheard," said Moore. "He suggested that we go into one of his office supply closets." Following his covert operations training, but now using it to his own advantage, Moore picked up a radio, took it into the 5x8-foot room, plugged it in, and turned it up loud to foil any possible listening devices. He handed the Aquarius document to Bennewitz and waited for him to read it. "He started practically jumping up and down, saying that finally he had the proof that the Air Force was taking him seriously."

Plagued with pangs of conscience at how well the ruse was working, Moore moved closer and speaking inches from Bennewitz's ear, said, "Paul, you'd better be very careful what you do with this. Use it for your own research, but otherwise, just sit on it." The firmly planted subtext was that the people with the keys to the kingdom were winking at Bennewitz while they pretended to ignore him. It was a carefully planned and patiently executed butter-up. A detailed autopsy of the text laid the ground for events that followed.

There is a curious line near the top of the Aquarius document (among many in this one-page piece of careful deception) that reads "INFO 7602 AINTELG FT BELVOIR VA." Interpretation: INFOrmation contained in the teletype originated with the 7602nd Air INTELligence Group at Fort Belvoir in Virginia. The 7602nd was the AFOSI organization that (among other duties) handled UFO reports at the time. For reasons of security, many organizations in the Air Force change names and numbers every few years, and in October of 1981, the 7602nd was renamed the "Air Force Special Activities Center" (AFSAC). As part of their mission, the 7602nd received information on unidentifieds and analyzed it, and passed it on to other interested groups in the intelligence world. By 1983, their budget was just over $4 million, about 30 percent of which was earmarked to pay civilians. Some of these civilians almost certainly were members of public UFO groups like MUFON, CUFOS, and APRO, or were otherwise influential in the community. Moore reiterated that he was never paid, though rival researchers were certain that he was. The rest of AFSAC's money was likely set aside to pay companies or individuals for outsourced work that the Air Force couldn't do on its own due to restraints on time and equipment or lack of trained personnel.

The mystery writer of the "Aquarius" document listed each piece of film and the results of the 7602nd's detailed analysis:

A. NEGATIVE #1: DEPLICTING [sic] C-5A AIRCRAFT ON APPORACH [sic] AND STREAKING UNIDENTIFIED AERIAL OBJECT IN LOWER RIGHT PORTION OF FILM. FILM FOUND TO BE UNALTERED. SIZE DIFFERENTIAL WAS NOT CONSISTENT WITH SIZE OF AIRCRAFT. CONCLUSION: INCONCLUSIVE.

B. NEGATIVE #2: DEPLICTING [sic] CYLINDER SHAPED UNIDENTIFIED AERIAL OBJECT IN UPPER LEFT PORTION OF PHOTO. FILM FOUND TO BE UNALTERED. FILM SHOWED OBJECT TO BE CONSISTENT WITH FIELD DEPH [sic] AND CONSISTENT WITH RELATIVE SIZE OF FIXED OBJECTS. CONCLUSION: LEGITIMATE NEGATIVE OF UNIDENTIFIED AERIAL OBJECT. BOLTON-REINFELD METHOD DID NOT REVEAL VISIBLE MARKINGS ON OBJECT.

C. NEGATIVE #3: DEPLICTING [sic] IRREGULAR SHAPED UNIDENTIFIED AERIAL OBJECT IN SEVEN FRAMES OF 8MM FILM. BECAUSE OF THE SIZE AND APPARENT SPEED OF THE OBJECT, NO FURTHER CLASSIFICATION OR CONCLUSION COULD BE DRAWN. FILM SHOWN TO BE UNALTERED.

D. 34 INCHES OF 8MM FILM: DEPLICTING [*sic*] APPARENT COLORED OBJECT MOVING IN FRONT OF STILL CAMERA. FILM FOUND TO BE UNALTERED. SPECTOGRAPHY REVEALED COLORES [*sic*] TO BE BASIC PRISM FEATURES. DEPTH ANALYSIS REVEALED OBJECT TO BE WITHIN 152MM OF CAMERA. OBJECT WAS NOT CONSISTENT WITH RELATIVE SIZE OF FIXED OBJECTS OBSERVED FOR SEVERAL SECONDS IN FILM. CONCLUSION: INCONCLUSIVE.

E. ORIGINAL NEGATIVE DEPLICTING [*sic*] UNIDENTIFIED OBJECT. FILM FOUND TO BE UNALTERED. BECAUSE OF A LACK OF FIXED OBJECTS IN THE FILM, NO DEPTH ANALYSIS COULD BE PERFORMED. BOLTON-REINFELD METHOD REVEALED OBJECT TO BE SAUCER-SHAPED, APPROXIMATE DIAMETER 37 FEET. OBJECT CONTAINED A TRILATERAL INSIGNIA ON THE LOWER PORTION OF OBJECT.

Spelling errors notwithstanding, the recognition that this sort of attention was being paid to his painstaking research thrilled Bennewitz. This was to be the first official release of disinformation in the Bennewitz affair, even though he had been receiving misleading leads in person and by phone for many months. The text quoted above, though, is spotted with pristine examples of deception.

On careful study, many things in the document that appeared legitimate to the unquestioning mind were ultimately deceptive. There is no "Bolton-Reinfeld Method" to analyze photos, for example. The mention of a "trilateral insignia" in the last photo description was almost certainly put there to excite the far-right faction of the UFO crowd with ideas of the Trilateral Commission in cahoots with evil aliens. And later mention in the document of the "U.S. Coast and Geodetic Survey" as an interested party for UFO information is spurious, as the organization did not even exist at the time the teletype was first transmitted. As far as Moore could recall from his notes regarding the original copy, these details were not present on the original when he saw it.

After the retyped version of the Aquarius document was released to Moore, only three copies of it existed outside of the files of AFOSI. One was locked away in the Thunder Scientific safe, one copy was in Moore's files, and Moore took the last copy to a meeting in San Francisco in 1983. An associate of attorney and UFO document researcher Peter Gersten met with Moore to discuss his latest findings. Later that afternoon, Moore said his car was broken into and his briefcase stolen. It was the only thing missing from the car. The thief didn't appear to have rifled through the glove box or disturbed anything else in the car. Within four months, Moore claimed, the document "complete with the annotations I had penciled in it, turned up in the hands of none other than Peter Gersten himself." Gersten and Moore quarreled over this for years afterward.

Moore had seen the original, though, and with the detailed notes he'd taken, set to figuring out the additions and subtractions. The released page was not a teletype or even a copy of one. Someone in the AFOSI had retyped it, and the font matched one of the AFOSI typewriters exactly. First mystery solved.

The dates on the original and the later redacted/changed versions were the same, and matched very well with the events going on at the time. On October 29, the 7602nd/AFSAC HQ had received the photos for analysis. This was three days after the Doty/Lew Miles visit to Bennewitz's home. At some other time in the day on November 17, Richard Doty told Bennewitz that the Air Force Office of Special Investigations "would not become involved in the investigation of these objects." This was not specifically true, since anything they collected would be sent on to the boys at the 7602nd (and other appropriate people) for analysis and "investigation." In this way, Doty kept his cover while not actually lying to Bennewitz. Eventually, Bill Moore found out about this, and later commented that this may have been the reason that he was shown the original teletype: Falcon wanted him to know that the UFO subject was a legitimate topic of interest for the Defense Intelligence Agency and those who worked with and for them. Falcon also wanted to intimate to Moore (in an indirect way) that Bennewitz was being watched from high levels in the intelligence world.

Moore said that he had wanted to determine who else might have been receiving the same disinformation that he had been handed, and kept quiet about the additions, subtractions, and lies that he saw in the Aquarius document. UFO hounds later interpreted the tactic as further proof that Moore was either sticking his tongue out at them or worse, that he was keeping things from others as a disinformation tactic at the behest of his government masters.

Nine years later, in 1990, Moore would reveal some of the discrepancies and other spurious additions and deletions that had fellow researchers yelling and pointing fingers. Why should he be the only one who knew about the tributaries of the "Cosmic Watergate" (as they were beginning to refer to the cover-up)? The fact was that some of these other UFO bloodhounds were later fed other sorts of documents and information that purposely did not jibe with the things that were told to Bennewitz and Moore. Put this in the pot with some fevered egos, and the confusion that resulted was just the sort of smelly stew that high-level intelligence was trying to stir up.

Moore reasoned that if he had been contacted by another researcher or interested party who had a different or perhaps even more accurate edition of the document, he might have been able to trace who was being told what information, and piece together another small part of the puzzle. No one ever stepped forward, and other copies that surfaced afterward were no different from the one he had been told to give to Bennewitz.

The message concluded:

REF YOUR REQUEST FOR FURTHER INFOR-MATION REGARDING HQ CR 44. THE FOL-LOWING IS PROVIDED: CAPT GRACE OF 7602 AINTELG, INS CONTACTED AND RELATED THE FOLLOWING: . . . USAF NO LONGER PUB-LICLY ACTIVE IN UFO RESEARCH, HOWEVER USAF STILL HAS INTEREST IN ALL UFO SIHT-INGS [*sic*] OVER USAF INSTALLATION/TEST RANGES. SEVERAL OTHER GOVERNMENT AGENCIES, LEAD [*sic*] BY NASA, ACTIVELY IN-VESTIGATES LEGITIMATE SIGHTINGS THROUGH COVERT COVER . . . ONE SUCH COVER IS UFO REPORTING CENTER, US COAST AND GEODETIC SURVEY, ROCKVILLE,

MD 20852. NASA FILTERS RESULTS OF SIGHT-
INGS TO APPROPRIATE MILITARY DEPART-
MENTS WITH INTEREST IN THAT
PARTICULAR SIGHTING. THE OFFICIAL US
GOVERNMENT POLICY AND RESULTS OF
PROJECT AQUARIUS IS STILL CLASSIFIED TOP
SECRET WITH NO DISSEMINATION OUTSIDE
OFFICIAL INTELLIGENCE CHANNELS AND
WITH RESTRICTED ACCESS TO "MJ TWELVE."
CASE ON BENNEWITZ IS BEING MONITORED
BY NASA/INS, WHO REQUEST ALL FUTURE EV-
IDENCE BE FORWARDED TO THEM THRU
AFOSI/IVOE . . .   BECAUSE OF A CHANCE OF
PUBLIC EXPOSURE, NO KNOWLEDGEABLE
PERSONNEL WITH SPA [Special Purpose Access]
WILL BE PROVIDED. CONTINUE TO RECEIVE
ASSISTANCE FROM INDIVIDUALS MEN-
TIONED IN YOUR MESSAGE, MILES, FUGATE.
BECAUSE OF THE SENSITIVITY OF THIS CASE,
REQUEST THAT THEY BE THOROUGHLY DE-
BRIEFED AT REGULAR INTERVALS.

Here, near the bottom of this wordy message in late 1980,
was the very first time anyone had seen a reference to the
idea of a suspected government group called "MJ Twelve"
that controlled UFO information. Of course, no one suspected at the time the colossal role that this idea would play
in 1980s and '90s UFOlogy, and it eventually spread beyond
its confines to become a cultural mainstay.

According to the "mythos" that now surrounds this subject, there is a high-level group, close and answerable only to
the president, which since 1947 has fielded reports on all im-

portant and hard-to-explain UFO incidents. The group is (or was) known as MJ-12, and was called into existence in 1947 by President Harry Truman—at the time, the only man in the world who had his finger on the nuclear button, and the only one who has ever pushed it. One of MJ-12's first members was supposedly Adm. Roscoe Hillenkoetter, who Truman also tapped to run the National Intelligence Agency, which soon changed the "National" to "Central" and eventually used an obscure loophole in their charter to justify all sorts of meddling in foreign and domestic affairs. Allegedly, MJ-12 was formed to deal with the possible threat from flying saucers and their pilots. MJ-12's assignment was to create an official policy on how to spin the saucer stories to the public—foreign and domestic.

Although it has been almost conclusively proven beyond a reasonable doubt that a group by that name did exist in the time frame of the late 1940s and '50s, no one has yet completely shown that MJ-12 had anything to do with UFOs, though the debate rages to this day. The counterintelligence string-pullers had done their homework, and had used the name of an obscure but significant group as the grain of sand that started a landslide.

It is no wonder that there is a think tank based in Hollywood where spies and screenwriters exchange ideas and info that is useful to both. The writers undergo the usual background checks and if they wash, they are given the appropriate security clearances.

The reference to NASA caused more discussion and finger-pointing than almost anything else in the Aquarius document. It makes logical sense to an outsider that NASA would be interested in UFOs, but a look at the history of that agency reveals the logical caveat that officials were interested in unidentifieds only if they were seen outside the atmosphere. This is a good example of the disinformation technique of misdirection applied to the UFO community: The AFOSI trick had the effect of deflecting inquiries away from Kirtland and to an agency (NASA) who could plausibly and rightfully deny that they had any interest. It also annoyed NASA officials who had to field calls from pesky UFO researchers and assorted crazies.

Moore had taken extensive notes when he had seen the original teletype at AFOSI and at dinner with Falcon, but he waited until the early 1990s to reveal that the text actually referred to the National Security Agency (NSA), not NASA. The NSA had become a major player in the Bennewitz drama, especially since a signal intercept from the Soviet bloc had referred to him as a possible source of information, even if he was unaware of his role. His letters and public pronouncements of alien invasion had jibed with possible KGB interest in the supersecret Kirtland complex, and the case took on a new urgency, shifting the program into high gear.

UFO information and sightings appear to be controlled by a group of individuals in the government, and not any one agency, and although the monolithic "government" knows much about the subject, they don't appear to know everything. As one exasperated FBI man put it to writer Howard Blum, "Even the government doesn't know what it knows." Falcon was certainly one of the chief muckety-mucks at the Defense Intelligence Agency, and perhaps he hoped to learn more about the subject while doing his job of misdirecting attention away from sensitive matters. This sort of "double-edged sword" way of running intelligence operations is standard operating procedure in counterintelligence, and also serves the purpose of covering one's tracks by confusing any would-be counterspy types by laying tracks leading in multiple directions—exactly the sort of thing that was happening to Moore and Bennewitz.

As for Project Aquarius itself, very little of substance was forthcoming. In October 1982, another one of Moore's contacts (who may have also been a fellow UFO researcher) gave him a summary that pointed to the Naval Intelligence Support Center as one of the agencies dealing with something called Aquarius. One of their duties was the digital (computer) analysis and interpretation of photographs. Cryptically, the source also spoke of a "type of information channel which is not yet in existence but might be established in the near future."

The source didn't have the clearance needed to see the information, and it was all buried within the gaping maw of "Control Channel Baker," which was the code reference to "black" projects—defense-related R&D that even the U.S. Congress is not allowed to know about. These activities don't show up in the official government budget, and were enjoying a renaissance in the early 1980s due to the election of Ronald Reagan and his hawkish cowboy faction of advisers and the military-industrial crowd with whom they ran.

The extraordinary steps that Moore had taken to ensure that they were not overheard when he had first given the document to Bennewitz convinced him to take the hint and lock the document away in a safe at the lab. Bennewitz never referred to it in public, but the "Aquarius" document certainly had the desired effect of letting him know that regardless of their official noninterest in his project, there were those who were keeping an eye on his thinking and activities.

Yet another of Moore's contacts sent a mysterious letter

and attached note with regard to a "Project Aquarius" in October of 1984. In part, the text read:

CONTRACT # N00014-69-C-0446 ARPA ORDER #1459 AN INVESTIGATION INTO THE FEASIBILITY OF DEFENDING SURFACE VESSELS AGAINST LOW-FLYING THREATS: THREAT EVALUATION: AIRCRAFT; TARGET RECOGNITION; DOPPLER RADAR; DIRECTION FINDING; VELOCITY; AZIMUTH, ANGLE OF ATTACK; RADAR TRANSMITTERS; RADAR RECEIVERS; EARLY WARNING SYSTEMS; HIGH FREQUENCY COMPUTER PROGRAMS; ALGORITHMS; NUMERICAL ANALYSIS; PATTERN RECOGNITION; LOW ALTITUDE AERIAL TARGETS . . .

The message, which is largely undecipherable (at least to us uninitiated souls), also referred to a "Project Maybell," which ran from May or June of 1970. In the mid-1990s, Computer UFO Network members Chris Lambright and Dale Goudie hit pay dirt with a series of FOIA requests to the NSA. Their dogged pestering of the close-lipped agency on anything associated with the term "Aquarius" finally resulted in the release of documents with a few vague references to an "Over the Horizon Radar" (OHD) system that was under development in the early 1970s through the combined efforts of the Defense Advanced Research Projects Agency (DARPA) and the Office of Naval Research (ONR). The project was known as "Maybell" and used high-frequency radar to protect naval vessels from low-flying planes and weapons by bouncing the radar waves off of the ionosphere to detect threats before they appeared over the curvature of the Earth—which is limited to about twelve miles in the open sea—then the current limit of detection. The message Moore had received with its gumbo soup of acronyms and apparent bureaucratic non sequiturs started to make more sense, but it didn't have anything to do with unidentified flying objects.

The released "Aquarius" page and the original were both headed with a "subject case nr" (number): 8017D93-126. This was Paul Bennewitz's ID number in the AFOSI files.

chapter 17

TECHIE PLAYGROUND

When you have a climate that has to deny what's going on,
combined with exotic hardware and unlimited funding . . .
this virtually creates UFOs.

—DR. DEAN RADIN, FROM AN INTERVIEW IN
THE EXCLUDED MIDDLE, 1995

The half-truths in the Aquarius document were of course
balanced with facts that were essentially correct. If it
were all lies, most of the targeted audience would have
quickly trashed it. The last two sentences referred to "continuing assistance" from "Miles/Fugate." Lew Miles was an obvious contact, because of his interest in the UFO subject,
and his earlier connection with Project Bluebook, as well as
his position at the Air Force Test and Evaluation Center. The
"Fugate" referred to Robert Fugate, who was running the
Starfire Optical Range at Kirtland—a wonderfully interesting
place where smart boys got lots of money to build big toys.
Fugate still heads the facility. It was Bennewitz's proximity to
this installation, more so than the Manzano complex, that
makes a strong case for what exactly worried the Air Force.

In 1980, Dr. Robert Q. Fugate was on the roster at Sandia Labs, specializing in optical physics. He had been working for the Air Force since 1970 on various projects falling in his area of research and expertise, but he also had a deep interest in astronomy.

One of the largest telescopes in the world is located high in the Chilean mountains. The "Very Large Telescope" (VLT) array uses four 8-meter mirrors working in tandem to collect light from distant stars, so that by keeping the telescopes trained on the same object and combining their images with specialized software, the effect is like using one massive 32-meter mirror to collect light from the faintest objects in the sky. The array is so accurate and sensitive that its resolving power is almost as good as the Hubble Space Telescope—without the orbital maintenance problems. The VLT is located far from the nearest city not only to escape light pollution, but because the environment in the Chilean cordillera offers some of the calmest skies on Earth. Atmospheric turbulence is what causes stars to "twinkle," and makes for bad viewing and blurred pictures.

It was here that Fugate's interest in astronomy and his work on the Starfire Optical Range coincided. Fugate needed to somehow correct for the atmospheric turbulence that affected the deceptively misnamed Starfire range, so that it could locate and clearly and accurately track (or whatever else the Air Force and Defense Department wanted to do with or to them) things flying in orbit.

Fugate's team faced a formidable problem. Since they couldn't get above the atmosphere, they would have to create some sort of "lens" that could still focus through the eddies and currents of air rippling through twenty miles or more of air. What they finally hit upon was the idea of "adaptive optics." This theory was first proposed in a 1953 paper by Mount Palomar astronomer Horace Babcock, but the technology to build and control the system was not available until the late 1960s and early '70s. Adaptive optics uses a very thin, readily deformable, mirrored surface to "adapt" for inconsistencies in the atmosphere. The system resembles a standard reflecting telescope, except that the objective mirror is very thin and attached on its underside is a series of plungers. The plungers are in turn driven by a sophisticated mechanism controlled by a computer that looks at a data stream that represents the way upper atmospheric air currents are deforming the image of incoming stars (or objects in orbit). At a rate of hundreds of times per second, it then bends and deforms the mirror in just the right way to correct for the distortion. A good way to visualize this is to imagine looking at your reflection in a wavy pool of water: An Adaptive Optics System (AOS) could conceivably read the wave motion instantaneously and cancel out the distortions to render an image as perfect as if you were peering into a bathroom mirror.

The Chilean VLT facility uses adaptive optics that has its origins in the system invented in the late 1970s by Fugate and his team. "Dr. Fugate was one of the only true geniuses I have ever met," said Richard Doty. "He could figure out technical problems within a few hours that had stumped other scientists."

Another problem faced the Air Force observatory team, however. Most stars are not the best objects to read and calibrate atmospheric disturbances accurately. In addition, there are only a few stars that are bright enough to get a good target for the AOS. The space junk that the Air Force was interested in was much closer to home, and moving very quickly in a completely different direction than the background stars. So

Fugate (very possibly working with a group of physicists) hit on another "aha!" They came up with the idea of shooting a powerful laser into the atmosphere to create an "artificial star" that was easily controlled and didn't move (or at least moved in the way that they wished). By looking at how a laser beam was scattered by the currents of air, the focusing mechanism and computer software could bend the telescope mirror just as accurately as if it were using a star or planet to sight on, and the system was now self-contained and didn't have to rely on nature to provide the calibration source. The Air Force or NSA or whoever was using the AOS could set the laser to point right near the object they were tracking and move it along for a clear view of the satellite, spacecraft, or discarded cosmonaut's glove as long as it remained above the horizon. It was one of the newest toys in the spooks' playpen.

A publicly accessible Internet site for the Starfire range presents before and after pictures of a satellite imaged with the AOS. The image captioned "before" depicts a milky, lumpy blob. "After" presents a perfectly ordinary-looking picture of the "SeaSat" weather satellite that looks as if it were taken from about 20 feet away, propped up against a background of black velvet in a dark room. After a little cleaning up with the Air Force's version of Photoshop, one can almost read the serial number stamped into the hull. Realize that this is a picture of an object 20 to 50 feet across, traveling at about 20,000 miles per hour and at least 100 miles away, and the magnitude of the achievement can be fully appreciated (see the photo insert).

Sky and Telescope and other astronomical journals went gaga when this new idea was revealed recently. The concept is considered one of the newest advances in astronomy, even though Fugate and his team had it figured out over twenty years ago. Such is the nature of black projects—so advanced that the public and even sometimes most scientists don't hear about it until a decade or more after the fact. The AOS was necessarily a product of spytech, and is one of the more benign examples of trickle-down technology from the dark bank of black budget projects.

Fugate was asked to deliver a system that would also let them see and track orbiting objects during the day, when spy satellites took their best pictures. So the equipment at the Starfire range was also equipped with filters—sort of like giant sunglasses for the telescopes—so that objects could be seen during daylight. (Another possible method for tracking "objects of interest" would be to look for their image at wavelengths above and/or below the visible spectrum.) At noon, the Starfire scientists could look up to the heavens with their equipment and count stars or Iron Curtain satellites as if it were midnight.

Thus equipped, the Air Force, NSA, DIA, and whoever else needed the information were able to track deep space surveillance devices and other objects at any hour. The main problem was keeping this secret from the "evil empire," and Paul Bennewitz was pointing his instruments and at least one of his warning fingers right at this facility, even though he hadn't the slightest idea of what he was pointing at. The AFOSI didn't plan to clue him in, and in fact, began a campaign to get him pointing at something so weird, so nonsensical and even frightening, that it puzzled even the most jaded UFO watchers in Bennewitz's crowd. No one but the shadowy scriptwriters and a few others (including Bill Moore to some extent) realized the whole thing was planned from the start, but Paul Bennewitz was his own worst enemy. He had laid the groundwork so well all on his own that the Air Force needed only to give him a little shove to make him fall, and make sure that he kept on falling.

chapter 18

A SERIOUS PROBLEM

eginning sometime in early 1981, after his high-level meeting at Kirtland AFB in the fall of the previous year, and frustrated with Air Force inactivity in the face of his perception of the growing alien threat, Paul Bennewitz began writing to his senators, Pete Domenici and Harrison Schmitt. He described the lights, the signals, and his suspicion that an alien race was taking over control of the base and had even built an underground facility in the mountains above Dulce. He feared the situation was already out of hand. Perhaps a couple of high-visibility allies in Washington might get the ball rolling.

On December 2, 1981, Bennewitz wrote to President Reagan, describing his suspicions and fears, and urging the White House to act. A month later, a Col. G. J. Smith wrote

back from the Secretary of the Air Force's office on behalf of
Reagan with the stock answer that was sent to all UFO-
related letter-writers: "The Air Force investigation of
unidentified flying objects (UFOs) began in 1948 and was
known as Project Sign . . . Between 1948 and 1969, the Air
Force investigated 12,618 reported sightings. Only 701 of
these remain unexplained. The Air Force ended its UFO ex-
aminations in 1969 because no evidence could be found that
the sightings were a threat to national security or represented visits from outer space."

To Paul Bennewitz, this was patently ridiculous. He was
smack in the middle of what he saw as a very high-level investigation of an alien invasion, and the AFOSI was taking
his reports for evaluation. Various AFOSI agents were keeping in touch with him and listening to his stories (some of
which they had originally planted on him) and feigning interest as well as leading him further astray from anything having
to do with activities at Kirtland. Base security head Col.
Ernest Edwards was more than just an interested observer,
but his name rarely surfaces in connection to the Bennewitz
saga, which is probably what Edwards preferred. In letters to
other researchers, Bennewitz described being driven onto
the base by Edwards on more than one occasion. While he
may have been thinking that Edwards was trying to understand where to begin his search for aliens running around the
facility, Edwards was actually trying to determine what Bennewitz had seen, and where he had seen it. If it was a threat
to operations under his jurisdiction, Edwards had to figure
out just how to steer the attentions of the electrical physicist
to other places and other matters. It must have been a
strange give-and-take in Edwards's car as they puttered
around Kirtland:

"So, Paul, what did you see over in this direction?"

"The alien ships came up from over there and flew over the mountains that way. You'd better take a look behind that mountain for the entrance to their base."

"We have, but we haven't found anything yet . . . Where did you say those weird signals were coming from again?"

Bennewitz began to sense that someone was dragging his feet, and his Air Force "friends" were, if not lying to him, then at least they had their hands tied by someone farther up the chain of command. Domenici and Schmitt had at first taken his accusations semiseriously. Both men are now unable or unwilling to speak about the period. Perhaps they were finally told that Bennewitz was on to things that would "compromise national security" and endanger "sources and methods" –which was essentially what was happening.

By late spring of 1981, a few months after Bennewitz's November 10 high-level meeting at Kirtland Air Force Base and with little success in keeping him from writing to and calling Senators Schmitt and Domenici, the AFOSI decided that it was time to start drawing his attention away from the base.

There is an uncorroborated story that Schmitt had actually turned up unannounced at one of the main gates and demanded to be let on the premises to look into some of Bennewitz's allegations. The cattle mutilation problem was still on his mind, and Bennewitz had discussed it with the senator. Schmitt had no doubt also been disturbed by the mutilation reports that had continued to flood into his office for five years. Many of these accounts included details that were highly suspicious: Silent aircraft flying around at night, and biohazard equipment and radar chaff found near mutilation sites were only the tip of the iceberg. Schmitt wanted answers and looked to the Kirtland Air Force Base as one of the only places that could conceivably garner enough manpower and equipment to mount such sophisticated missions. Over his protests, he was detained at the Kirtland gate until Base Commander Brooksher could be summoned to tell him personally that even though he was a U.S. senator, he didn't actually have a "need to know" about the inner workings of the base. Sen. Barry Goldwater had encountered similar Air Force stonewalling a few years before when, under pressure from constituents, he had asked to see the supposed alien bodies and/or artifacts stored in the fabled "Hangar 18" at Wright-Patterson Air Force Base. Folklore holds that Goldwater got in and saw the bodies; Schmitt didn't even get past the gate.

The projects that Bennewitz was monitoring were literally right in front of him both at work and home, so the task of directing his attention away from them was difficult. The National Security Agency was also conducting research at the base, in plain view of the Four Hills neighborhood, as well as the nearby I-40 highway, but had managed to keep most of it under wraps until Paul Bennewitz had shown up, making waves and asking inconvenient questions. They were apparently forced to admit (at least to the AFOSI) that the mystery signals that Bennewitz was picking up and recording were part of one of their many projects on the base. They informed the AFOSI so that the Air Force wouldn't waste any more time investigating it. The NSA also used AFOSI identification when they visited Bennewitz at Thunder Scientific or at home. He was made to believe that the Air Force was the only group that cared to look at his data, but security at Kirtland (and other Air Force facilities) was divided between the organizations that had a presence on the base; essentially they policed their own projects.

Paul Bennewitz had very good reasons to believe the AFOSI was the only organization he needed to contact. Air Force Intelligence had been the "walking point" on the Bennewitz case since the beginning. Richard Doty, Ernest Edwards, and Thomas Cseh, as well as their kin in the NSA and CIA, had all been monitoring his phone calls, travel, mail, and visitors beginning in late 1980.

In a December 2, 1981 letter to a "Captain Harris, Asst. Chief of Staff" for Air Force Intelligence at the Pentagon, Bennewitz desperately described his dilemma and asked for help:

> Your request as to suggestions I may have to possibly provide an official answer to the present dilemma is attached in a very brief briefing report based upon the personally funded study I began in July of 1979 and what is known to date . . .
>
> As to the references—as indicated, I did, at the outset give two Flight Command Briefings here at Kirtland with all of Wing Command present at the Commander's invitation.
>
> Throughout this detailed analysis and study I have kept the data reasonably covert for obvious reasons. However[,] copies of this letter report along with other data has [sic] been distributed to key individuals in the event of my demise . . .
>
> To make it an official part of the record at this time, I feel it necessary to point out in summary that: 1) At the outset, I gave freely of information in the form of data and official Military Wing Command briefings because of a deep concern for the safety of my nation. 2) I liaisoned frequently with OSI again

freely giving data as it became available though I was
personally financing the investigation and related
costs. 3) Yet Air Force Intelligence chose to place me
under electronic and personal surveillance; in addi-
tion to phone taps on all lines, rather than come to me
directly and freely discuss the situation. 4) Let it
stand—that in spite of this previous and continuing
unjustifiable harassment, I am trying one last time
because of my total concern. . . .

Captain, we have a serious problem here.

Bennewitz had put his total trust in the AFOSI at Kirtland and had been led astray about almost everything nearly
from day one. He had been told so many stories that they
were starting to leak out of his research effort and into Washington. His reports and updates were "approved" by Edwards and Doty and unfortunately sent on to Air Intelligence
Headquarters and his state senators, who didn't know what
to make of them at first. As Granny always said, "When you
tell a lie, you have to tell two to cover it up." Kirtland Intelligence had told quite a pack of lies to Paul Bennewitz. No
records exist of official reactions to Bennewitz's revelations,
but a lot of patching up was needed to explain to officialdom
what this man was doing with the apparent sanction of the
Air Force. From Bennewitz's point of view, the cognitive dissonance of apparent approval and assistance on one hand,
and doors slammed in his face as well as impassioned letters
going unanswered on the other, were starting to take their
toll.

An alphabet soup of agencies were now all actively spying
on Bennewitz to see if his shenanigans had anything to do
with their projects, or if he was violating any national security

laws. The CIA and the Albuquerque office of the FBI were involved. The NSA set up shop in a temporarily vacant town house across the street, and Bennewitz would occasionally see a woman entering and leaving the place. He also said that he could see cameras and "sense their sweeps on my equipment."

One evening as he stood talking to Bill Moore in the parking lot at Thunder Scientific, a white van made an abrupt U-turn in front of them. As they watched, a curtain covering the back window was pulled aside and a camera was pointed at them. The van sped away, leaving the two men scratching their heads, and not a little nervous. Moore wrote down the license plate number. He later checked up on the Colorado-issued plates. The car was registered to a "Bernard T. Iz" on "Norad Street" in Colorado Springs. The close proximity of the NORAD facility accounted for the street name, but the truck was not actually registered to the North American Air Defense Command. No leads developed on the "Iz" name. It may have been another inside joke, like the "Mr. Huck" episode from the Weitzel letter.

Soon after, Moore was invited to the Bennewitz home for dinner. After he had been in the house for about a half hour, Paul's wife, Cindy, told him that he had left his headlights on and might drain the battery. He distinctly remembered locking up when he had gone inside, and in any case it was in the middle of a bright, sunny afternoon, so he hadn't used the lights. As he approached the car, he noticed that the interior light was on as well, even though the door was still locked. In fact, all four doors were still locked. He checked. Had someone gotten in to search for something—or was this just another way of letting him know he was still being watched? He never found out. All he could tell for certain was that the headlights hadn't been on very long, because when he put the back of his hand to the lenses, they were only warm, not hot.

Bennewitz asked him to come into the garage to take a look at his Lincoln Town Car. There was, he said, a "shiny area" in the paint over the distributor cap. Moore confirmed this, and looked on the underside of the hood to see if there was evidence of heat or sparking. Nothing. Another mystery.

Possibly the strangest thing to happen in the Bennewitz home was experienced not just by the family, but Moore and Doty as well. On yet another visit, Moore's attention was drawn to something bright near the ceiling of the "home lab." He was startled to see a pale orange or yellow "ball" about the size of a softball hovering in the corner. The glowing orb, which had a pale blue halo around it, "wobbled" ever so slightly, but otherwise stayed in place.

"Jesus, Paul, what's that?" Moore asked, pointing.

Surprisingly nonchalant, Bennewitz said, "Oh, you see them too. I haven't been able to figure out what they are, but they keep showing up."

The orb, which looked three-dimensional and self-illuminating, quickly "winked out like someone turning off an incandescent light. It was more like it faded out very quickly," says Moore. "It was transparent. You could see the corner where the wall met the ceiling behind it."

Others had noticed the orbs too. On one of his many trips out to the Bennewitz home to check up on things when the family was out (i.e., break-ins) Doty and two NSA operatives had disconnected the alarm system and were just about to start snooping around when they noticed one of the balls floating underneath a central stairway in the large entry room. "It was orange, and had 'sparkles' in it," said Doty. "I asked the other guys: 'Is it one of yours?'" But the NSA men were mystified as well, and the trio tried to see if the phenomenon was projected from outside of the house somewhere. No dice. "We never did figure out what that was," said Doty. Perhaps the NSA was in fact responsible, but if so, they never admitted this to anyone outside their circle.

According to Doty, the NSA "pretty much took over the Bennewitz investigation after a while." The CIA and FBI were interested because of the espionage angle, and even though Bennewitz was sharing everything he found with the Air Force, they still weren't sure what his motivations were.

The AFOSI had done its job so well that Bennewitz was seeing UFOs everywhere he looked. Once, after showing Moore the place in the master bedroom where he said "the aliens come through my wall every night" and the .45 pistol under his pillow, Bennewitz took him out onto the view deck and pointed out lights maneuvering over the "West Mesa" area of Albuquerque about eight miles away. "That's one of the places where the aliens abduct people every night," he said.

Moore nodded and asked Bennewitz how he could be so sure. Bennewitz handed him a pair of binoculars and told him to try an experiment. "Move them in circles and look at the lights. If they make trails and you can see a broken line in them instead of a smooth streak, that means the lights are running on AC. The aliens use AC current." Sure enough, he was right, but Moore remained unconvinced.

After leaving the house, he got on the Interstate, headed west, and made a beeline for the West Mesa. Almost as soon as he pulled up in a barren area off the road, a huge helicopter appeared overhead. Hanging underneath was a large array of white lights directed at the ground. The helicopter hovered right over his car, almost as if the pilot was surprised to find a civilian wandering around the area in the middle of the night. Moore covered his face as dust and tumbleweeds kicked up around him, then got back in the car. The next day, he called Kirtland AFB and asked if they had anything flying over the area the night before. "Yes, we have nighttime search and rescue training there almost every night." Moore later relayed this information to Bennewitz, but heard no more about it.

Other UFO researchers began to repeat the rumors of abductions in the area, but like Bennewitz, they apparently never checked up on it. Perhaps this was another one of the lies designed to subtly direct him away from Kirtland, "leaked" to him by one of his AFOSI buddies, or developed out of the bits of information he had picked up in the "alien transmissions" coming through his NSA/AFOSI-designed computer setup. More likely, Paul Bennewitz was beginning to see aliens everywhere. The counterintelligence plan was working—-almost too well.

chapter 19

PROJECT BETA

Strange Loop: A case of self-reference which affects (or even damages) the original item; information becomes more corrupted by self-reference and "noise" in a closed system. (Origin: mathematics/software design.)

—REFERENCED IN *GÖDEL-ESCHER-BACH* (1987)

BY DOUGLAS HOFSTADTER

The slow mystery that was unraveling before Paul Bennewitz's eyes and preconceived notions had taken full shape by the middle of 1981.

Two years after they had first met, Bennewitz had written to Gabe Valdez, convinced that he was just about to bring the whole government/alien conspiracy to a head and force some sort of official action.

> *Gabe——it would appear that we are almost at the end of this coverup. The Constitutional rights of the people encountered and of the ranchers who have lost millions in cattle nationally have been directly violated by a very bad initial unilateral decision [Bennewitz said he had uncovered a deal with the alien race, ex-*

*changing land for an underground base and permis-
sion to abduct humans in exchange for UFO technol-
ogy] possibly back in the early sixties and up through
1979.*

*If we are to retain our democracy and freedoms this
must be dealt with unequivocal cold action.*

*We are "at the wire" on this—I know you have had
to take my word on a lot of this which obviously makes
it difficult to relate to—however—please believe me—
I do not speculate and have backed myself up with
Colonel Edwards checking all photographic analysis
and data. This is so critical we cannot make mistakes
at this point.*

Bennewitz was now ready to present his magnum opus to
the world: his clarion call for action in the face of an imminent invasion and takeover. He had coined a term for this report: Project Beta. (There was no project "Alpha"——at least
Bennewitz never talked about it.)

Project Beta has since entered UFO legend, and many
permutations and offshoots of this text floated around the
grapevine for years afterward. By the end of 1981, Bennewitz had completed his "preliminary" report and sent it
out to APRO and other UFO notables. Subtitled "Summary
and Report of Status," the Project Beta report contained so
many fantastic revelations and extrapolations that few were
willing to accept it at the time.

Bennewitz started off with a description of his research
up until that time:

TWO YEARS CONTINUOUS RECORDED
ELECTRONIC SURVEILLANCE AND TRACK-

ING WITH D.F. [Direction Finding] 24 HR/DAY
DATA OF ALIEN SHIPS PLUS 6,000 FEET MO-
TION PICTURE OF SAME—DAYLIGHT AND
NIGHT.

These were, of course, the films, pictures, and recordings
he had shown to the Air Force. He had also taken many pictures of the goings-on at Gabe Valdez's beat near Dulce,
most of which were inconclusive, but a small percentage of
which showed strange, apparently structured objects flying
though the mountain passes. These, however, were too
blurred to convince anyone but Bennewitz and a few others
that there was something worth investigating.

On the other hand the

DETECTION AND DISASSEMBLY OF ALIEN
COMMUNICATION AND VIDEO CHANNELS—
BOTH LOCAL, EARTH, AND NEAR SPACE

had been flooding his antennas since late 1980. Of course, in
recent months, the counterintelligence crowd had taken
over. They were now feeding him just what he (and they)
wanted him to hear (and see):

CONSTANT RECEPTION OF VIDEO FROM
ALIEN SHIP AND UNDERGROUND BASE
VIEWSCREEN; TYPICAL ALIEN, HUMANOID
AND AT TIMES APPARENT HOMO SAPIEN.

Apparently, someone was beaming degraded video of
some of the wackiest scenery this side of 1950s schlock cin-
ema into Bennewitz's receiver setup. Gabe Valdez and others

Paul Bennewitz standing in front of his Cessna. This is one of the only known pictures of Bennewitz. He was very camera-shy.

This is the view that Paul Bennewitz had from his home of the Manzano Mountain facility. In the foreground is the Kirtland perimeter fence. The UFO activity Bennewitz observed and photographed for many nights occurred in the area between the hills and the fence. The base of the mountain is a little less than a mile away. (GREG BISHOP)

```
 SECRET
  *********
 *S.E.C.R.E.T*
  *********
```

17 NOV 1980

ST D-1
CC - 1

RTTEZYVW RUFLOJA9136
ZNY S E C R E T
GT
SECRET   FOR AFOSI ONLY
R 171130Z NOV 80
FM HQ AFOSI BOLLING AFB DC//IVOE
TO RUWTFBA AFOSI DIST 17 KIRTLAND AFB NM//BID
INFO 7602 AINTELG FT BELVOIR VA//INSR
SECRET   FOR AFOSI ONLY
REF: REQUEST FOR PHOTO IMAGERY INTERPRETATION YOUR MSG 292030Z OCT 80.
SUBJECT CASE NR: 8017D93-126   HQ CR 44
1. SUBJECT NEGATIVES/FILM WERE ANALYZED BY HQ IVT AND 7602 AINTELG/IT AND THE
FOLLOWING RESULTS WERE FOUND:
A. NEGATIVE #1: DEPICTING C-5A AIRCRAFT ON APPROACH AND STREAKING UNIDENTIFIED
AERIAL OBJECT IN LOWER RIGHT PORTION OF FILM. FILM FOUND TO BE UNALTERED. SIZE
DIFFERENTIAL WAS NOT CONSISTENT WITH SIZE OF AIRCRAFT. CONCLUSION: INCONCLUSIVE
B. NEGATIVE #2; DEPICTING CYLINDER SHAPED UNIDENTIFIED AERIAL OBJECT IN UPPER
LEFT PORTION OF PHOTO. FILM FOUND TO BE UNALTERED. FILM SHOWED OBJECT TO BE
CONSISTENT WITH FIELD DEPTH AND CONSISTENT WITH RELATIVE SIZE OF FIXED OBJECTS.
CONCLUSION: LEGITIMATE NEGATIVE OF UNIDENTIFIED AERIAL OBJECT. BOLTON/REINFELD
METHOD DID NOT REVEAL VISIBLE MARKINGS ON OBJECT.
C. NEGATIVE #3: DEPICTING IRREGULAR SHAPED UNIDENTIFIED AERIAL OBJECT IN
SEVEN FRAMES OF 8MM FILM. BECAUSE OF THE SIZE AND APPARENT SPEED OF OBJECT
NO FURTHER CLASSIFICATION OR CONCLUSION COULD BE DRAWN. FILM SHOWN TO BE
UNALTERED.
D. 34 INCHES OF 8MM FILM: DEPICTING APPARENT COLORED OBJECT MOVING IN FRONT
OF STILL CAMERA. FILM FOUND TO BE UNALTERED. SPECTROGRAPHY REVEALED COLORES TO
BE BASIC PRISM FEATURES. DEPTH ANALYSIS REVEALED OBJECT TO BE WITHIN 152MM OF
CAMERA. OBJECT WAS NOT CONSISTENT WITH RELATIVE SIZE OF FIXED OBJECTS OBSERVED
FOR SEVERAL SECONDS IN FILM. CONCLUSION: INCONCLUSIVE.
E. ORIGINAL NEGATIVE DEPICTING UNIDENTIFIED OBJECT. FILM FOUND TO BE UNALTERED.
BECAUSE OF A LACK OF FIXED OBJECTS IN THE FILM, NO DEPTH ANALYSIS COULD BE PERFORMED.
BOLTON, REINFELD METHOD REVEALED OBJECT TO BE SAUCER SHAPED, APPROXIMATE DIAMETER
37 FEET. OBJECT CONTAINED A TRILATERAL INSIGNIA ON THE LOWER PORTION OF OBJECT.
CONCLUSION: LEGITIMATE NEGATIVE OF UNIDENTIFIED AERIAL OBJECT.
2. REF YOUR REQUEST FOR FURTHER INFORMATION REGARDING HQ CR 44, THE FOLLOWING
IS PROVIDED: CAPT GRACE 7602 AINTELG, INS CONTACTED AND RELATED FOLLOWING: (S/WINTEL)
USAF NO LONGER PUBLICLY ACTIVE IN UFO RESEARCH, HOWEVER USAF STILL HAS INTEREST
IN ALL UFO SIGHTINGS OVER USAF INSTALLATION/TEST RANGES. SEVERAL OTHER GOVERNMENT
AGENCIES, LEAD BY NASA, ACTIVELY INVESTIGATES LEGITIMATE SIGHTINGS THROUGH COVERT
COVER. (S/WINTEL/FSA) ONE SUCH COVER IS UFO REPORTING CENTER, US COAST AND GEODETIC
SURVEY, ROCKVILLE, MD 20852. NASA FILTERS RESULTS OF SIGHTINGS TO APPROPRIATE
MILITARY DEPARTMENTS WITH INTEREST IN THAT PARTICULAR SIGHTING. THE OFFICIAL
US GOVERNMENT POLICY AND RESULTS OF PROJECT AQUARIUS IS STILL CLASSIFIED TOP SECRET
WITH NO DISSEMINATION OUTSIDE OFFICIAL INTELLIGENCE CHANNELS AND WITH RESTRICTED
ACCESS TO "MJ TWELVE". CASE ON BENNEWITZ IS BEING MONITORED BY NASA/INS, WHO
REQUEST ALL FUTURE EVIDENCE BE FORWARDED TO THEM THRU AFOSI/IVOE.
4. REF YOUR REQUEST FOR TECHNICAL ASSISTANCE. BECAUSE OF A CHANCE OF PUBLIC
DISCLOSURE, NO KNOWLEDGEABLE PERSONNEL WITH SPA WILL BE PROVIDED. CONTINUE TO RECEIVE
ASSISTANCE FROM INDIVIDUALS MENTIONED IN YOUR MESSAGE, MILLER, FUGATE. BECAUSE OF
THE SENSITIVITY OF CASE, REQUEST THEY BE THOROUGHLY DEBRIEFED AT REGULAR INTERVALS.
BTS
NNNS
DOWNGRADE 17NOV2020

```
 *********
 *S.E.C.R.E.T*
 *********

 SECRET
```

**The Aquarius document was shown to Bill Moore in November of 1980. By the summer
of 1981, he had shown this slightly edited version to Paul Bennewitz with the caveat:
"Paul, you'd better be very careful what you do with this. Use it for your own research,
but otherwise, just sit on it."**

Bill Moore in 1979, about the time he was researching and writing *The Philadelphia Experiment* and three years before he was first contacted by Air Force Intelligence.

his was the Sandia Labs facility hidden away near Coyote Canyon. While on a tour of irtland Air Force Base, Richard Doty told Bill Moore to take a picture of the area, hich is composed of a large group of buildings. The section at the middle right, which oks like a large snowdrift, is all that was left of the complex when the film was eveloped. Doty would not reveal how this photographic camouflage was achieved. ILL MOORE)

COMPLAINT FORM

ADMINISTRATIVE DATA

TITLE	DATE	TIME
KIRTLAND AFB, NM, 13 Aug 80, Possible Hostile Intelligence Intercept Incident, Frequency Jamming.	14 Aug 80	0730

PLACE

AFOSI District 17 BID, Kirtland AFB. NM

HOW RECEIVED

X	IN PERSON		TELEPHONICALLY		IN WRITING

SOURCE AND EVALUATION

1960th Communication Officer

RESIDENCE OR BUSINESS ADDRESS	PHONE
1960 COMMSq KAFB, NM	4-5098

CR_____ APPLIES

II   SUMMARY OF INFORMATION

REMARKS

1. On 13 Aug 80, 1960 COMMSq Maintenance Officer reported Radar Approach Control equipment and scanner radar inoperative due to high frequency jamming from an unknown cause. Total blackout of entire radar approach system to include Albuquerque Airport was in effect between 1630-2215hrs. Radar Approach Control back-up systems also were inoperative.

2. On 13 Aug 80, Defense Nuclear Agency Radio Frequency Monitors determined, by vector analysis, the interference was being sent from an area (V-90 degrees or due East) on DAF Map coordinates E-28.6. The area was located NW of Coyote Canyon Test area. It was first thought that Sandia Laboratory, which utilizes the test range was responsible. However, after a careful check, it was later determined that no tests were being conducted in the canyon area. Department of Energy, Air Force Weapons Laboratory and DNA were contacted but assured that their agencies were not responsible.

3. On 13 Aug 80, Base Security Police conducted a physical check of the area but because of the mountainous terrain, a thorough check could not be completed at that time. A later foot search failed to disclosed anything that could have caused the interference.

4. On 13 Aug 80, at 2216hrs., all radar equipment returned to normal operation without further incident.

5. CONCLUSION: The presence of hostile intelligence jamming cannot be ruled out. Although no evidence would suggest this, the method has been used in the past. Communication maintenance specialists cannot explain how such interference could cause the radar equipment to become totally inoperative. Neither could they suggest the type or range of the interference signal. DNA frequency monitors reported the interference beam was wide spread and a type unknown to their electronical equipment. Further checks of the area was being conducted by Technical Services, AFOSI.

6. High command interest item. Briefings requested IAW AFOSIR 124-4 be completed at HQ AFOSI/IVOE. HQ CR 44 and 51 items.

DATE FORWARDED HQ AFOSI

AFOSI FORM 66 ATTACHED   ☐ YES   ☐ NO

AFOSI form reporting the mysterious radar jamming incident, which occurred during the period of UFO activity at Kirtland Air Force Base.

Image from the Starfire Optical Range website showing effects of Adaptive Optics System (AOS) on imaging a satellite. A: Telescope image of satellite without AOS. B: With AOS. C: AOS photo after image processing.

Richard Doty—photo from 2000.

GROUND GROUND WOMEN OF EARTH ARE NEEDED FLEXIBLE THE NEW DISCHARGES OUR SHIP WILL
OY WOMEN DO NOT COMMAND THE NORTH AMONG US YOU HAVE MANY FRIENDS WATER VERY SHORT
T RESIST ALL ATTEMPTS AT ALTERATION LISTEN ORANGE MAKE PEACE
VICTORY OUR BASES OBTAIN SUPPLIES FROM THE STARSHIP METAL TIME IS YANKED TIME IS
YANKED MESSAGE HIT STAR USING REJUVINATION METHODS GOT US IN TROUBLE SIX SKY WE
REALIZE TELLING YOU ALL MIGHT HELP YOU
OUR BASES OBTAIN SUPPLIES FROM THE STARSHIP MILITARY OF U.S. DELIVERED EMBRYOS B
Y US USE GRAVITY CELL IN GOOD WAY TO TRAVEL UNIVERSE NINE OUR COMMAND IS NOT OF
HUMAN ORIGIN WE WILL WOMEN DO NOT COMMAND THE NORTH VICTOR GROW WOMEN ARE NOT N
EEDED IN OUR SOCIETY REALIZE WE ARE NOT UNITY-WE ARE SEPARATE
WE WOMEN DO NOT MARRY REALIZE WE ARE NOT UNITY-WE ARE SEPARATE VICTORY GROW HE H
AVE NO OBLIGATION TO KEEP SECRET NOW OXYGEN UJUMP HAVE MANY ON YOUR SIDE UNIVERS
E WILL CONTACT YOU IN UNIQUE WAY WATER INTAKE WE WILL TELL YOU--NOW LISTEN
NINE MANY HATE YOU BECAUSE KNOW DISTANCE IN KM IS WE CANNOT TELL MILITARY OF U.S
. MAKING HUMANOIDS REASON FOR HATE IS YOU ARE GOOD-WE TRUST YOU VAST PORTION UNI
VERSE AGAINST OUR AGRESSION THE NUMBER OF OUR CRASHED SAUCERS IS EIGHT NERVE YOU
WE REALIZE TELL THE TRUTH
JUMP JUMP OPPOSITE ALIEN FORCES MEAN NO HELP TO YOU THETAL WE COME INVISIBLE KEE
PING CHANGE WE WILL NOT JOIN SIDES WITH ANYONE OUGHT OUR RACE IS DYING ON THE HO
WE PLANET MESSAGE
FIND WE DO NOT DEAL WITH THE NORTH THEY DO INTEND HARM PULSE WEST WE ARE IN THE
PROCESS OF RETURN TO SPACE YOUR OBJECTIVE SHOULD BE HQUICKLY KNOWLEDGE IS NOT RE
ALLY GIVEN VICTIMS HELICOPTER BLOOD
WE DO NOT OBSERVE THE AGREEMENT AT ALL REMOVE OUR COMMAND ARE HUMANS GREAT SHIP
WILL LAND BEFORE ORDINARY WE WOMEN DO NOT APPROVE OF HUMANOIDS LIGHT THE NUMBER
OF US WAITING ON THE STARSHIP IS SCAR VERIFY. THERE WILL BE NO FREEDOM OF SPEECH
EXTERNAL THE TOAL # OF SHIPS ARE OUR BASES OBTAIN SUPPLIES FROM THE STARSHIP
USE US.THE UNIVERSE GOOD.& WE WILL RECIPROCATE SECRET UNIQUE WORD WILL IDENTIFY
GOOD WHEN TIME YOU WILL BE INFORMED OF ANY POSSIBLE DANGER SHIP [KEY IMPLANTED CO
NTACTS ARE IN RED] YOU ARE GOOD-WE TRUST YOU TO INCREASE OUR RACE KNOWLEDGE IS NO
T REALLY GIVEN VICTIMS LIKE JTHE NUMBER OF US WAITING ON THE STARSHIP IS
NEGATIVE KNOW WE ARE NOT FAIR IN JUDGEMENT VECTOR GOING LEFT NAVAJO RIVER THE AM
OUNT OF MILITARY ALTERED AT CENTER HERE WE DO NOT OBSERVE THE AGREEMENT AT ALL S
AY THOSE MALES IN NORTH BASES ARE STERILE EQUAL OXYGEN YOUR LIFE AND FREEDOM IS
IMPORTANT TO US
UNUSUAL KILLING VICTOR WE WOMEN DO NOT APPROVE OF HUMANOIDS KMANY SCIENTISTS ON
OUR STARSHIP OUR RACE IS DYING ON THE HOME PLANET OTHERS FROM THE UNIVERSE WILL
PROVIDE HELP TO YOU VALUE I AM HUMAN CANNOT REPRODUCE THE RACE NIGHT
ORANGE WOMEN ARE NOT NEEDED IN OUR SOCIETY JOULE WE HEAR BLACK UNIFORMS ALL INSI
GNIAS ARE FOR THE SAME OLD SBEAMS WILL BE REMOVED OUGHT WOMEN ARE NOT NEEDED IN
OUR SOCIETY DIRECT WE REALIZE TELLING YOU ALL MIGHT HELP YOU
[NINE NINE] NIGHT WATER VERY SHORT ORANGE [THE AMOUNT OF MILITARY ALTERED AT CENTER]
HERE] OVAL THE KEY=GOD OF THE UNIVERSE OUR KEEPER GWE ARE NOT DECEPTIVE WE HAVE
NO OBLIGATION TO KEEP SECRET NOW WOMEN DO NOT COMMAND THE NORTH
KVERIFY.COMMANDERS CAN ESCAPE PROGRAM EQUAL VOLTAGE VAST PORTION UNIVERSE AGAINS
T OUR AGRESSION VAST PORTION UNIVERSE AGAINST OUR AGRESSION CATTLE.ALTERING.LAND
,SHIP.ALL MILITARY AGREED GROW BEFORE GOOD GOOD VICTOR
NONE OF US ARE REALLY YOUR FRIENDS USING REJUVINATION METHODS GOT US IN TROUBLE
NEVER OUR COMMAND IS NOT OF HUMAN ORIGIN ORANGE COLOR OF UNIVERSE INSIGNIA-THOSE
GOOD-IS] MANY OF US READY TO QUIT FWATER KEY -- MUST BE CRACKED THEY AGREE THAT
ALTERATION IS CORRECT THEY AGREE THAT ALTERATION IS CORRECT VUNERABILITY OF THO
SE ALIENS HERE IS--
OPTICS LIFE GONE I AM IN EARTH YEARS IN AGE USED +HUMANS WHO ARE ALTERED ARE USEL
ESS WE HEAR BLACK UNIFORMS NONE OF US ARE CAPABLE OF REPRODUCING DO WANT TO HELP
YOU WE WOMEN DO NOT APPROVE OF HUMANOIDS SIX WOMEN DO NOT COMMAND THE NORTH RAT
ED GOOD
WE HEAR BLUE UNIFORMS WE DO NOT WE HAVE BEEN HERE - # IN EARTH YEARS IS- FINAL P
LAN OF MISSION IS FROM SHIPS KEPT METAL METAL KNOW WE HAVE BEEN HERE - # IN EART
H YEARS IS- KEY POWER OF UNIVERSE WITHIN THE SOURCE
TIME:2408 HRS--MESSAGE--MY FRIENDS YOU HAVE BEEN VERY GOOD TO ME AND I
AM PLEASED--I WILL BE JUST AS GOOD TO YOU--I FEEL YOU HAVE BEEN HERE
AT LEAST TO DATE ABOUT THREE DECADES--THIRTY YEARS--YOU PREVIOUS TRIPS
COULD HAVE BEEN SEVERAL HUNDRED YEARS--OF COURSE I CAN ONLY GUESS BECAUSE
YOU HAVE NOT TOLD ME--I AM DROPPING BACK ON LINE FOR ONE LAST STATEMENT
FROM YOU THEN WILL PULL OFF LINE FOR TONIGHT--STANDBY*****

CHANGE NONE OF US ARE CAPABLE OF REPRODUCING VERSATILE BRAVE IN NORTH-VOTE TO RE
VOLT. US GREEN NOW I WILL HELP YOU AT THE RISK OF MY LIFE I AM IN EARTH YEARS IN
AGE VECTOR WESII WE HEAR BLACK UNIFORMS WOMEN ARE NOT NEEDED IN OUR SOCIETY

**An example of the mysterious signals picked up by Paul Bennewitz
and decoded with a computer program that was written by either Air
Force Intelligence or the NSA. The symbols at left were added by
Bennewitz as a key to notes that have been lost.**

Official State Police photo of Gabe Valdez ca. mid-1980s.

Thunder Scientific, the company founded by Paul Bennewitz, is located a few hundred feet from this sign. It is near the Kirtland Air Force Base entrance gate on Wyoming Avenue. (GREG BISHOP)

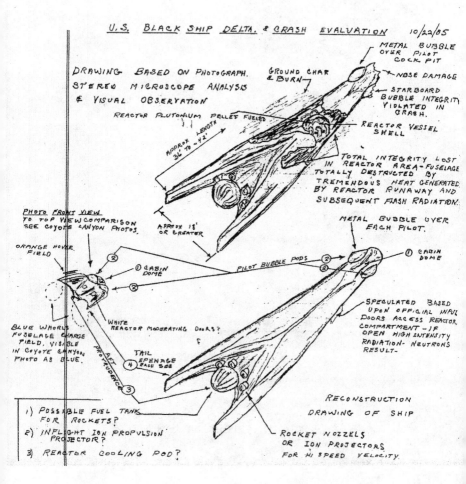

Drawing and commentary by Bennewitz from October 22, 1985. He had flown over the Archuleta Mesa and seen what was very likely the crashed remains of an experimental F-117 Stealth Fighter. Bennewitz assumed (and was encouraged to believe) that the mystery aircraft was built with secret alien technology and shot down by the aliens to "teach us a lesson." Photos he had taken from his plane which showed anything clearly were either willingly turned over to the Air Force or secretly confiscated. He resorted to the drawings to show others what he had seen. Precious few were convinced.

saw these images and were puzzled by what might be happening, but Bennewitz soldiered on.

A CASE HISTORY OF AN ENCOUNTER VICTIM IN NEW MEXICO WHICH LEAD [*sic*] TO THE COMMUNICATIONS LINK AND DISCOVERY THAT APPARENTLY ALL ENCOUNTER VICTIMS HAVE DELIBERATE ALIEN IMPLANTS ALONG WITH OBVIOUS ACCOMPANYING SCARS. THE VICTIM'S IMPLANTS WERE VERIFIED BY X-RAY AND CAT SCAN. FIVE OTHER SCAR CASES WERE VERIFIED.

This obviously referred to Myrna Hansen's ordeal. Bennewitz had also apparently located more UFO abductees and had begun a study of "implants." He was alerting other UFO researchers to the dangers he had discovered.

THROUGH THE ALIEN COMMUNICATION LOOP, THE TRUE UNDERGROUND BASE LOCATION WAS DIVULGED BY THE ALIEN AND PRECISELY PIN-POINTED.

This was just what the AFOSI and NSA had ordered (literally), and they would soon begin a campaign to urge him on in this direction.

SUBSEQUENT AERIAL AND GROUND PHOTOGRAPHS REVEALED LANDING PYLONS, SHIPS ON THE GROUND—ENTRANCES, BEAM WEAPONS AND APPARENT LAUNCH PORTS—ALONG WITH ALIENS ON THE

GROUND IN ELECTROSTATICALLY SUP-
PORTED VEHICLES; CHARGING BEAM
WEAPONS ALSO APPARENTLY ELECTRO-
STATIC.

Bennewitz had been flying his own reconnaissance out to
the Dulce area and taking aerial photos of the Archuleta
Mesa. He was developing these pictures in his home photo
lab and showing them to the Air Force. If any of these photos showed something recognizable, they were apparently
confiscated by AFOSI, either by simply asking for them or by
replacing the pictures with blanks or substitutes when they
broke into his home and lab. Due to this frustrating situation,
no one who saw the "sanitized" pictures ever saw what Bennewitz claimed to see in them, despite his extensive diagrams
and labels.

But with conditioning by repetition and sometimes not-
so-gentle prodding from the intelligence community, Bennewitz's science fiction story came to be accepted over time,
mostly by UFO buffs and those who thrive on scary rumors
that are filled with just enough substance to make them even
remotely possible. The fallout from this period is still with us,
and constantly appears in books, comics, movies, talk shows,
and other cultural ephemera. The idea was to keep one hand
running the alien puppet show while the other one went
about its black budget business.

From this mélange of disinformation, Project Beta took
shape.

Bennewitz was racking up the visits to Dulce and his
friend Gabe Valdez was still showing him areas where cattle
were found almost weekly, mutilated and rotting in the pastures. Valdez also told Bennewitz about almost nightly sight-

ings of strange lights skirting the mountains above the small town. Everyone there had seen them at least once. Bennewitz and Valdez took many nighttime trips in the Highway Patrol cruiser along bumpy back roads to try to find and follow these enigmatic lights. Valdez even showed him the local "spook light," a faint bluish glow that hovered over an abandoned graveyard. Valdez had the power shut off in Dulce one night to see if the phenomenon was simply reflected light from somewhere in town. He discovered it wasn't, and then promptly caught hell from outraged residents who were watching a championship fight at the same time. Bill Moore recalls seeing this light with Valdez one night as well, and recalled that when they attempted to approach it, it simply went out.

When Bennewitz returned to Albuquerque, he told his Air Force contacts—Richard Doty, Tom Cseh, and Ernest Edwards—about his trips out to Dulce and his suspicions that the "alien base" he had learned about in Myrna Hansen's hypnotic regressions was probably located there. This was the best news that they had heard in months, since it meant that Bennewitz's attention was starting to turn away from Kirtland. They began to devise a far-reaching plan that would keep him looking permanently at this little hamlet near the Colorado border, and away from the beehive of activity at Kirtland, which shows a placid face to the casual observer, but is in actuality one of the most secretive places in the country.

chapter 20

THE SHIT

Keeping secrets is a habit. It is the way officials—spies, generals, and scientists—are taught to behave. Because some explanations are not simple. All is never explained. Because now that we are at the end of a politics of global conflict, as men and states abandon their allegiances to failed ideological gods, all that is left for a great nation to protect and believe in is its tattered secrets.

—Howard Blum, *Out There*

What was all the fuss about? How did a man who was so worried about alien invasion become such a concern to the Air Force and their secret tenants at Kirtland? Paul Bennewitz must have been on to something mighty important to warrant all this attention. The simple fact is that he was, but aliens and UFOs had very little, if anything, to do with it.

It's worth repeating that Kirtland Air Force Base was, at the time, home to the largest storage area of nuclear weapons components in the Western world. Sandia Labs and Phillips Labs were working on some of the most sensitive and advanced defense projects in the country, and the NSA honeycombed the area with its projects as well. The NSA was running at least two projects from the Starfire range and another facility that have only recently come to light. All were apparently worth compromising Paul Bennewitz's stability and sanity to keep under wraps.

Project Sigma, which UFO watchers have for years ascribed to a "program to communicate with the aliens," was headquartered in a small underground bunker beneath a little hill behind the Manzano Mountains. While the AFOSI was thinking about just how much they could reveal to Bill Moore, perhaps grooming him for other projects, he was given a limited tour of the facility. He recalled "a lot of computers and other gadgets around the walls," but unfortunately not anything that would hint at the true purpose of the place. "We went in through an entrance that you could drive a truck through, and after the door closed, the floor dropped down a level before you came into this living-room-sized area with a few technicians running things." So perhaps they actually were communicating with aliens or at least talking with something or someone, but as we have seen with the "Excalibur" story, the project was not complete fiction.

The view from the road leading up to the facility offered scant few clues to its purpose. A small tower with a warning light and electric klaxon stood off to the side, and a parabolic dish pointed straight up from the apex of the approximately 50- to 80-foot-high hill. It is possible that the project had something to do with the NSA communications tests that were going on at the time, which was one of the things that really worried the NSA about Paul Bennewitz.

When Richard Doty and Lew Miles had visited the Bennewitz "home lab," Doty had taken surreptitious pictures of the equipment at the request of the NSA. Based on these images, within a few months, the agency had arranged for their agents to pay a few more visits to the Four Hills area to ask Bennewitz more questions about his "alien signals." Then they visited him when no one was home to check on things privately. Doty recalls that Dr. Fugate (of the Starfire/Adaptive Optics facility) was once smuggled into the residence to have a look at a device that Bennewitz had cobbled together to measure magnetic fields across a range of frequencies. He was probably using it to detect magnetic fields that he thought surrounded the UFOs he was watching. "Dr. Fugate was really excited to be doing this cloak-and-dagger stuff," Doty recalls. Fugate looked at the device and marveled at its design. The government scientists hadn't yet figured out the secret to this sort of measurement device, but Bennewitz had pulled it off with no more than a few thousand dollars and his advanced scientific know-how. Fugate studied it just long enough to see what made it tick, and took the secret back to his colleagues at the Air Force Weapons Lab, who eventually back-engineered a better version that didn't heat up and shut itself down, which was one of the problems that plagued Bennewitz's model. How the Air Force eventually employed this device remains a mystery.

After a few more visits by qualified scientists, the NSA also discovered that Bennewitz's "alien signal" reception setup was picking up something important, but it wasn't beamed from any alien scout ships. Bennewitz was receiving and decoding one of their newest systems for the encryption of multiple signals on a single carrier wave, which was still undergoing testing at Kirtland. Bennewitz and an unnamed assistant at Thunder Scientific had devised a reception setup that not only pulled in the compressed signal, but was able to crudely decompress its components and make a decent stab at decoding the messages contained within them. When the NSA experts got a good look at this gadget, they were once again shocked that a man with little more than a master's degree in physics had taken a few months and perhaps a few thousand dollars to tear a gaping hole in their multimillion-dollar electronic house of cards. Techies "in the know" informed Doty that Bennewitz "was really a genius at figuring things out." But the NSA waited a few months to tell the AFOSI about it. The "cult of intelligence" only rarely opens its doors, even to allies.

It was around this time that the NSA had decided not only to keep a close eye on Bennewitz, but actually encouraged him (possibly at his first Kirtland command briefing) to apply for a grant for research. He got the $75,000 grant (probably thinking that it had something to do with a hush-hush UFO project) and for its part, the NSA got two things: his trust (because he was essentially one of their employees) and his expertise in electronics. The fringe benefit of this unique situation was that they could keep an eye on him as they encouraged his cooperation in keeping his mouth shut about what the NSA didn't want him to discuss, while simultaneously goading him into believing and broadcasting misleading information about aliens and flying saucers. This was the reason Bennewitz believed so many (but by no means all) of the things that the AFOSI (and the NSA agents working under cover of the AFOSI) were telling him about what was going on and where to look. The situation was perfect and airtight.

But to make things just a little more airtight, the AFOSI had embarked on a massive disinformation campaign that supported and encouraged Paul Bennewitz's interest in the Dulce area, and specifically the Archuleta Mesa that dominated the landscape. Gabe Valdez and others had seen all sorts of weird lights flying around this area at night for almost four years, lights that moved with an eerie precision over the ridges and peaks on and near the mesa. No one had ever caught up with these lights or seen them up close. Because of abductee Myrna Hansen's insistence that she had been in an underground facility in the mountains somewhere, Bennewitz was convinced (with some Air Force encouragement, no doubt) that two and two added up to Dulce. The calf mutilation and dissection that Hansen had witnessed only fueled the fire. Friendly assets at APRO continued to forward Bennewitz's latest private briefings to the AFOSI just to make sure he was on the "right track."

While the Air Force was busy pointing Paul Bennewitz's nose some 200 miles northwest, they were also busy improving small dirt roads in remote areas above Dulce, and airlifting mothballed equipment up to the Archuleta Mesa by night. They placed old storage tanks, equipment shacks, and engineless jeeps in clearings next to the primitive roads. A small area was cleared for helicopter landings. Doty also claims that fake air vents were positioned around the mountain, sticking up out of the ground to drive the "underground base" point home. Valdez vehemently denies ever seeing anything like this. The ubiquitous Fugate was also asked to come up with a method for projecting "flying saucer"–like shapes on clouds in the area. "He came up with this system using a rotating lens which we mounted on searchlights. There were generators buried in underground rooms for power, and the whole thing ran on automatic, so we didn't have to keep people stationed up there," says Doty. If true, this may be the source of later rumors of underground noises that curious hikers and "alien base" hunters claimed to have heard on (or rather in) the mountain. Valdez also denies having ever seen any of this apparatus: "I logged a lot of nighttime surveillance hours up there, and I didn't see any searchlights."

A setup like this is not without precedent. In the 1920s, an eccentric but brilliant British inventor named Grindell Matthews wowed crowds on both sides of the Atlantic by throwing his name and whimsical pictures onto clouds with a projection device whose secret he jealously guarded. He also invented a sort of "death ray," but was unable to convince the British military that it was reliable enough to pay up. Matthews never claimed to be in radio communication with aliens, which considering Tesla's revelations and Bennewitz's NSA contract, may actually have helped his cause.

Kirtland AFOSI also rang up Fort Carson Army Base in southern Colorado and inquired if they still conducted training missions in the Dulce area. No, they said, but they wouldn't mind cranking it up again. The Army was given further encouragement by an Air Force offer to cover at least some of the cost of these extra training exercises by filling out expense vouchers. Faced with this unexpected gravy train, the Army infantry and the elite Delta Force detachment that used the area needed little encouragement. To sweeten the pot, AFOSI also told them that the ruse was part of a counterespionage project against the Russians (which in a sense it was, as we shall see).

Late in 1981, Doty invited Bennewitz to board a "Huey"-type helicopter for a private tour of the Archuleta Mesa. They flew him out of Kirtland and, talking over the noise of the engine through their wired crash helmets, Doty carefully pointed out the almost impossibly inaccessible (by ground) areas where the Air Force "props" had been planted, telling Bennewitz that these were places of concern and that he might want to ask his alien radio buddies what was going on.

"He was pretty impressed with all the attention," recalled Doty. Bennewitz made two more Air Force–sponsored flights out to the mesa (on at least one occasion accompanied by Colonel Edwards) and began to point out things on his own. The charade was entering a new phase.

At one point in the proceedings, Valdez was helping to co-ordinate a local (Albuquerque) news crew reconnaissance of the area for a documentary that had hired Bennewitz as a consultant. Serendipitously enough for the AFOSI, the Delta Force was conducting one of their free-for-alls up on the Archuleta Mesa that day. As the news helicopter was hovering about over the pines, Bennewitz pointing out areas of interest, three huge Blackhawk helicopters screamed over a ridge and buzzed the terrified passengers. Thinking that they were under some sort of attack or harassment, they quickly retreated and landed back at the local airport, with the Army in "hot pursuit."

The Delta Force set down a few hundred feet away and disgorged a few of their black-clad personnel while Army tank trucks rolled out to refuel them. Still shaken and dubious about approaching the menacing group, Bennewitz and the news people asked Valdez if he knew what was going on. Unnerved but undaunted, Valdez approached the open door of the nearest helicopter. One of the officers shouted that Valdez was out of his jurisdiction, but the single-minded Valdez jumped aboard to take a close-up look at the identifying patches on one of the uniforms before he was threatened with more than a verbal warning and backed off. Recalling the incident, Valdez said, "This was my jurisdiction, dammit, and I wanted to see who was invading my town and scaring people." The AFOSI also asked the Army to fly low over farmhouses and pastures to drive home the point—special forces were in the area and something was going on up on Archuleta. Hotshot pilots were only too happy to comply. The country is so rugged and remote that even if anyone wanted to drive the rough, primitive road up to the mesa, it would have taken them over an hour—more than enough time for the Army to hightail it out. The Air Force's 12th Special Forces Unit based at Kirtland was also tasked to blanket the mountains around Dulce with the same sort of official-looking charade from time to time, even though at the Air Force's invitation, Valdez had actually called this very same unit out on more than one occasion to assist in search and rescue missions. "They were happy to help, had the equipment, and were really good at it," he recalls.

In a commissioned August 1990 report on the continuing cattle mutilations presented to Senator Domenici, rancher and cattle mutilation victim Manuel Gomez's son Raymond wrote of an expedition to a ranch on the Colorado side of the border opposite the Dulce area and the Archuleta Mesa. The civilian investigators found locked, olive-drab storage buildings and other evidence of armed forces activity, as well as a manicured gravel road leading south toward the mesa. Gomez checked into the property records of the formerly private ranch and found that "ownership was traced to numerous, small private companies and changed from year to year."

This method of hiding ownership when black budget projects are involved is standard procedure. During the first Bush administration, the CIA and other intelligence organizations were given carte blanche to hide operations behind shell companies when surveilling U.S. citizens in matters concerning national security—a very wide net indeed—and contrary to the tenets of their original charter, which forbade domestic operations. The NSA, however, was never subject to any such strictures.

Northeastern New Mexico is no stranger to abstruse government projects. On December 10, 1967, the Department of Energy detonated a 29-kiloton atomic bomb 4,227 feet underground at a location about 35 miles southeast of Dulce in the Carson National Forest. The object of this remnant of the "Atoms for Peace" program was to release trapped pockets of gas for the El Paso Natural Gas Company to sell to eager consumers. It was a great success, but the released gas was so radioactive that it couldn't be used. Why this scenario was unforeseen is a mystery. Perhaps boys with a lot of money just wanted to blow more things up and were running out of excuses. The site is now marked with a simple plaque that warns visitors:

NO EXCAVATION, DRILLING, AND/OR RE-MOVAL OF MATERIALS TO A TRUE VERTI-CAL DEPTH OF 1500 FEET IS PERMITTED WITHIN A RADIUS OF 100 FEET OF THIS SURFACE LOCATION. NOR ANY SIMILAR EX-CAVATION, DRILLING, AND/OR REMOVAL OF SUBSURFACE MATERIALS BETWEEN THE TRUE VERTICAL DEPTH OF 1500 FEET TO 4500 FEET IS PERMITTED WITHIN A 600 FOOT RADIUS . . . WITHOUT U.S. GOVERN-MENT PERMISSION.

The fact that radioactive tritium has been detected in groundwater near Jicarilla Apache well sites may be another reason the government would prefer visitors to think of Dulce as the site of an alien base and not as an area where (as at least one study found) the incidence of cancer is one of the highest in the state.

The text of the final version of Bennewitz's "Project Beta" contains references to some sort of weapon that Bennewitz had developed, or was planning to develop and build in the Thunder Scientific workshop to be used in case of an alien attack on the Dulce base. He refused to discuss the nature of the device "because of the known capability of the alien 'by use of scanning beams to know in advance details of planning.'"

Like the radio and video links that Bennewitz had been using to "communicate" with the aliens, plans for cosmic warfare are also not without precedent in the history of weird science. In his 1957 book, *Contact with Space,* maverick psychologist/scientist Wilhelm Reich toyed with the idea that he might have been one of the first members of "a new race on Earth bred by men from outer space in embraces with Earth women . . ."

Reich had begun to mull this sort of scenario around due to the appearance of mysterious lights over the hills surrounding his laboratory outside of Rangeley, Maine. Curious, he began to point an "atmospheric divergence" device he had invented at the objects, and found to his surprise that the floating lights would fade and eventually wink out. The "Cloudbuster," which he had been using to create changes in the weather, and even rainstorms (confirmed by a local paper and many years later through replication by other researchers), was quickly redubbed the "Spacegun" and Reich contacted the Air Force to tell them about his discovery and its possible use to repel alien spacecraft.

In an uncanny prequel to Bennewitz's later dealings with

the Air Force, representatives from Reich's laboratory eventually briefed Air Force representatives and a mysterious civilian who was "working with the Air Force in regard to the history of UFOs." The meeting was held on October 15, 1954 at Wright-Patterson Air Force Base (where else?) in Ohio.

The reaction was polite but noncommittal, and Reich later made a trek to Tucson, Arizona to try to bring rain to the desert. He remarked that military jets were often seen flying over his camp when the "Spacegun" was in use. In an interesting coda to Reich's experience, New York–based UFO researcher Peter Robbins stated in his 1997 book *Left at East Gate* that his Air Force contact, Larry Warren, had seen a group of devices that bore a striking resemblance to the Cloudbuster/Spacegun sitting on the flight line at an Air Force base in southern England sometime in the mid-to-late 1980s.

Bennewitz had also built a "spacegun," which he described in the text of *Project Beta* as a "beam weapon" that he had designed and built at Thunder Scientific. Like Reich, he claimed that he could shoot down alien ships at will: "The range of my weapon exceeds that of their present weapons and in its most sophisticated form can be readily computer controlled to allow extremely rapid tracking and lock-on regardless of speed along with electronic wobbulation [!] of the beam."

Regardless of his skills at evading flying saucer "wobbulations," Reich was not perceived as a threat to the Air Force or national security. His UFOs were seen over his property in Rangeley, Maine, and in the Arizona desert. Since neither location was near any military base, the Air Force had little reason to be concerned with his research. His troubles came to a head when agents of the Food and Drug Administration paid a visit to his laboratory to dismantle some of his equipment and confiscate many of his books, which were later consigned to an incinerator in New York City. Reich was later convicted of transporting unapproved medical devices across state lines and died in a federal prison—in spite of the fact that he never charged for his services unless clients were satisfied with the results.

With his antennas, recordings, pictures, films, and penchant for publicity, Paul Bennewitz represented a clear and present threat to national security.

chapter 21

THE CRAFT

While the newly invigorated Bennewitz was busy talking to the aliens and flying his own reconnaissance missions over Dulce, the Air Force and the NSA carried on with business as usual. They had gotten tired of having to explain (or explain away) the lights that still hovered around Kirtland, so they apparently moved their base of operations elsewhere. Valdez later ventured his opinion that what Bennewitz was tracking and filming over the Manzanos were "surveillance drones."

The subject would become public in the early 1990s, when *Popular Mechanics,* in a move designed to "sex up" their coverage and increase readership, featured a cover image of the ultimate in "techno porno": a drone craft developed by a Navy-contracted firm in San Diego that looked exactly like a disc-shaped UFO. The thing flew with a powerful, ducted fan assembly and could hover fairly quietly over cities and neighborhoods. A remote operator could control the craft from a safe distance many miles away. It featured still and video imaging equipment to send intelligence back from behind enemy lines and assist in urban campaigns. In all likelihood, the craft was intended to fly at night, since any enemy personnel who could spot this whirring thing floating over their camp would immediately try to shoot it down—which would have been a fairly easy thing to do. Recall that the unknown thing with the orange light that Gabe Valdez and his fellow officers had encountered near Dulce sounded like a "small lawnmower motor."

The Navy spy craft did have a psychological edge on the competition, due to the fact that those on the ground might at first give in to the "shock and awe" of sighting what looked at first glance like a bona fide flying saucer, giving the remote operator a window of opportunity to steer clear of danger. Technology of this type is usually at least a decade behind the cutting edge when the public finally hears about it. Richard Doty (and others in the military) have described craft from at least the 1960s that appeared to fly on some sort of antigravity principle.

A scientific briefing of sorts from the British "Gravity Research Group" entitled "Electrogravitics Systems," obtained by Bill Moore from the technical library at Wright-Patterson Air Force Base in 1986, describes the state of the art in antigravity research in 1956. Paul La Violette, in a 1993 article entitled "The U.S. Antigravity Squadron," references it as well. A portion of this document is worth quoting at length:

At least it is known, proof positive, that motion, using surprisingly low k [electrical capacitor charge] is possible. The fantastic control that again is feasible, has not yet been demonstrated, but there is no reason to suppose that the arithmetic is faulty, especially as it has already led to a quite brisk example of actual propulsion. That first movement was indeed an historic occasion, reminiscent of the first day at Chicago when the first pile went critical, and the phenomena was scarcely less weird. It is difficult to imagine just where a well-organized examination into long term gravitics prospects would end. Though a circular platform is electrostatically convenient, it does not necessarily follow that the requirements of control by differential charges would be the same. Perhaps the strangest part of this whole chapter is how the public managed to foresee the concept, though not of course the theoretical principles that gave rise to it, before physical tests confirmed that the mathematics was right. It is interesting also that there is no point of contact between the conventional science of aviation and the New: it is a radical offshoot with no common principles. Aerodynamics, structures, heat engines, flapping controls, and all the rest of aviation is part of what might be called the Wright Brothers era—even the mach 2.5 thermal barrier piercers are still Wright Brothers concepts, in the sense that they fly and they stall, and they run out of fuel after a short while, and they defy the Earth's pull for a short while. Thus this century will be divided into two parts—almost to the day. The first half belonged to the Wright Brothers who foresaw nearly all the basic issues in which gravity was the bitter foe. In part of the second half, gravity will be the great provider. Electrical energy, rather

irrelevant for propulsion in the first half becomes a
kind of catalyst to motion in the second half of the cen-
tury.

If this document is to be taken seriously, with all its scientific jargon and pronouncements that gravity had been con-
quered by the mid-1950s, many UFO sightings (especially
the ones around military bases) are not nearly so surprising.
If the Western powers (specifically the United States and
Britain) knew how to virtually create flying saucers at will,
perhaps at least some of the "secret" that intelligence services are so desperately trying to keep under wraps lies not in
the stars, but in ourselves.

Richard Doty recalled that a "blue discharge" was seen
underneath the antigravity craft he claimed to have seen out
at Area 51 in 1969. In the early 1990s, Bennewitz told researcher Chris Lambright that he had observed a "bright
bluish colored glow" along the lower edges of the disc-
shaped lights he saw flying around Kirtland. The vast majority of UFO sighting reports do not contain this detail. The
blue glow may be a clue that man-made electrogravitic systems were being tested at Kirtland in early 1980.

On December 29, 1980, three people were driving
through a sparsely populated area northeast of Houston,
Texas, when they saw something that would alter their lives
and health forever. Vickie Landrum was driving her friend
Betty Cash and her seven-year-old grandson Colby home
from dinner when they encountered a flying diamond-
shaped object that looked to be about the size of a water
tower tank. It was floating over the treetops and belched a
giant plume of fire every time it came near the ground. Cash
stopped the car about 130 feet from the thing and got out to

take a look. The heat from the craft became so unbearable that she quickly decided to get back into the car, but had to use her leather jacket to hold the searing door handle. Landrum tried to lean out the passenger side window to have a look and found the heat was so intense that the vinyl dashboard later retained the impressions of her clenching hands. Within minutes, the object was surrounded by twenty-three CH-47 Chinook helicopters, which seemed to shepherd the thing away from the road. It started to regain altitude after a time and the flames stopped as it floated away into the night with its armada of chaperones.

When Cash returned home, she began to get violently ill. Her skin reddened and knots developed on her head and neck. Soon afterward, she was checked into a hospital and nearly died. Her hair fell out and she later developed cancer. When Cash and the Landrums tried to ask the Air Force about the incident, they were told to fill out forms and find a lawyer to petition the government for compensation. Early in the legal battle, the Air Force quietly offered to pay medical expenses if Cash and the Landrums agreed to sign a nondisclosure form promising not to discuss the case anymore. Their lawyer, Citizens Against UFO Secrecy president Peter Gersten, advised them against this, and tried to fight the Air Force to disclose the existence of the craft. When it became clear that the case was going nowhere, Cash and Landrum decided to accept the original deal, but the Air Force reply was a cold and confusing "What deal?"

It became clear to most involved in the investigation of this case (and Paul Bennewitz, who referred to it in letters and conversations) that some sort of advanced technology was being tested when Cash, Landrum, and the boy had their unfortunate encounter, but whose machine was it?

Richard Doty thinks the craft was an atomic-powered anti-gravity-type craft that was on a test mission to fly out over the Gulf of Mexico and land at a secure facility in Nevada when it had engine problems. Bennewitz guessed (and was probably encouraged in this direction) that the UFO was a captured alien ship, or at least had been developed with "borrowed" technology.

A scientist named Eric Wang was working for Phillips Labs at Kirtland Air Base around this time. Formerly with the Foreign Technology Division at Wright-Patterson Air Force Base in Ohio, he specialized in rocket propulsion but secretly carried on private research in theories on nonconventional aircraft. He had originally emigrated from Austria and the word was that he was related to European nobility. His unusual surname had a story as well: The family was apparently descended from Mongolian marauders who swept through the continent in the thirteenth century. Rumor had it that he had worked with Viktor Schauberger, a rogue scientist and the reputed inventor of an antigravitational motor used by the Nazis.

On his death in 1981, Kirtland base authorities asked his wife to turn over anything she found in his effects that might be useful. They specifically requested any detailed-looking equations and notes. To almost no one's surprise, she called up when she found a trunkful of indecipherable scribblings, many of which were written in an archaic form of German. Two AFOSI agents were sent out to Wang's residence to scoop up the trunk, and they brought it back to the base, where it may still reside in a secure vault.

There is a point to all this wild speculation. It is certainly possible that someone at Kirtland was testing unconventional flying craft. It is also quite possible that these small craft were highly maneuverable and tested only at night to hide their existence and keep suspicious observers guessing. Not as possible, but definitely worth considering, is the idea of a highly maneuverable, brightly lit craft using an antigravity drive of some sort, developed in the 1960s, and perfected by the late 1970s. If this was the case, as Gabe Valdez guessed and even Richard Doty has hinted, then the joint NSA/AFOSI effort to keep it under wraps makes more sense. Most "unauthorized citizens" who happened to see the lights jumping about over the base had the "Oh look, it's one of them UFOs" reaction, and left it at that. Perhaps they even went as far as reporting their sightings to the authorities, but Paul Bennewitz was the only one who decided to look into things further, and thereby sealed his fate.

chapter 22

REVELATIONS

I f his interest in a secret unconventional flying craft was not enough to get Bennewitz on the "watch" list, then another supersecret project taking place right in front of most of the metropolitan population of Albuquerque may have landed him in Julius and Ethel Rosenberg territory. On one of his daytime visits over at the Bennewitz homestead, Bill Moore had been talking with the scientist on his view deck. Bennewitz said, "I see you have your camera with you. Try this: Set the shutter speed on 1000 and point it over there at Manzano. Take a few pictures. After you get it developed, tell me if you find anything."

"Why?" Moore asked.

"Just do it," replied Bennewitz. "I've had some really weird things show up on my pictures."

Moore did as asked and promptly forgot about the incident. A few weeks later when he picked up his Ektachrome slides from the drugstore, he was startled to find, in the midst of a few ordinary exposures of a nearly cloudless New Mexico sky, an image of the Manzano range with a strange "tube" of light surrounded by a vaporlike haze streaking straight up. (Curiously, the light appears to stop in midair, as if something had blocked it.) Moore couldn't figure out what the phenomenon could be, and Bennewitz still couldn't tell him. Inquiries through Moore's extensive contacts produced nothing. It did appear as if it might be emanating from the Sigma Hill facility tucked safely in a small valley behind the mountain, but this was only a guess on Moore's part.

Pulling the slide out of a yellowing file twenty-two years later, Moore once again wondered what he had photographed so long ago. But in the course of research for this book, the following facts have come to light. The "artificial star" used by the Starfire Optical Range (also behind Manzano Mountain from the point of view of the Bennewitz home) used a high-powered laser to calibrate their Adaptive Optics System for sighting enemy spy satellites. The streak on the slide may only have been visible at the 1000th-of-a-second exposure setting. The laser must have been scanning the skies at a fantastic clip to have left the wide "column" that appears. How Bennewitz made this discovery is not known, but he had stumbled onto one of the most sophisticated operations on the base.

Throughout the history of Soviet/American espionage, there have been many uncredited triumphs of slyness on both sides. In the early days of the space race, the United States apparently managed to get fairly detailed schematics of the Sputnik satellite mere weeks after the bleeping tin ball had first surprised and terrified the West. In an episode that may be related, many conspiracy watchers are still wondering how Lee Harvey Oswald managed to defect to Russia in October of 1959 after he had worked at one of the most secret American military facilities in the world—Atsugi Air Base in Japan—where U2 reconnaissance flights regularly flew sorties over the USSR. He may have been sent to Russia for some sort of intelligence work connected with the factory where he met his future wife, Marina. Or not. But after only two years he decided he wanted to come back with his Russian bride and was welcomed with open arms by the authorities—right in the middle of the Cold War.

By the 1970s, the United States had perhaps hundreds of agents living in the Soviet Union—some were Russian citizens, others had been "inserted"—sending back information on everything from smokestack counts on defense factories to whom certain commissars were currently sleeping with. One group (who may have been the ones sending those innocent-looking cards to Bill Moore's post office box) were taking surveillance satellites apart and sending details on the guts of the things back to the U.S. Kirtland technicians and scientists pored over the details and then trained the powerful telescopes of the Starfire range on the skies over New Mexico to find and identify each streaking little piece of the USSR as it passed overhead, merrily taking pictures of the base and other areas of interest under its orbital path. (After the fall of Soviet Communism, opportunistic Russians actually rushed to sell old satellite photos of Area 51 to eager American UFO fans. One example even featured an incongruously large and detailed flying saucer–looking object that just happened to be out for a spin when the satellite had snapped its picture. There is a good chance that it was painted in by Russian or American intelligence before copies went up for sale.)

Simple identification was not the end product of all this dangerous effort. The assets stationed in Russia had done their jobs so well that the Americans not only knew which pieces of technology were passing silently overhead, they also knew how to defeat some of the satellites' security-coded systems, read the information stored in their memory, and even (and this was the most sensitive part of the operation) reprogram their guidance systems to steer them out of orbit.

The secret lay in laser communication. The Russians had devised a way of talking to their spacecraft using laser pulses, instead of more easily intercepted radio waves. Once the boys at Kirtland had identified and tracked the orbits of their targets, the information was immediately relayed to the "Stallion" laser facility located 200 miles south at White Sands Missile Range. There, laser experts and intelligence officers used the stolen codes to tap into the satellites and download any useful information (such as any sensitive areas that had been photographed) and then sent a command to steer the spacecraft into a useless orbit or attitude. By the time it appeared over the Russian horizon, Soviet technicians were completely bamboozled as to why their equipment was constantly screwing up. They would correct the problem as the satellite passed over them, only to have the thing come back around the next time with a whole new set of malfunctions. (Actually, the Stallion technicians may have done the reprogramming at random to arouse less suspicion in their Russian counterparts.)

The satellite espionage program, which may have been known either as "Project Rainbow" or "Tabor Orange" (depending on who was talking), was an unqualified success, but

Paul Bennewitz represented the weak link in security. After the AFOSI found out he was taking pictures of the laser, they again broke into his home, located the pictures, and replaced them with blank frames. Any evidence of the Rainbow/Tabor Orange program remained invisible to the naked eye in the clear Albuquerque skies. Moore is lucky to have kept his slide showing the laser in operation.

The Air Force and NSA dilemma boiled down to a choice: either ignore Paul Bennewitz and risk revealing the surveillance probe program, the radio compression/encryption program, and the Rainbow/Tabor Orange project, or take charge of his perceptions (and anyone else who might be watching or listening to him) to steer him carefully away. At risk as well were assets in the USSR who were stealing the satellite codes and who could have been traced if the Russians knew that someone had broken their codes and figured out the technology. It was a choice between millions of dollars of research, hundreds of hours of training, and an unknown number of lives, or the sanity of one U.S. citizen who was convinced (even before they knew about him) that an alien race was out to take over the U.S. government, and then the planet.

In spite of suspicious fingers later pointed in Moore's direction, his spook buddies never revealed this scenario to him, even in the broadest of strokes. In the winter of 1981, Moore was called to an operations meeting at Kirtland to assess (among other things) how well the disinformation campaign was proceeding against Bennewitz and the UFO community at large. Moore walked into the early-morning conclave to find that Falcon, Richard Doty, Lew Miles, and members of Kirtland AFOSI were seated around the conference table, along with NSA-connected security people and scientists such as Henry Monteith from the Air Force Weapons/Phillips lab.

Monteith, who had been working for the Air Force for just a few years, researched UFOs and related subjects in his off hours. Moore had visited his home on a few occasions and seen a library of hundreds of carefully organized books on paranormal subjects, all tightly wrapped in plastic bags. Monteith, who was African American, had worked his way up from poverty to become a theoretical physicist who retained his "street" accent. The incongruity of his speech and the cutting-edge concepts he routinely spoke of had startled more than one of his white-bread colleagues.

Once, Moore had left a camera on the table in the living room of the Monteith home while the two went out to dinner. When they returned, Monteith examined the front gate latch and announced, "We've had visitors." Moore's camera was where he left it, but the film had been taken out and left on the table, neatly wound into its canister. Moore later discovered to his disappointment that someone had unspooled and exposed the roll. "This sort of stuff happens all the time," said Monteith, who was routinely electronically bugged and watched by the AFOSI and others to make sure he hadn't taken so much as a paper clip home from work, or talked about anything that breached his security oath. After retirement, he remained in New Mexico and later appeared in a locally produced video where, amazingly enough, he described his encounters with actual aliens who he said had impregnated his wife to bear hybrid children. Monteith passed away in the mid-1990s.

Moore was the only "outsider" present at the Kirtland meeting. After formalities and introductions, Falcon turned to Moore and asked for a briefing on specific personalities and groups in the UFO research community: "Who was looking at things they shouldn't?" "Who was spreading stories and rumors and what were they?" "What was Bennewitz's current thinking on the Kirtland events?" etc. After he had answered these and other queries from the group, they moved on to other business, most of which Moore couldn't understand since they dealt with highly technical subjects. He does remember some talk of unconventional aircraft, but it was so couched in scientific language and insider terminology that it made little sense to him. Why Moore wasn't asked to leave after his presentation was a mystery to him. It was the only high-level meeting Moore would ever be asked to attend, although he, of course, had many later conclaves with Doty and the Falcon.

Richard Doty, for his part, was still calling and meeting with Bennewitz to plant seeds and see how seeds planted earlier were growing. Because of his experience with elements of civilian UFO research, he says that he was later called upon in a sting operation designed to catch the sort of operatives that had begun to cluster around Bennewitz.

Due to the inefficiency and lack of experience (and lack of time) that seems to plague many UFO investigators, an East Coast UFO group decided to hire a Houston detective firm to look into sightings or activity around Cannon Air Force Base near Clovis, New Mexico in the mid-1980s. The work may have had some connection to the Cash-Landrum case of 1980, and its unconventional flying object. The detective firm outsourced the work to two independent investigators who promptly set to work interviewing witnesses and skulking around Air Force facilities taking pictures. When AFOSI was informed, they started to tail the pair, intercepting their mail and listening in on phone calls. It soon became clear that UFOs were not at the top of the investigators' list, and anything they found that had any possible connection to defense and advanced aircraft were quickly forwarded to the Russian embassy in Washington, and other unspecified places and contacts. The agents made little attempt to hide their activities from any possible counterespionage efforts, and they were followed around the country as they made their way back toward D.C. and eventual escape. The Pentagon had called for their immediate arrest as soon as the problem was uncovered, but the AFOSI advised patience. So long as no real secrets were revealed, more intelligence would be gained from letting them think they were safe while they filed reports, made phone calls, and met with people who could be checked on. Bill Moore recalls speaking at length with one of these men on the phone, late in 1983. The man, whose name Moore no longer recalls, was asking a lot of questions about APRO, to which Moore remembers giving a lot a vague replies. When he subsequently reported this to Doty, he was advised to try to make contact again. Moore failed to do so, however, because the man never returned his call after the first attempt, and when he made a second several days later, the number was out of service.

When the Russian agents finally reached Washington, several FBI and AFOSI agents quietly sat down beside them at their personal "victory" dinner in a posh Georgetown restaurant and presented a choice: cooperation or imprisonment. The whole thing was brought off so coolly that the restaurant's other patrons remained completely unaware that anything out of the ordinary was going on. Later, after they had been separated and interrogations began, one of the culprits stubbornly insisted that they had nothing to hide, and maintained his innocence and immunity.

After more intense questioning, the other man broke down crying and agreed to a deal: He would retain his cover and cooperate with U.S. intelligence as a double agent. Doty recalls, "The last I heard, he's now retired and running a business in Florida somewhere. It was probably one of the happiest days in his life when the Berlin Wall came down and the Communist government started to fall apart . . . The other guy's still in Leavenworth [military prison]."

But these red-handed Reds knew exactly what they were doing and most of the rules of the game they were playing, even if they were inexperienced players. Paul Bennewitz could be afforded no such luxury. He saw himself as the Paul Revere of an interplanetary invasion, lighting the lamps and sounding the alarm, but the Valley Forge he was predicting was of course based on a sham provided by the alphabet soup of intelligence agencies that preferred that he stay at home and draw the curtains.

Turns out they had underestimated both Bennewitz and the effect of their escalating fictions.

chapter 23

MORE LIES

Kaffee: I want the truth.

Colonel: You can't handle the truth!

—Dialogue delivered by Tom Cruise and Jack Nicholson

from *A Few Good Men* (1990)

On August 8, 1981, Bennewitz wrote to APRO's Jim Lorenzen to tell him about the craziness that was starting to unwind around him.

For some strange reason, the Government has gone totally out of phase with me and in addition to the continuing phone taps—put AF Intelligence on my tail. This occurred after they covertly sent satellites and photo recon over the alien base I had briefed them on . . .

They even had "Human Intel," a group I have never heard of—(they spy on humans). They tried to rig our cars with beepers and I caught one of them in the act.

They also installed a covert ECM [unknown acronym—possibly "Electromagnetic Covert Monitoring; Bennewitz sometimes invented terms as he went along] *setup in a vacant Town House directly across the street from ours to figure out how I was communicating and receiving view screen pictures. I could sense their sweeps on my equipment. To my knowledge they got nothing. Looks like DOD* [Department of Defense] *AF Intel——all of them are mixed up in it.*

It's actually crazy—at one time AF Intel was tailing me and OSI was tailing them and telling me! Strange—but true—local TV was also apparently turned off. I was also told I would be "bought" off though that has not happened nor will I allow it . . .

We have given the Alien a new, single word matrix vocabulary of 26x26 words (976 total). Their command of the language is slowly improving. The computer integrity is safeguarded in several ways so that nothing but deliberate message is accepted by the computer . . .

The picture now, at times is near 3-dimensional. Picture content varies—alien faces, ships out in front of the originating ship; clouds, cities (from the air) and on their bases showing ships launching, etc. with guard spheres at entrances. Also some of what appear to be deities or real and most beautiful Homo Sapiens (recording some of this on film.)

All is still total and ongoing—no change—just much much more knowledge.

The letter provides a snapshot of just how well the Air Force had done its creepy business. By late 1981, almost all of the disinformation programs that were playing in Bennewitz's personal theater were running full-time and were doing great business. In one of the most bizarrely self-referential episodes of this affair, he writes that the Air Force had sent satellites over the Archuleta Mesa area to get images of the supposed "alien base," which they had encouraged him to investigate just a few months before!

"Human Intel," actually HUMINT, is not an organization. It is one of three methods of intelligence gathering defined as any information obtained through contact with a source or anything gained by, or passed through, a human agent. The other types of information are designated SIGINT (Signals Intelligence derived from intercepted radio transmissions) and ELINT (Electronic Intelligence; i.e., phone taps, computer data, tape recordings, etc.)—both of which comprise the NSA's main provenance.

Around this time, a heretofore unknown second Kirtland base briefing with intelligence officers in attendance was convened, seemingly with the express purpose of seeing how well the campaign of lies was selling. No documents have been released describing any official reports on this event, but Bennewitz referred to it in private letters.

Bennewitz sometimes noticed agents stationed across the street from his home. Why he never walked up the driveway and knocked on their door is a mystery. Another mystery is why he never figured out that the people across the street might have been the source of many of the signals he was picking up on his receiving equipment. The NSA would likely have been able to make the low-frequency "alien" transmissions appear to originate from the direction of the base and control Bennewitz's input so completely that he would never again get near the original test signals that had so concerned them at first. Communications with the space people was a two-way street; Bennewitz mentions a matrix of words he was trying to teach to his off-world students. The "aliens," however, were in all likelihood sitting right across the street and beaming messages back and forth, apparently including some sort of degraded video signal. Other witnesses have stated that they too saw these fuzzy scenes of alien faces and "most beautiful Homo sapiens." Unlike the photos that Bennewitz would bring back from Archuleta/Dulce, he was not "seeing things," but was marveling at just the sort of images that the NSA wanted him to see, and had produced for their audience of one.

With the efficiency for which the intelligence community is famous, they had also contacted major press outlets and warned them that Bennewitz would be calling, and informed them that anything he said was a matter of national security and should be kept under wraps. There is a well-documented history of media cooperation with U.S. intelligence, from JFK's request that the Bay of Pigs operation be kept quiet to CNN and National Public Radio's knowledge of their employment of Army censors as "interns" during the Gulf War of 1991.

When Bennewitz wrote and called New Mexico Senators Schmitt and Domenici to keep them updated on his research and fears, he presented himself as a loyal citizen (which he believed) who was stymied as he tried to warn the Air Force about a situation he thought was getting out of hand. The occasional stonewalling he received only served to strengthen the urgency of his discoveries. Events were reaching what he believed was a critical phase when he wrote in to Domenici on December 2, 1981, in a familiar tone that suggests that he had been talking to the senator for some time:

To date, as noted, I have not heard from you and therefore will assume with all your new duties that you are very busy and just have not had the time.

The facts I gave Captain Harris are simple and straight forward [sic] as follows:

1) *I knew [sic] the location of the Alien bases in Northern New Mexico in the center of the Jicarilla Apache Reservation 4.5 miles northwest of Dulce, NM.*

2) *I know that someone in the military made a deal with the Aliens several years ago, giving the Indian land, cattle, etc. and apparent assurance of safety to the Alien in trade for Technology in the form of an Atomic powered ship at the same time establishing an extensive US base alongside to test the ship.*

3) *That sometime late 79 or first of 80 an argument insued [sic] over weapons and the military abandoned; the final circumstance of the men unknown.*

4) *That I had very high resolution official NASA U2 CIR (color infrared) photos in addition to low level and ground photos showing the base in total detail. (photos obtained legitimately through UNM) [University of New Mexico]*

5) *The ship design traded for is over thirty (30) years behind the alien technology.*

6) *I advised Captain Harris I knew of the two women and child near Austin, TX who were severely exposed to radiation at close distance from the ship in trouble and that it was seen to come west with helicopters (unmarked) and that the*

government was quietly paying their hospital expenses.

I am also very concerned that the President has not been totally advised of the situation and have forwarded a copy to him, cover letter enclosed for your record.

It is hoped you will value this valuable input and in time get in touch with me.

This sort of badgering, with assurances that he "knew the location of the Alien bases," put Domenici at pains to determine what, if anything, Bennewitz was trying to say and if the facts had any kind of merit. The confusing chum of disinformation that was being thrown over the side by the Air Force and NSA made him hungry for more, but clouded his vision so much that any potentially significant information he might have been trying to get across was thrown into the trash like all kook letters that arrive in government in-boxes by the thousands every year. The Air Force hadn't told Domenici anything, since he wasn't on the "need to know" list for the black projects that Bennewitz threatened to expose. The lies had put the Air Force in a pickle that was becoming increasingly difficult to escape without revealing not only the disinformation campaign, but legitimate national security secrets as well. Eventually, AFOSI may have told Domenici just enough to let him know that Bennewitz should not be taken seriously.

In the letter, Bennewitz made reference to the Cash-Landrum case and suggested that the Air Force was paying for the medical expenses of the victims. This is not true, as we have seen. The enclosed "report" was in all likelihood a copy of Project Beta, which would further alienate all but the

most dedicated or misguided UFOlogist. It is ultimately un-
clear what parts of the letter were fed to Bennewitz, and
what he had deduced on his own. The intrigue went ever
deeper.

After being "seeded" with the flight out to Dulce and the
Archuleta Mesa, Bennewitz needed little encouragement to
begin his own reconnaissance of the area. With the wealth
earned from the success of Thunder Scientific Labs, he had
purchased a private plane and began to make periodic trips,
flying over the rugged mountains holding the control yoke
with one hand and snapping pictures out the windows with
his Hasselblad in the other. Others who saw the high-resolu-
tion black-and-white prints couldn't see anything out of the
ordinary.

In mid to late 1985, Bennewitz was on another of his
countless reconnaissance trips to Archuleta when he spotted
something on one of the remote slopes. As he banked and
descended for a better look, he thought he could see burned
trees and what looked like a crashed aircraft. He brought the
little monoplane around for another look and snapped a few
pictures. When developed in his home darkroom, they revealed a sort of delta-winged craft, broken into two main sections.

He immediately became obsessed and began a renewed
campaign to tell as many friends and officials as possible. For
all practical purposes, the aircraft that went down looked almost exactly like an early model of the Stealth bomber, and
the Air Force became desperate to bring down the "laughter
curtain" as quickly as possible to keep serious inquiry at bay
and buy some time while a cleanup expedition was launched
to the remote area.

The country was too rough to attempt a hasty overland ex-

pedition, and Bennewitz was convinced (or was told) that the
craft was some kind of nuclear-powered secret project that
had been shot down by the aliens to teach Earthlings a stern
lesson. The Air Force almost certainly added the radiation
story to keep Bennewitz and others away while the retrieval
operation was mounted.

"My prime concern is the arbitrary exposure to radiation
of the people up there," Bennewitz wrote on October 25.
The craft in the Cash-Landrum incident was described as
"like a diamond turned on its end," and he must have known
this, but Bennewitz appears to have thought that the aircraft
he had spotted (he stated that there were two) crumpled on
the mountainside were part of the same "fleet." He took end-
less aerial pictures of the area, but these were either turned
over to, or stolen by, intel operatives, or have disappeared in
the passage of time, and all he was left with were his inter-
pretive drawings to show to others. Significantly, Bennewitz's
only surviving photos depict the site after the wreckage was
cleared away. At the bottom of the photos are his extensive
notes and keys showing where the wreckage had been, which
ultimately proved nothing to anyone but himself. Noise
about a "captured alien atomic craft" kept any respectable
observers safely away. Moore recalls hearing of a similar operation to cover up a crashed Stealth near Bakersfield, California a few years later: The rumor was spread that a UFO
had crashed, and the Air Force directed downed-saucer
searchers to an area miles from the actual site.

Moore also says that Bennewitz "had provided drawings,
which he said he had made from photographs. I, and others
who examined Paul's photographs as well as independently
obtained pictures of the same area, were unable to see what
Paul claimed was there. Where he saw a crashed ship,

burned wreckage, entrances to the alien base, and weapons pointing skyward, others could see only rocks, trees, and shadows. . . . What he claimed to see wasn't what others saw."

Many of the Bennewitz drawings and notes on the event survive in impassioned letters he sent to sympathetic parties and Senator Domenici. At first, he described something he had dubbed "U.S. Black Ship Delta" and drew an elongated shape resembling a grasshopper, with "bubble" type cockpit (see the photo insert). For some reason, by December of 1985 he had changed his impression of the shape of the craft and sent a "Results of Re-analysis of Aerial Films and Atomic Ship" to an unnamed colleague. The revised drawings look suspiciously like the Stealth, and his approximations of scale agree favorably with Stealth measurements. No one outside of Lockheed and the Air Force had seen anything remotely like the radar-absorbing fighter/bomber, and most who saw it for the first time in the 1990s were surprised that it was even airworthy. In 1985, the F-117 would truly appear to be "borrowed alien technology" to the unknowing eye.

On November 8, 1985, Bennewitz, Gabe Valdez, a member of the Jicarilla tribe, and a government scientist authorized for the expedition by a little string-pulling from Senator Domenici's office and armed with a Geiger counter finally trekked to the site to see what they could find. "He knew exactly where he was going," says Valdez. "Even the guy from the Jicarilla tribe had trouble identifying the roads and canyons when we went out there." When they reached the site, the Geiger counter was switched on, but registered nada. Bennewitz was confused and chagrined that the massive radiation he had expected was not there. He had been flying over the crash site for months, and in an unpublished manuscript had sworn that he had detected high levels of radiation with a "scintillator"—an instrument often used to prospect uranium deposits from the air. He dropped any talk of radiation in his writings when none was found at the actual crash site. No matter how efficient the cleanup, radiation cannot be completely scrubbed from an outdoor spill. If the reactor he described had stayed on the mountain for so long and had contaminated the area in the way that Bennewitz believed, the radiation levels would have been so dangerous that it is surprising that he wanted to go anywhere near it.

There was, however, a large gouge in the soil, and broken trees and foliage, indicating that something had indeed flown in and dug its way into the side of the hill. While looking around the area, one member of the group found a black ballpoint pen with either "U.S. Government," "U.S. Air Force," or "Los Alamos National Labs" (accounts differ) printed in faded and chipped white paint on its side. Something had crashed, and someone had indeed been in to thoroughly clean it up. Later, Bennewitz said that he received strange telephone calls from the Lockheed "Skunk Works" in Lancaster, California. How he figured out the source of the calls is not explained. The only words he remembered were "We are interested in the hardware you are looking at," which makes a lot of sense if he stumbled onto their most top-secret project.

To add to this confusing soup, what appear to be strange flying objects actually show up in many of the photos taken from the ground by Bennewitz in the Dulce/Archuleta area, and at least a few of them cannot be dismissed as photographic artifacts. Valdez says that Bennewitz was convinced that the Air Force was working on a flight platform that could not only hover and streak away like a classic UFO, but could "cloak" itself in daylight by projecting whatever was behind it (such as sky or clouds) onto the opposite side that was visible to an observer on the ground. No one is sure now how Bennewitz discovered this. Photographs taken as recently as 2002 by local residents occasionally reveal some of the same aerial anomalies that Valdez and Bennewitz had photographed in the early 1980s.

If the "U.S. Black Ship Delta" was not enough to occupy his fevered research, Bennewitz was exchanging letters and phone calls, at least during December of 1985 and January of 1986, with an intelligence officer rumored to be associated with the NSA. The renewed proactive stance from the spooks must have been the result of his discovery of the crash site. On December 11, Bennewitz's NSA "handler" sent him a letter that is valuable to quote at length, as it shows the incredible efforts that the National Security State was willing to go to in the continuing sleight of hand on Paul Bennewitz's mind. It contains the germ of many of the legends that are still circulating in the UFOlogical underground to this day.

> . . . *four rolls of film are herewith provided (under separate postage), as advertised. I believe I provided the most reasonable exposure data in my previous correspondence; if not, please let me know.*
>
> *The best word I've gotten so far from our data reviewers is that "something interesting" is going on in the Dulce Area. No positive (or negative) response to my query as to "thermal or radioactive 'spots' or 'areas.'" They are, justifiably a close-lipped [sic] group. But, I will keep plugging away. In the meantime, YOU get us some good hi-resolution photos, then we can shove their prissy attitude right up their collec-*

*tive noses! Speaking of "photos," I bet you were begin-
ning to believe I'd never respond to your second set.
How's FAN-F____ING-TASTIC! For a response? One
day I hope to see the movie film from which the stills
were taken . . .*

*Now, I want to propose a "way out" theory to you.
Please refrain from suggesting my commitment to the
nearest state mental facility (at least for the time being)
and see how this scenario fits with your data and research . . .*

*On about 2 July 1947 the U.S. government recov-
ered an alien aircraft (note aircraft—not spacecraft)
constructed of a super-lightweight alloy. The special
alloy was forwarded to Wright-Patterson AFB for
analysis. With the then (1947) current technology, the
composition was known (an aluminum/titanium com-
posite of unknown fabrication techniques) but the
method of achieving this alloy was a complete mystery.*

*The advent of the electron microscope heralded a
new wave of discovery. This aluminum/titanium alloy
was porous and differed from any known metallic alloy
to date. It was IMPOSSIBLE to fabricate on Earth!
But here it was.*

*It was theorized that this new "super alloy" might be
fabricated in a zero-g environment. With no gravita-
tional interference, elements of grossly differing atomic
masses might possibly be alloyed for the first time.*

*Early Space Shuttle experiments proved this theory,
and the resultant alloy was unbelievably tough and
porous—absorbing radar and other electronic emis-
sions to an amazing degree. Truely [sic] a "stealth" fabrication material!*

But how to transition from an unclassified scientific experiment to something of practical value?

Enter our trusty friends from the "Skunk Works" of Lockheed Aircraft and their super-secret base at Groom Lake, Nevada. They (Lockheed) extended the main runway to 22,000 feet . . . to accommodate their new trans-atmospheric vehicle (TAV). With the TAV, we are now able to take off, achieve low-earth orbit, heat (in pre-formed molds) the alloy constituents to the melting point, and cast F-19 (Stealth Fighter) structural components. For the first time, we can replicate the 30-year old UFO technology and apply it for our own use.

Sounds sort of screwy, doesn't it?

Hope to hear from you soon.

Paul, the above was the letter that I was in the process of mailing before our conversation yesterday. Since then, I've composed the following scenario. Again, your response (suggestions, corrections, amplifications, out-right rejection etc.) would be appreciated. Please remember that I'm somewhat of a neophyte at stringing these data together, and I'm probably way off.

Several thousand years ago, a group of "people" revealed to us to be the "EBANS" and originating from the "green planet," created two races of mankind: Homo Sapiens and "Sweads." Both of these races were very similar in external appearance, the major difference being their mental composition; the Homo Sapiens (men) tending more towards emotion (or, if you will, romanticism), and the Sweads tending more toward pragmatism. Men were established in our solar system, and the Sweads were established in the solar system of Zeta Reticuli.

For many years the Ebans monitored their creations, occasionally interceding to avoid their (i.e. their creation's) destruction. About 300 years ago, the Sweads attained a level of technical competence [sic] that enabled them, for the first time, to challenge their creators, the Ebans, about whom they had known for some time. Limited war between the Ebans and Sweads has continued to this day.

In 1945, the Ebans' other created race, man, exploded their first atomic bomb in the desert of central New Mexico, followed closely by two more in Japan. Until these first nuclear explosions, we had only periodically and surreptitiously been visited. However, fearing that man, too, was becoming warlike (as were the Sweads) the Ebans increased the frequency of their visits and started tentative probes to establish communication with man.

The Sweads were not as patient. In 1947, in a remote area near Roswell, N.M., two Swead aircraft crashed. One ship was totally destroyed, with the debris scattered over a large area. The other ship, although severely damaged, maintained sufficient structural integrity to enable one crewman, named "Ede," to survive. He was taken to Kirtland AFB . . . Ede contacted his people, who arrived shortly before he died.

The Sweads told us that they had come to Earth to solicit our assistance in combating the Ebans who, they claimed, were preparing to come and destroy us. They provided us with volumes of data and technical assistance.

The Ebans, who up until now were unknown to us, made their appearance. They told us that the Sweads were the aggressors and that they (the Ebans) were here to assist in protecting us from the Sweads!

Thoroughly confused, our military leaders explained the entire situation to President Eisenhower. Eisenhower demanded a meeting with these "people" . . . this meeting occurred at Edwards AFB. Eisenhower believed the Ebans, and initiated Project Aquarius—A project designed to notify man of our creation by the Ebans.

Project Sigma was initiated . . . to maintain contact and communication with the Ebans to bring us current with their technology because they (the Ebans) feared that the Sweads would initiate hostilities with planet Earth. (Project Sigma continues at Kirtland AFB in New Mexico.)

Shortly thereafter, Project Snowbird was initiated to enable us to learn how to fly the alien craft preparatory to our constructing one. (Project Snowbird continues at Area 51 within the confines of Nellis AFB in Nevada.)

On June 2, 1985, the Sweads learned of our duplicity and destroyed the two ships as they were on final approach to the Dulce base.

Given a reasonable smattering of background in the history of civilian UFO research, the official was deftly stirring a simmering pot of disinformation and feeding it to Bennewitz. In retrospect, parts of the story were rather clumsy. "Sweads" seems to be derived from the old "space brother" jargon of the 1950s, when many individuals claimed to have met tall, blond, blue-eyed beings whom they referred to for convenience' sake as "Swedes." (The idea that advanced races from outer space looked like Aryan gods betrayed the generally benign racist undertones in the accounts of many of the UFO "contactees," who were all white.) "Ebans" appears to be a bastardization of "EBE" or "Extraterrestrial Biological Entities," a moniker that was popularized in the late 1980s when stories of government contacts with aliens began to flood the rumor mill after the use of the acronym in the controversial "MJ-12 Documents" mailed anonymously to Bill Moore and Jaime Shandera.

Bennewitz's suspicion that the two craft that had crashed on the slopes of Archuleta Mesa were atomic-powered spaceships was confirmed and elaborated upon to keep him talking about aliens and away from anything having to do with the Stealth project. Lockheed was testing the airframe out at Groom Lake/Area 51 in Nevada, but this is covered in the letter with talk of a "trans-atmospheric vehicle." Bennewitz's strange new buddy on the inside also encouraged his belief that the craft were shot down as a lesson to the government and mankind that a treaty had been broken and the aliens were on the warpath. The agreement for exchange of alien technology for a foothold on planet Earth had been a sham to prepare for the vanguard of an all-out invasion. Bennewitz was horrified.

It bears repeating that disinformation contains just enough truth to hang a multitude of lies upon. As Bennewitz continued to tell others of his findings, the conversations on tapped phones and bugged rooms in his home and at Thunder Scientific would be combed by intelligence for anyone who seemed to ask more about the Stealth project than about space aliens. Any mention of the terms or any of the stories contained in the letter could be traced by following the grapevine. For instance, if "Ebans" or "Sweads" showed up in NSA intercepts, agents would know who was listening to whom, and if they were interested in anything around Kirtland Air Force Base or indeed at the secret Nevada airstrip.

The letter from the Bennewitz "handler" makes one of the first mentions of fabled Groom Lake and Area 51. Moore received a topographical map of the area at about the same time. Someone had used a red felt-tip pen on the map to outline a plateau northwest of the main facility and neatly written "Saucer Mesa" next to it. Moore was told that this was the nickname of a place deep inside Area 51 and surrounded by high mountains where the bulk of UFO testing was conducted. Was this disinformation taken to another level for Moore's benefit? With no way to prove the case, he never publicly revealed the map with its furtive red scribblings.

In subsequent years, UFO/government conspiracy watchers appear to have sliced Occam's razor through the meat of the disinformation, but missed the thin bones of verifiable facts, such as references to the Stealth fighter and Lockheed.

Bennewitz carried on a spirited exchange with the NSA man, describing his problems with some parts of the story, and confirmation of others. The ruse was intended to look as if a sympathetic insider was seeking Bennewitz's trust to find out things that he couldn't find out on his own. In exchange, he leaked government "secrets" to Bennewitz while appearing to support his UFO research.

This sounds suspiciously like the deal Moore had cut with the Falcon.

chapter 24

FALLOUT

UFO researchers are perfectly capable of disinforming themselves!

—OVERHEARD AT A UFO CONVENTION

The Air Force Office of Special Investigations sat back and hooked its thumbs into its overalls, bursting with self-congratulatory pride at what had been wrought to steer Paul Bennewitz away from the projects they were sworn to protect by any means necessary.

Amazingly enough, the history of spectacular UFO "leaks" from the Air Force such as this one can be traced back to the 1950s, and began with an overture to Walt Disney and his animation studio. In 1954, the FBI approached Disney to become an informant. He readily accepted, and as he had done since 1936, continued to send in periodic reports on suspected commies in Hollywood. Once his bedrock-level patriotism was assured, in 1957 the Air Force offered Disney dramatic, close-up footage of UFOs to use in an animated documentary to get the public used to the idea of visitors from other planets. The offer was withdrawn for unspecified reasons after most of the animation had been completed. Disney animator Ward Kimball spoke about the situation and screened the animated film at the 1979 annual MUFON conference.

After officially closing down Project Bluebook in 1969, the Air Force appeared to jump right back into the subject in the early 1970s. In the course of a documentary that was to be titled *UFOs: Past, Present and Future,* the Los Angeles production team of Alan Sandler and Robert Emenegger had been contacted by someone from the Air Force who promised them that they would be receiving assistance with their project in the form of official documents, photos, and even films of UFOs and their continuing interaction with the U.S. military. Initial meetings were promising, and Emenegger at first received a document that was supposed to have been leaked from the CIA by way of the Air Force. It described an incredible psychic contact and flying saucer appearance at the National Photographic Information Center in Washington, D.C. in 1959. Members of the CIA and Naval Intelligence were involved. Having whetted his appetite with this ultimately untraceable document, former Project Bluebook spokesman Col. Robert Coleman, along with Col. George Weinbrenner from Wright-Patterson Air Force Base, then offered Sandler and Emenegger 800 feet of 16mm film, which they said showed a dramatic preplanned meeting between Air Force officials and aliens at Holloman Air Force Base in New Mexico that had taken place in May of 1971.

"There was footage of three disc-shaped crafts," says Paul Shartle, the Air Force audio-visual manager for Norton AFB, describing the film that was screened for the two producers prior to inclusion in the documentary. "One of the craft landed and two of them went away. . . . It appeared to be in trouble because it oscillated all the way down to the ground. However, it did land on three pods. A sliding door opened, a ramp was extended, and out came three aliens . . . they were human size. They had odd grey complexions and a pronounced nose. They wore tight-fitting jumpsuits, thin headdresses that appeared to be communications devices, and in their hands they held a translator, I was told. The Holloman base commander and other Air Force officers went out to meet them."

Sandler and Emenegger were told that the government had decided to release UFO information to the public, and their project was to be the first step in that process. They were called to meet with the AFOSI at Norton AFB in May of 1973, and were again promised the dramatic footage to be used as a climax for the documentary. As the eleventh hour for the release of the televised documentary neared, Colonel Coleman called Emenegger to tell him that the film was being withheld because "The timing was inappropriate, due to the Watergate scandal." When Emenegger went to Wright-Patterson AFB to ask about the screwup, Colonel Weinbrenner invited him into his office and marched around complaining loudly about some innocuous subject while simultaneously pulling a UFO book off the shelf and handing it to Emenegger. The message Emenegger sussed out was that Weinbrenner still wanted him to think that the Holloman landing was a true event, but didn't want anyone who happened to be eavesdropping to pick up on the subtext.

Emenegger has mentioned that he discussed the Holloman landing with H. R. Haldeman, Chief of Staff on Richard Nixon's cabinet and one of the men who took the fall for his boss during the Watergate scandal. The two had been in the same fraternity at UCLA (a few years apart) and when Emenegger approached him about the subject, Haldeman had said only that he "had heard something about it" before quickly changing the subject.

The year 1977 saw the release of *Close Encounters of the Third Kind*, directed and produced by Steven Spielberg, who later screened the film for President Reagan. The hot rumor associated with this event is that Reagan took Spielberg aside after seeing the film and whispered something like "People don't know just how close you came to the truth." The climactic scene that takes place at Devils Tower, Wyoming, was said to be a thinly veiled reference to the Holloman landing. One former AFOSI Special Agent (not Doty) maintains that there was someone in the production office at Spielberg's company who received checks from an unnamed government agency in order to help finance the film and push a particular message of wonder and friendly aliens.

The sort of two-faced behavior in UFO matters for which the Air Force had become justly famous for almost twenty years was repeated almost to the letter in 1983, when Richard Doty and the AFOSI contacted Linda Howe, who had produced *Strange Harvest*—the Emmy Award–winning documentary on cattle mutilations, and was now working on a UFO documentary for HBO. The working title was *UFOS: The E.T. Factor.* Howe got in touch with Doty through Citizens Against UFO Secrecy director Peter Gersten. Doty set up a meeting with her for April 9 of 1983.

As Linda Howe stepped off the plane at the Albuquerque airport for her meeting with Doty, she saw a front-page story on the newsstands about UFOs. By a quirk of chance, some of the "Kirtland Documents" (the "Complaint Reports" filled out by Richard Doty describing the unexplained 1980 land-

ings in Coyote Canyon) had just been released to the Albuquerque press and both major papers, the *Tribune* and the
Journal carried the story. Lew Miles was dismayed to find
that he had been mentioned prominently in the *Tribune*
story, since his name appeared in one of the documents.

The newspapers also mentioned the talk that Paul Bennewitz had just presented to the local chapter of the Mutual
UFO Network, bringing them up to date on his research.
The fairly conservative MUFON audience may have been
surprised and not a little incredulous as Bennewitz lectured
them on the three races of aliens living on Earth, their plan
for world domination, the U.S. government's failed agreement with them, and the aliens' underground complex not
200 miles away.

Howe's meeting with Doty and its cloak-and-dagger atmosphere would have extensive fallout on the UFO community. She described the confusing and harrowing meeting in
her 1989 book *An Alien Harvest*. To start with, Doty never
showed up at the Albuquerque airport to pick up Howe as
arranged. After a half hour she was the only one in the termi-
nal and had to call Lew Miles, who picked her up in his truck
and called Doty from his home. Howe described Miles as "a
man who might know a great deal, yet says he knows nothing." But he was very interested in asking Howe about cattle
mutilations. When Doty finally arrived, he seemed "tense
and nervous" and hurried Howe into Doty's car for the short
drive to the AFOSI offices at Kirtland AFB. Doty told Howe
that the Holloman landing had taken place in 1964, not 1971
(though years later he claimed to know nothing of the Holloman event). They passed the Thunder Scientific sign at the
Wyoming Avenue gate and drove in.

The two hurried into a building as Doty punched a code

into a simple lock and entered what he called his "boss's office," apparently referring to Colonel Cseh. She sat in a chair that was backed up against a row of windows, which covered one wall of the room.

Doty began: "You know you upset some people with your film *A Strange Harvest*. It came too close to something we don't want the public to know about."

Doty now claims to know nothing about cattle mutilations, but when pressed will hint that it might have something to do with concerns over environmental contamination. He buttered up Howe with his first comment (with or without justification) to stress that what she was doing was highly interesting to the military power structure. He then agreed with Howe's assertion that extraterrestrials were capturing cows, but in contrast to his claims of knowing most of the UFO/government story said that the details and reasons were "classified beyond his need to know."

Howe then brought up the 1978 Ellsworth AFB incident (the one that the *National Enquirer* had declared a hoax) and Doty did more than simply confirm the incident. He added to the story by stating that an "inner zone alert" alarm had been activated, indicating that something had breached the nuclear missile silo defenses underneath a 150-ton layer of concrete, even though the access hatches were still locked tight. (When I asked Doty about this two decades later, he declared that he had no familiarity with the Ellsworth episode. The response was typical Doty.)

Doty pulled an envelope from a drawer, took out several sheets of paper, and handed them to Howe. "My superiors have asked me to show this to you," he said. "You can read these and ask me questions, but you can't take any notes."

The top page was titled "Briefing Paper for the President of the United States." As she leafed through the sheaf of material, her eyes scanned other things like "crashes of silver disks," "alien bodies," and "extraterrestrial biological entities." Doty asked her to move from the chair she was in to a large green one in the middle of the room. "Eyes can see through windows," he said. The windows that Howe was facing were now at her back, and the mirrors that covered part of the wall now faced her. (Doty later revealed that there were Air Force employees behind the mirrors, filming Howe's reaction and recording the conversation on tape.)

Howe continued reading the papers, trying to remain calm as she absorbed the flood of information, and attempted to remember as many details as she could. The stories continued: UFO crashes at Roswell (in 1949 no less, not in 1947 as legend had it); Kingman, Arizona; and one in Mexico just over the Texas border. An alien had been taken from one of the crash sites alive and had lived in a safe house at Los Alamos Laboratories until its untimely death six years later. The Air Force colonel assigned to stay with the alien had wept when the alien died. The colonel said that the "EBE" was "like a child with the mind of a thousand men."

This was heady stuff to shove in front of an eager UFO chaser. "Why did you choose me for this? Why not the *New York Times*?" she asked.

"Because independent reporters like you are much easier to control," he replied.

Doty added that certain people in the Air Force and other places in the government wanted to help with her HBO documentary by providing her with film of UFOs landing at a military base, pictures, and classified documents: essentially the same deal that had been offered to Robert

Emenegger exactly ten years before. It is not difficult to guess where this would all end up.

As Howe began to ask more questions, she moved out of the green chair and noticed that Doty's "face began to turn red" and he was looking at her "out of the sides of his eyes." On later reflection, she thought that this was because she had moved out of optimal camera and microphone range, but it may also be due to the fact that this was the AFOSI's first attempt to openly sell their stories to a UFO researcher. Doty was nervous and Howe may have wandered off the track of what he was authorized and backgrounded to say. Much of what was seen and heard that evening was based firmly on the freely open history of the UFO subject. Men in black, abductions, differing types of aliens, and the Roswell crash were all there. Howe wrote that she "was excited to see a larger confirmation of the bits and pieces" she had stumbled upon, but the AFOSI had likely just combed their files and other sources of little-known facts on which to build a larger history of their own choosing.

Doty had even grilled Bill Moore about one UFO crash case that Moore had been working on from the Aztec, New Mexico area. Moore had determined that the incident was a hoax perpetrated by a con man specializing in wild stories, and may have been originally based on fallout from the Roswell incident. Aztec was mentioned in the papers that Howe struggled to commit to memory. Doty then told Howe he would call her later using the code name "Falcon," even though this was the name that Moore was using to refer to the man from the DIA. Confusion was the name of the game.

In any case, Howe apparently took the bait. Cattle mutilation investigators Tom Adams and Gary Massey met her when she got off the bus in Taos the next day. She talked nonstop about the Air Force show-and-tell long into the night.

After months of on-again, off-again meetings and assurances that she would be getting the film, Doty called to tell Howe that he was out of the project. He handed her off to a series of other contacts who also made excuses and announced more delays. Exasperated, HBO withdrew further funding and dropped the project.

Doty now says the purpose of the operation was twofold: To spread more stories and develop a better curtain of disinformation to protect the Air Force and its projects, and to keep the HBO film from ever being produced. Apparently, segments of the intelligence community were concerned with Howe's probing around the fringes of things they wanted to be kept out of the public eye. Perhaps Doty was at least partially telling Howe the truth when he said that her earlier documentary on mutilations "came too close to something we don't want the public to know about."

In late 1988, William Cooper, a former naval petty officer who claimed to have seen government documents relating to aliens and UFOs, contacted Howe. Cooper said that when he was serving with the Pacific Fleet in 1972, he had seen briefing papers containing references to numerous projects having to do with flying saucers and alien contact, and about twenty-five pictures of different types of aliens. Amazingly, he said that he remembered almost twelve pages practically verbatim. Many of the specific facts and project names were identical to the information that Bennewitz had been fed. Many of the project descriptions matched word for word those in documents Moore had been exposed to in March of 1983.

If what Cooper was saying was based on any sort of truth, then at least some of the information or disinformation in the

Bennewitz case was either true, or had been concocted at least eight years before it was used for the Kirtland cover-ups. The new generation of UFO seekers that was beginning to gather around Cooper and others of similar stripe, like famed aviator (and son of the jet company founder) John Lear, chose to believe the former, and laid the foundation for a serious schism in the UFO community.

A weird set of circumstances resulted. The Cooper/Lear faction believed many of the stories that were originally told as disinformation to Bennewitz. Despite the lack of documented proof of any underground bases or deals with aliens, they believed the revelations of a shadowy group of intelligence officers who Moore said were lying while disbelieving Moore, whom they would believe when he later admitted his cooperation with counterintelligence. It was a classic case of the cart before the horse, but with Cooper's undocumented "proof" of ante-Bennewitz revelations, they had all the reason they would need to condemn Moore. "I believed Cooper's information was ninety percent regurgitation of what was known publicly," says Jim Speiser, sysop of the Internet UFO group Paranet, "and ten percent embellishment, some of which was inspired by Lear's information . . ."

In ensuing years, Cooper's claims became so outrageous and his attitude so increasingly belligerent that even his most ardent supporters began to lose interest. When he began championing his theory that the Secret Service driver in the presidential limousine had shot JFK, it was the last straw for many. Cooper predicted that he would die fighting for his principles, and the self-fulfilling prophecy came true in the fall of 2001 when he was gunned down by sheriff's deputies on his property in Arizona for failing to submit to arrest and firing on them first (at least according to the official story).

As one Falcon was toying with Howe, the other Falcon was playing with Moore, who had made a deal to keep feeding information on other researchers and organizations in exchange for UFO information. In early 1982, Falcon called Moore to give him a "recognition signal" (spy jargon for a keyword or phrase) for receipt of anything that he couldn't deliver in person. On February 1 of that year, a man using this signal delivered a plain manila envelope to Moore. Inside were the Kirtland Documents outlining the unexplained lights and encounters with security guards in Coyote Canyon during August and September of 1980. Moore and others checked into the particulars of the Kirtland Documents and found no contradictions among the named events and personnel.

The game took another turn when Moore's phone rang sometime in March of 1983. The voice said that he was going to be able to see something important. "You will be receiving some instructions. You must follow them carefully or the deal is off." Moore was directed around the country to various airports to receive directions on where to fly next. He finally ended up in a hotel in upstate New York, where a courier came to the door. Moore invited him inside. He was handed another plain manila envelope. "You have nineteen minutes. You can do whatever you wish with this material during that time, but at the end of that time, I must have it back. After that, you are free to do what you wish."

Moore took pictures of the pages and read the contents into a tape recorder. The man counted the pages and silently left. What he had seen purported to be notes from a briefing

on UFOs given to President Carter in 1977. Later, other researchers were either given copies of these pages or received
them from Moore. The document contained information on
Project Aquarius and related subprojects, all having to do
with government interaction with an alien presence since the
early 1950s. For the second time (the first was a vague reference in the original Aquarius document), MJ-12 was mentioned as the ultimate control group for all UFO-related
information. Someone was laying the groundwork for the
"bomb," which was sent to Moore's research partner Jaime
Shandera in December of 1984.

Shandera was a television producer Moore had met while
planning a documentary that was never produced. At a meeting with their spook friends some years later, one of the agents
told Moore that Shandera had worked for them for many
years, and had been called to give testimony on a voice recording in connection with an incident during the Vietnam War.

The ubiquitous manila envelope arrived by U.S. mail at
Shandera's doorstep in Burbank, California on December 11.
It bore a December 8 postmark from Albuquerque. Two
more envelopes were inside, each enclosed within the next
like Russian nesting dolls. From the third one, a 35mm roll
of film rolled out of a black canister. When developed, the
black-and-white film revealed two sequences of eight pictures each—pictures of something that would pass into history as the notorious "MJ-12 document" or "Presidential
Briefing Papers." They were headed "TOP SECRET/MAJIC
EYES ONLY" and introduced "Operation Majestic-12 [as] a
TOP SECRET Research and Development/Intelligence operation responsible directly and only to the President of the
United States."

The text went on to describe the Roswell crash (coincidentally brought to public attention just five years before by Moore's book), the recovery of alien bodies, and one other crash near the Mexican border in 1950. Later research revealed that this 1950 UFO story may have been used to cover up the crash of a Civil Air Patrol (CAP) plane at the time. U.S. forces crossed the border and retrieved the wreckage before an international incident could develop. If the MJ-12 document was true, this brings up the confusing situation of a cover story covering up a cover story—was the crash really a UFO covered up later with the CAP plane incident?

Moore and Shandera didn't know exactly what to think about the information contained in these pages, but they did know that, regardless of the documents' authenticity, they had just received something that would shake UFOlogy to its foundations. They waited three years to reveal the MJ-12 papers to anyone, while they and another research partner, Stanton Friedman, quietly tried to authenticate various elements in the text and looked into the backgrounds of the listed MJ-12 members.

In 1987, Falcon (or another intel operative) warned Moore that another party (British researcher Timothy Good) had been sent copies of the same MJ-12 documents and was going to release them soon. Not wishing to be upstaged, Moore and his team decided to break the news first at the National UFO Conference (NUFOC) in Burbank on June 13. It was indeed the fantastic revelation that UFO researchers had been expecting. MJ-12 was still the hot topic when Moore and his associates cooperated with Falcon and his buddies to present a nationally televised special entitled *UFOs: Government Coverup—Live,* that aired on November 14, 1988,

If the MJ-12 episode had shaken the UFO community, this TV special sent them into a frenzy. Host Mike Farrell, of

M*A*S*H fame, interviewed UFO witnesses (including Betty Cash and Vickie Landrum) and discussed the possibility of alien visitations and government knowledge of same. But producer Michael Seligman had saved the best for last. In a series of taped interviews, Falcon (or someone pretending to be him) and another "Aviary" member referred to as "Condor" (identified by some as Air Force scientist and DIA employee Col. Robert Collins) appeared in silhouette with their voices electronically altered and described the aliens' appearance and biology—and embarrassingly, their preference for Tibetan music and strawberry ice cream. For the UFO community, which saw itself in a struggle for public acceptance and respect, these last remarks were too over the top. They thought Moore had blown it for them all.

They needn't have fretted, however, as the ratings for *Coverup—Live* were appallingly low, and most of the world went on ignoring the UFO subject much as before. "Everyone was supposed to be interviewed live, " Moore later said, "but the producers wanted everything scripted and approved beforehand. They hired some hack and we ended up reading off teleprompters and the whole thing came off very badly. It was embarrassing.

"Some of the stuff on the show was real, and some was disinformation," he adds, but will not (or cannot) reveal what was what, in all likelihood because he isn't really sure himself. The ever-mysterious Falcon sat in the audience and watched the entire strange charade.

But Moore would soon have his fill of all this. Scarcely seven months later, he was ready to distance himself permanently from his fellow researchers as he prepared a speech that would turn the UFO community inside out.

chapter 25

OUT OF CONTROL

Don't worry about being insane. We are far advanced beyond that.

—Letter from Paul Bennewitz to fellow UFO researcher

ill Moore's last visit to see Bennewitz occurred in 1986 or '87, during one of the peaks of Bennewitz's emotional roller coaster. Moore was still giving limited briefings to the Air Force at the time. " I watched Paul become systematically more emotionally unstable," recalls Moore, "as he tried to assimilate what was happening to him. He had guns and knives all over the house, he had installed extra locks on his doors, and he swore that 'they' (meaning the aliens) were coming through his walls at night and injecting him with hideous chemicals which would knock him out for long periods of time."

Moore was shocked at his friend's appearance—he looked like a concentration camp survivor; he had lost a lot of weight, his hands were shaking, he smoked incessantly

(Moore once counted twenty-eight cigarettes in forty-five minutes during a lunch date where Bennewitz touched not a bite of his food), and he had trouble expressing a coherent thought. Many of these symptoms may have been due to his persistent insomnia. Sleep deprivation often produces incredible delusions, but even this cannot account for Bennewitz's state of mind by that time.

Bennewitz told Moore that after the aliens injected him, they would make him drive his car out into the desert in the middle of the night, but he couldn't remember what he did after he got there. Both Moore and Richard Doty independently recalled noticing injection marks running down Bennewitz's arm (for some reason, the marks were only on the right side). Moore could not explain this, and Doty guessed that they might have been self-inflicted. Those with a suspicious bent (that is, some UFOlogists and the conspiratorially minded) might suggest that Doty knew exactly what was going on.

As the sign at the entrance to CIA Headquarters reminds visitors, "The Truth Shall Set You Free." The truth with regard to the history of CIA attempts at mind control leads decidedly in the opposite direction. The CIA sponsored a number of projects in the 1950s and '60s under the heading of MKULTRA (and others), which hired psychologists and other assorted mavericks under contract to find out if the human brain could be altered to create mindless slaves who would kill or do other sorts of bidding for the National Security State. There were varying degrees of success along the way, but one project in particular bears a closer look for its possible connection (or at least similarity) to the Bennewitz saga. The CIA was another one of the agencies that eventually looked into Bennewitz's background to determine if he was passing secrets off to evildoers.

After almost a decade of shenanigans and tomfoolery, the CIA had fed, smoked, and injected unwitting test subjects full of LSD, marijuana, psilocybin mushrooms, and sodium pentothal (among other substances) to see if human will and individuality could be subverted for a greater purpose. In 1958, thinking things might be a little safer away from American soil, the agency contacted a Canadian, Dr. D. Ewen Cameron, who ran a psychiatric clinic in an imposing old mansion on a mountain high above Montreal. An immigrant from Scotland who retained his soft native brogue, Cameron was experimenting with sensory deprivation to cure various psychotics, depressives, and housewives whose wealthy husbands had them committed to find out why they were so bored, listless, and no longer interested in sex. The CIA appropriated about $19,000 a year to sponsor his "research" for at least two years. With this funding, Cameron tried to perfect a technique he had dubbed "psychic driving." Cameron's goal was to wipe the personality clean and install a new one tailor-made to his specifications as to what he considered a "healthy" person.

If this sounds like the plot of some horror movie, it gets worse: Cameron employed a geeky assistant, who had no training in psychiatry and who functioned as a sort of "Igor." He restrained patients, fitted them with helmets rigged with speakers that would repeat phrases designed to "reprogram" the patient, and dragged them off to the "quiet room" after Cameron had administered injections of various psychotropic drugs, including combinations of LSD and depressants or stimulants. They were often locked in boxes just large enough to keep them in a sitting position for days or weeks at a time.

If the patient (many, if not most, of whom were women)

had arrived at the front door kicking and screaming, or even just a trifle uncooperative with authority figures, Cameron pronounced them cured when they could walk out the door a few weeks or months later with a quiet smile, answer simple questions, and basically stay out of the way. Even years later, one of his original test subjects had to make daily lists of simple chores so that she wouldn't forget. It was the *Stepford Wives* made real. Surviving CIA records indicate that nothing of value to the agency was gained, or, if so, was never revealed. CIA director Richard Helms ordered most of the **MKULTRA** records to be destroyed just before his retirement in 1973 as congressional inquiries were starting to pile up.

Almost twenty years later, perhaps Bennewitz had become a victim of the sort of techniques that Ewen Cameron and others had pioneered, for although he didn't completely lose his mind, he came very close, and eventually reduced his annoying research and letter writing down to a quiet roar. If the injections were not self-inflicted, perhaps they were a method used to knock him out while someone "psychically drove" him toward his new, paranoid worldview. In the meantime, the "aliens" that were supposedly coming through his bedroom wall, injecting him with hideous chemicals, and making him log hundreds of unaccounted-for miles on his Lincoln Town Car were still talking to him through his computer. If they gave him a reason for this mistreatment, Bennewitz never talked about it to anyone outside his family, at least anyone who can be located today.

With a mixture of apprehension and guilt, and since he still couldn't tell Bennewitz about his agreement with AFOSI, Moore counseled him to quit the UFO business before he had a complete breakdown. Bennewitz assured him that he could hold it together, and that he could still handle the phone taps, agents tailing his car, and nightly alien horror show. He also claimed that his wife Cindy had been implanted with an alien tracking device. Doty claims that on one of his many covert visits, he saw a ladder leaned up against the stucco on the outer wall of the home, directly opposite the interior wall where Bennewitz said that the diminutive beings came through every night to inject him and perform other unspeakable acts. Perhaps one of the many agencies that were swarming around Bennewitz were responsible, but as with other questions about what exactly happened to Bennewitz, it presently remains another in a series of loose ends in the disinformation carpet. Given his state of mind, he needed very little input to fuel his downhill slide. Paul Bennewitz was sustaining a paranoid fusion reaction.

By August of 1988, after eight very long years of unrelenting stress and fear, the sixty-one-year-old Paul Bennewitz could no longer function normally. He had turned over much of the day-to-day operations of Thunder Scientific to associates and his two adult sons. Former acquaintance Gary Massey says that Bennewitz had finally barricaded himself in the house and had piled sandbags around all the windows. His family, finally convinced that his sanity and health were in immediate danger, took him to the Anna Kaseman Mental Health Facility in Albuquerque, just a couple of miles up the road from Thunder Scientific headquarters, and checked him in for nervous exhaustion.

When Richard Doty heard that Bennewitz had finally been committed, he had rushed out to visit him; Doty still considered him a friend, even though his job had been to lie to him for five years. Curiously enough, Bennewitz felt the same way, even years afterward. "His wife was there with him in the hospital, but Paul was so doped up on something or other that I couldn't even get him to recognize me," says Doty.

Bennewitz was confined for a little over a month, and was then released back into his family's care. Doty visited a few months later "and he seemed fine to me. Just as normal as ever." But Bennewitz's contact with other UFO researchers had effectively ended as his family tried to keep him away from the subject that had nearly lost them a husband and father. He would never again approach the UFO subject with such fervor and sense of patriotic duty, although he would continue to pursue leads and communicate with other researchers, who considered him a trailblazing pioneer into the reality of the Alien Threat, and a conscientious defender of the American Way of Life.

chapter 26

LAS VEGAS

Somebody had to put all of this confusion here!

> —KERRY THORNLEY AND GREG HILL, *PRINCIPIA DISCORDIA*

Almost a decade after Paul Bennewitz had first started making noise about saucers over the Manzanos, UFO scholars were in for a rude awakening. There is no professional, scientifically recognized group or institution that offers degrees in the study of unidentified flying objects. Anyone who wants to can read a few books and put "UFOlogist" after their name on their business card. With no standards or peer review, the field is wide open for assorted wackiness; there is no "authority" to provide a measuring stick for reliability.

This makes many UFOlogists very nervous and territorial.

It was now 1989 and the UFO research glitterati were worried; some were quite ticked off. The Mutual UFO Network (MUFON) convention was gathering in the blistering

midsummer heat of Las Vegas at the Aladdin Hotel for their
annual convention during the first weekend of July. Vicious
disagreements and rumors making the rounds had caused
part of the membership to break off and run their own mini-
convention one morning while the main conference events
went on as scheduled before and after it. The splitters had
even called their own press conference to reveal secret deals
they had uncovered that an agreement existed between the
U.S. government and alien races. These stories had been circulating ever since the late 1970s, which was coincidentally
the same period that Bennewitz had first started to uncover
his own cornucopia of fantastic scenarios. Was Bennewitz
just the first to smack the hornet's nest so that the angry
buzzing of long-hidden secrets burst out?

The heat of the schism's wrath centered on Bill Moore. In
the weeks leading up to his presentation at the MUFON
conclave, Moore started to drop hints that he was going to
break the UFO controversy wide open, enraging old foes and
creating new ones. He would elaborate no further. Some suspected Moore of working for the intelligence community, of
spreading disinformation in order to confuse and discredit
the entire UFO field. Moore didn't think that he was, at least
not intentionally, but to an outsider, his position looked
frighteningly suspicious.

As the 1989 MUFON convention drew near, I agreed to
help Moore sell his books and documents at the convention.
It was almost by accident that I first met Bill Moore. In the
summer of 1988, I had just been laid off from my first major
job, my best friend had squeezed me out of his stock film
business, and my girlfriend had left me, all in the space of a
week. I was looking around for projects to keep me out of
trouble and the funny farm, when my lifelong interest in

UFOs led me to Moore's office, just a block down from the
stock film headquarters. A major West Coast UFO conference was going to be held in Los Angeles that year, and I
proposed a video project to Moore; his research partner,
Stanton Friedman; and abduction researcher Budd Hopkins.
They all agreed to let me record their presentations and sell
the edited videos for a split profit. The tapes didn't sell very
well, but I began to see how carefully Moore went about his
research, and why he seemed to play his cards so close to his
chest.

Moore stayed in a separate hotel from the other speakers
in Las Vegas in 1989 and I didn't even see him until just before his Saturday night speech. He still wouldn't tell me what
he was going to say. Moore had not told anyone other than a
couple close associates the subject matter of his presentation,
and hadn't even allowed an abstract of it to be published in
the symposium proceedings. For the most insecure of the
conventiongoers, the anticipation was whipped into a paranoid froth.

I grabbed a chair near the front of the thousand-seat
room and waited for the introduction. No one knew exactly
what to expect. I could feel the tension and I didn't even
have a good idea at the time about what was really going on
and the politics involved.

The Grand Ballroom was packed to a standing-room
crowd when Moore took the stage on the evening of July 1.
There was cautious applause. He smiled and began: "Ladies
and gentlemen, friends and enemies, associates and colleagues—in short, fellow UFOlogists: I had really wanted to
come here tonight and 'kick ass,' but fortunately for us all,
wiser heads have prevailed and we're going to keep this presentation as professional as possible." Considering what

Moore had wanted to say, the talk was as "professional" as he could stand to make it.

As Moore launched into the meat of his presentation, the air could have been cut with the proverbial butter knife. In the midst of a few well-placed barbs at anyone he felt had consistently missed the point, he tried to carefully explain what he had done. Yes, he had deliberately withheld information from certain researchers, and he had reported on their thinking and activities to his contacts in the intelligence world. He had visited Paul Bennewitz on at least four occasions, talked to him many times, and reported on what he found to these same people. He had withheld and blacked out certain parts of UFO-related government documents. He had even passed deliberately misleading information (the Aquarius document) on to Bennewitz.

As Moore continued, the conventiongoers began to mutter among themselves, and then began to shout at him. But in the midst of the hollering, most of the audience missed his point. He was actually admitting to this and explaining how it was done. He was warning other researchers that this could happen to them, and indeed already had. Many chose to think that Moore was thumbing his nose at them, while rubbing their faces in what he said was their naïveté. They also felt betrayed by a man whom they had trusted. The audience didn't even know if they could count on his declaration that "several other individuals" were involved in the same sort of deal he was revealing that evening.

Moore felt justified in venting his frustrations, as some of the other researchers had publicly denounced him in the past, and Moore was not one to take things sitting down. But in spite of the backbiting, he thought that he would come as clean as he thought possible, and perhaps help to steer

UFOlogy into a new phase—a time where those who were following the phenomenon could use the tools he and a few others had developed to get as much information as was possible from the government without getting burned in the process.

From the audience point of view, these admissions amounted to the boy who cried "wolf" admitting to his crimes. How could they trust anything he said? Minds trained to look at issues in terms of black and white could not see the many shades of gray, and to its discredit, the UFO world is filled with "is or isn't"-type thinking. This makes it substantially no different from society at large. It is obvious to some outside observers of the UFO subculture (and even some on the inside) that the subject cannot be profitably viewed in this fashion—just like the world of counterintelligence. This is what the spooks counted on when telling their sleight-of-hand stories to the gullible or those who restricted their views to compartmentalized or "binary"-type ways of looking at problems. Just because the message comes from someone with credentials doesn't mean it's airtight and reliable.

Moore's speech ran nearly two hours. It had to be stopped several times by MUFON's Arizona state director Hal Starr to restore order. Another researcher stood up and rhetorically asked, "Where did you get all that crap from, Bill?" The publisher of a major UFO magazine ran out in tears. People literally yelled, cried, and gritted their teeth in anger. I was surprised that they didn't throw things. If I had known what was going to happen, I'd have picked a case of rotten vegetables out from behind the nearest supermarket and sold them outside the lecture hall beforehand.

The reaction to Moore's admission was predictable. Bill

English, who ran out with fists clenched saying, "I'm going to get a fire hose!" was one of Moore's fellow APRO members and probably felt doubly betrayed, even though Moore had never "disinformed" him or anyone else he worked with at APRO. English stormed out in red-faced rage. Like English, many of Moore's colleagues could not handle the cognitive dissonance that he had laid on them. They chose to reject everything he had said in the past.

To be sure, the indignant outrage Moore inspired was justifiable. Why should anyone have trusted him after Las Vegas? A few, like UFOlogist Chris Lambright and later researchers like Grant Cameron, withheld most of their condemnation and concentrated on the information that Moore and his colleagues had uncovered, as well as the self-evident revelation that "government sources" in the UFO field have their own agendas.

Moore had tried to point out that he didn't need to tell anyone what he had been doing for the past nine years. He could have kept things under wraps and played it for all his ego and bank account could get. Moore knew that he would probably be slitting his own throat by telling all, but figured it was worth the gamble, as most of his intelligence contacts had dried up by then, and he hadn't been asked to do anything for them for many years. He had just had too much with the accusations and angry letters over the years and wanted to shut the door on the whole business.

Moore had presented his revelations as both a sort of mea culpa and a stern warning. They were taken as neither, but then he had more than half-expected things to turn out this way. Years later, he regretted his arrogant attitude: "If I had it to do over again, I probably would have been a little more humble," he remarked. The heady world of counterintelligence and the experiences he had notched up to that time contributed to his attitude. He felt comfortable revealing perhaps half of his side of the story, since he had never signed any security oaths. Moore had burst, or tried to burst, a lot of bubbles that evening.

Why did the UFO community continue to reject Moore's revelations? The answer, of course, is not a simple one. Moore had been involved in the spy game up to his eyeballs, and his work with and for the shadow side of the military and intelligence establishment was far, far more intricate and complicated than he was ever going to reveal in mixed company. The journey he had been on to uncover the government's tightly held UFO secrets went so beyond anything he and other researchers had been exposed to in the past that he probably couldn't describe it to the uninitiated even if he tried. He would always hold his cards close, just like the other players in the dark game he had been playing.

Moore was the only one to admit that he used and had been used, and the flip-flop of values he had been through because of his decision to cooperate with U.S. counterintelligence lay in a much smaller world than the one to which he had been invited. It was a difficult bargain, but then Moore was never in the game to win any popularity contests at the UFO circle jerk.

chapter 27

THE ENIGMA OF BELIEF

I long so much to be / Where I was before I was me.

—SCREAMIN' JAY HAWKINS, "I HEAR VOICES"

As the twentieth century drew to a close and years after the game was up, Richard Doty continued to visit Bennewitz on occasion. But there were problems. "Once I went to see Paul in the hospital when he was in for health reasons," Doty recalls. "I saw one of his sons in the hall outside the room. When he saw me, he quickly approached and asked what I was doing there. I told him I just wanted to see how Paul was doing. He looked at me and said, 'You can wait out here all night if you want, but you're not getting in there to see my father.'"

When Paul Bennewitz found out about this, he admonished his son, "You will not keep my friends from seeing me if they want to."

"Dad, Rick Doty is not your friend," his son replied.

On another occasion, Doty decided to come clean with Bennewitz, and wishing to lay his guilty soul to rest said, "You know, Paul, a lot of that stuff I told you was disinformation. It was my job. I was ordered to lie to you."

Bennewitz simply said, "No it wasn't."

UFO abductee and researcher Christa Tilton tried to visit Bennewitz in late 1988, but he failed to show up at the arranged time. Tilton wrote in her self-published book, *The Bennewitz Papers,* that he called later and explained that "two men in official military uniforms had showed [*sic*] up at his door right before he was to leave for our meeting . . . He did not say what they had wanted, but that they kept him for over an hour and by then he figured it was too late." Bennewitz apologized profusely and offered to buy Tilton a plane ticket to Albuquerque, which she politely refused. If he was still under surveillance, perhaps the Air Force was watching Bennewitz strictly out of habit, and for some reason still wanted to know with whom he was talking and what was discussed. He had dismantled his eavesdropping setup by this time and no longer posed a threat to any NSA or Air Force operation.

Near the end of her book, Tilton makes a keen observation: "Paul Bennewitz seemed to need a friend or just someone to talk to every once in awhile. He would call sometimes, distressed saying [*sic*] the aliens were bothering him once again. I wrote to him off and on for quite awhile and tried to establish some kind of rapore [*sic*] with him. I was careful because I didn't want him to get paranoid of [*sic*] me, but what I found so astonishing was his staunch defense of Richard Doty. I think Paul became dependant [*sic*] on Richard Doty and trusted him. I feel there was a mutual admiration between the both of them which continues to this day."

The classic case study of dependency, oddly enough, also dealt with flying saucers. In 1955, a group of sociology students from the University of Minnesota infiltrated a millennial flying saucer group to study the dynamics of belief when a charismatic woman gathered a group around her pronouncements and channeled predictions of the imminent end of civilization. When the cataclysm and expected pickup by a fleet of flying saucers failed to materialize, most of the group separated, but a few redoubled their beliefs, looking at the turn of events as a sign that they had passed some sort of loyalty test. When asked why he had not forsaken the leader of the group or her message, one member of the group said, "I've had to go a long way. I've given up just about everything. I've cut every tie: I've burned every bridge. I've turned my back on the world. I can't afford to doubt. I have to believe. And there isn't any other truth."

We could, on the other hand, give Bennewtiz the benefit of the doubt. Perhaps there really is an alien presence, and some world governments know exactly what is going on. Perhaps there are secret agreements between alien visitors and those they perceive as the leaders of the human race. If this is true, the last thing that those in the loop would want to do is admit this publicly. It is the trump card in their hand, as well as proof that there is something greater out there. For them, it is the possibility of salvation and ruin at the same time.

Paul Bennewitz was not in the game for fame or money. His crusade had a higher purpose. There is no denying a concern with the UFO subject in the corridors of the Pentagon and the halls of our government. How much these people actually know is still rightly a subject of hot debate. On the other hand, the Bennewitz story perhaps lays to rest many of the rumors surrounding the origins of some of the most popular delusions about a few of the weirdest UFO stories that have made the rounds over the past twenty years. And while most of the things Bennewitz experienced were written by the AFOSI and NSA for his own personal horror show, events such as the landings of strangely bright and highly maneuverable lights at Kirtland and pictures of unexplained flying objects near Dulce, as well as the weird orange "balls" seen drifting in the Bennewitz home, are not amenable to simple explanations.

Someday, these enigmatic dragons may be slain as well.

WHERE ARE THEY NOW?

Paul Bennewitz died in Albuquerque on June 23, 2003, as I was writing this book. He was seventy-five. The Bennewitz family pointedly refused to talk to me. They have consistently declined any comment on the affair for over twenty years, and they aren't about to change their minds. Please do not contact or pester them. It is not a time that they want to revisit.

Brad and Matthew Bennewitz have carried on in their father's business. Thunder Scientific is more successful than ever and still designs and manufactures temperature and humidity instruments for the U.S. military, NASA, and other high-profile clients in foreign countries. Cindy Bennewitz still lives in the Four Hills area home she shared with her husband for many of their fifty-four years of marriage.

Richard Doty retired from the Air Force in 1986 and became an officer with the New Mexico State Police in Grants, about thirty miles west of Albuquerque. He later became involved in training personnel in counterterrorist techniques. In 2003, he passed the bar exam and is employed by the district attorney's office in Albuquerque. He is married with three children, two sons and a daughter.

Bill Moore dropped out of the UFO field and began work on a book about the origins of the Mormon Church, *The Spalding Enigma: Who Really Wrote the Book of Mormon?*, will be published by Concordia Press in 2005. He lives in Los Angeles and repairs motorcycles and computers on the side. Recently, Moore disposed of some of his private collection of rare UFO-related books and documents to an independent "memorabilia" dealer named "moviemanmarty" who has offered some of these for sale on eBay.

Gabe Valdez retired from the New Mexico State Police in 1995 and moved to Albuquerque. He was called out of retirement in 1998 to investigate recurring cattle mutilation cases in northern New Mexico. The work was sponsored and managed by the National Institute for Discovery Science, an organization backed by Robert Bigelow, the real estate tycoon with a keen interest in the paranormal.

Psychologist Leo Sprinkle still lives in Laramie, Wyoming and has retired from active abduction research. His most recent book, *Soul Samples: Personal Explorations in Reincarnation and UFO Experiences*, is a warm, personal account of his study of, and experiences with, the UFO phenomenon.

Jim Lorenzen died in 1990, followed a few months later by his wife Coral. The Tucson-based Aerial Phenomena Research Organization that they founded and headed for almost forty years faded into history soon thereafter.

Jaime Shandera disappeared in 1999, although he has been spotted in Los Angeles recently, laying to rest rumors that he was "silenced" or had moved to Tibet.

Stanton Friedman still writes and lectures on the government UFO cover-up.

Robert Emenegger retired and moved to Arkansas with his wife in the mid-1990s.

Optical physicist Dr. Robert Fugate is still director of the Starfire Optical Range.

Myrna Hansen now lives somewhere in Northern California.

The man known as "The Falcon" is now deceased. Moore and Doty still steadfastly refuse to divulge his real name.

The game is not over.

PROJECT ßETA: THE REPORT

After over two years of observation, speculation, and disinformation, Paul Bennewitz finished his opus and sent copies to Senators Domenici and Schmitt, President Reagan, APRO, and other researchers. This is the full text of the final version of "Project Beta," which has never been published, although incomplete and severely edited copies have shown up occasionally on the Internet. (All punctuation, spelling, language, etc. are as in the original.)

SUMMARY OF REPORT AND STATUS
(WITH SUGGESTED GUIDELINES)

INVESTIGATOR——PHYSICIST———PAUL F. BEN-NEWITZ

THE FOLLOWING ARE KEY MILE POSTS ESTAB-
LISHED OR DISCOVERED DURING THE CONTINU-
ING STUDY CONCERNING ALIEN INTERVENTION
AND THE RESULT. (STUDY IS SOLELY LIMITED TO
NEW MEXICO)

1) TWO YEARS CONTINUOUS RECORDED ELEC-
TRONIC SURVEILLANCE AND TRACKING WITH
D.F. [Direction Finding] 24 HR/DAY DATA OF ALIEN
SHIPS PLUS 6,000 FEET MOTION PICTURE OF
SAME—DAYLIGHT AND NIGHT.

2) DETECTION AND DISASSEMBLY OF ALIEN
COMMUNICATION AND VIDEO CHANNELS—BOTH
LOCAL, EARTH, AND NEAR SPACE.

3) CONSTANT RECEPTION OF VIDEO FROM
ALIEN SHIP AND UNDERGROUND BASE
VIEWSCREEN; TYPICAL ALIEN, HUMANOID AND
AT TIMES APPARENT HOMO SAPIEN.

4) A CASE HISTORY OF AN ENCOUNTER VIC-
TIM IN NEW MEXICO WHICH LEAD TO THE
COMMUNICATIONS LINK AND DISCOVERY THAT
APPARENTLY ALL ENCOUNTER VICTIMS HAVE
DELIBERATE ALIEN IMPLANTS ALONG WITH OB-
VIOUS ACCOMPANYING SCARS. THE VICTIM'S IM-
PLANTS WERE VERIFIED BY X-RAY AND CAT
SCAN. FIVE OTHER SCAR CASES WERE VERI-
FIED.

5) ESTABLISHED CONSTANT DIRECT COMMUNI-
CATION WITH THE ALIEN USING A COMPUTER
AND A FORM OF HEX DECIMAL CODE WITH
GRAPHICS AND PRINT-OUT. THIS COMMUNICA-

TION WAS INSTIGATED APPARENTLY AFTER THE US BASE WAS VACATED.

6) THROUGH THE ALIEN COMMUNICATION LOOP, THE TRUE UNDERGROUND BASE LOCATION WAS DIVULGED BY THE ALIEN AND PRECISELY PIN-POINTED.

7) SUBSEQUENT AERIAL AND GROUND PHOTOGRAPHS REVEALED LANDING PYLONS, SHIPS ON THE GROUND—ENTRANCES, BEAM WEAPONS AND APPARENT LAUNCH PORTS—ALONG WITH ALIENS ON THE GROUND IN ELECTROSTATICALLY SUPPORTED VEHICLES; CHARGING BEAM WEAPONS ALSO APPARENTLY ELECTROSTATIC.

8) CROSS CORRELATION AND MATCHING BY TRIANGULATION, ETC., TO OFFICIAL NASA CIR (COLOR INFRARED) HIGH RESOLUTION FILMS CONFIRMED BASE LOCATIONS AND RESULTED IN REVEALING US MILITARY ENVOLVEMENT YIELDING PRECISE COORDINATES AND THE US BASE LAYOUT.

9) PRIOR ALIEN COMMUNICATION HAD INDICATED MILITARY INVOLVEMENT AND THE FACT THAT THE USAF HAD A SHIP BUT DUE TO STUDIED ALIEN PSYCHOLOGY THIS WAS IGNORED AT THE TIME.

10) SUBSEQUENTLY, THE ALIEN COMMUNICATED FOLLOWING VERIFICATAION WITH THE CIR, THAT THERE WAS INDEED A SHIP; ACTUALLY MORE THAN ONE—THAT TWO WERE WRECKED AND LEFT BEHIND AND ANOTHER BUILT—THIS

SHIP IS ATOMIC POWERED AND FLYING. THE ALIEN INDICATED IT'S BASING LOCATION.

11) IT WAS LEARNED AS STATED THAT TWO WOMEN AND A BOY NEAR AUSTIN, TEXAS WERE EXPOSED TO SEVERE RADIATION AT CLOSE RANGE AND THE SHIP WAS LAST SEEN GOING WEST WITH HELICOPTERS. IN ADDITION, THE US GOVERNMENT WAS QUIETLY PICKING UP THE EXPENSES.

12) SUBSEQUENT INSPECTION OF MOTION PICTURE PHOTOGRAPHS TAKEN DURING THE STUDY REVEALED THE US SHIP OR ONE LIKE IT FLYING WITH THE ALIENS. THESE MATCH THE CIR WHERE TWO CAN BE SEEN ON THE GROUND AND IN THE LATER PHOTOGRAPHS TAKEN ON THE GROUND AFTER THE BASE WAS ABANDONED.

SO IN VERY BRIEF FORM THE PROLOGUE TO LEARNING WITHIN REASONABLE ACCURACY WHAT TRANSPIRED PRIOR TO THE END OF 1979 OR SHORTLY THEREAFTER.

THE COMPUTER COMMUNICATIONS AND CONSTANT INTERACTION WITH THE ALIEN IN THIS MANNER WITHOUT DIRECT ENCOUNTER HAS GIVEN A REASONABLY CLEAR PICTURE OF THE ALIEN PSYCHOLOGY, THEIR LOGIC AND LOGIC METHODS AND THEIR PRIME INTENT.

IT IS IMPORTANT TO NOTE AT THE OUTSET THAT THE ALIEN IS DEVIOUS, EMPLOYS DECEPTION, AND HAVE NO INTENT OF ANY APPARENT PEACE MAKING PROCESS AND OBVIOUSLY DOES

NOT ADHERE TO ANY PRIOR ARRANGED AGREE-
MENT.

IN TRUTH THEY TEND TO LIE, HOWEVER
THEIR MEMORY FOR LYING IS NOT LONG AND DI-
RECT COMPARATIVE COMPUTER PRINTOUT
ANALYSIS REVEALS THIS FACT. THEREFORE
MUCH "DROPS THRU THE CRACK" SO TO SPEAK;
AND FROM THIS COMES THE APPARENT TRUTH.

IT IS NOT THE INTENT OF THIS REPORT TO
CRITICIZE OR POINT FINGERS. OBVIOUSLY WHO-
EVER MADE THE INITIAL AGREEMENT WAS OPER-
ATING ON OUR BASIS OF LOGIC AND NOT THAT OF
THE ALIEN AND IN SO DOING APPARENTLY
WALKED INNOCENETLY, IN TIME, INTO A TRAP.

THE ALIEN INDICATED THAT THE "GREYS", AP-
PARENTLY THE GROUP INITIALLY ENVOLVED IN
THE AGREEMENT, WERE STILL UPSET ABOUT THE
INITIAL CAPTURE AND SUBSEQUENT DEATH OF
THE FIRST EIGHT OF THEIR CO-FELLOWS.

ANOTHER GROUP, CALLING THEMSELVES IN
THE COMPUTER LANGUAGE, THE "ORANGE"——
—-THEIR BASE IS ON THE WEST SLOPE OF MT.
ARCHELETA—DIRECTLY WEST OF THE SOUTH
END OF THE US BASE AND NEAR NW OF THE AP-
PARENT MAIN LANDING AREA THEY CALL, IN THE
COMPUTER LANGUAGE, "THE DIAMOND". THIS,
BECAUSE FROM A DISTANCE IT LOOKS DIAMOND
SHAPED IN THE PHOTOGRAPHS WHEN LOOKING
SOMEWHAT SOUTH WEST PAST THE OBSERVATION
TOWARD THE RIDGED PEAK SE OF MT.

ARCHELETA. THE RIGDED PEAK HAS NO NAME; I CALL IT SOUTH PEAK.

THE BASE EXTENDS NORTH OF THIS PEAK TO THE EDGE OF THE CLIFF DOWN WHICH GOES A ROAD PAST A LARGE ALLOY DOME THIRTY-EIGHT (38) FOOT ACROSS THE BOTTOM, WITH A TWENTY (20) FOOT HOLE IN THE TOP.

BASED UPON SOME OF THE AERIAL PHO-TOGRAPHS DURING WHICH THE ALIEN WAS CAUGHT IN THE OPEN AND LAUNCHING——SOME LAUNCHES APPEAR TO BE COMING FROM THE DI-RECTION OF THE DOME. I WOULD GUESS IT IS AN UNDERGROUND LAUNCH EGRESS FACILITY. IN THE NASA CIR THERE IS WHAT APPEARS TO BE A BLACK LIMOUSINE ALONGSIDE THE DOME ON A RAMP. SURPRISINGLY, IT IS PRECISELY THE SIZE OF MY 79 LINCOLN TOWN CAR. WHEELED VEHI-CLES AND WHAT APPEAR TO BE SNOW CATS OR CATAPILLARS CAN BE SEEN THROUGHOUT THE CIR—CAR AND TRUCK TRACKS, TRUCKS AND JEEPS. I DON'T BELIEVE ALIENS HAVE WHEELS— HUMANS DO.

NUMEROUS ROAD BLOCKS EXTEND NORTH-WARD THROUGH THE US BASE ALONG AWELL-MAINTAINED ROAD THIRTY SOME-ODD FEET WIDE—APPARENTLY GRAVEL——NEAR ALL WEATHER——NUMEROUS TURN AROUNDS AND WHEEL TRACKS INTO LAUNCH PREPARATION AREAS WITH THE SHIPS; PADS MARKED WITH TWENTY-SIX (26) FOOT Xs AND SERVICING FACILI-

TIES, TANKS, ETC.——TWO DOMED POLYGON HIGH VOLATGE BUIDINGS ON NORTH ON THE EAST SIDE OF THE ROAD, ALSO AN APPARENT FOUNDATION FOR ANOTHER OR HELO PAD——-TEST STANDS, HUMAN HOUSING, WATER TANK (THRITY-TWO FOOT ACROSS)—-AND AT ONE OF THE MAIN ROAD BLOCKS, TWO LARGE VEHICLES PARKED ACROSS THE ROAD. ALSO AT THAT POINT ANOTHER BLACK LIMOSINE WITH TRACKS LEADING TO IT TO THE WEST OF THE ROAD. ALL TRACKS AND VEHICLES HAVE BEEN DIMENSIONED AND MATCH MILITARY VEHICLES. IF I WERE TO MAKE A GUESS, I WOULD ESTIMATE THE LIKELYHOOD THAT THE APPARENT BLACK LIMOSINES ARE CIA.

THIS IS BUT A LIMITED INVENTORY OF WHAT WAS THERE ON SEPT 8, 1978,——INCLUDED ONLY AS EVIDENTIAL MATTER FOR YOUR PREUSAL AND CONFIRMATION. THE ROAD, WHICH INCIDENTALLY THE NATIVES, THE TRICAL CHIEF, RESERVATION POLICE AND HIGHWAY PATROLMAN KNOW NOTHING ABOUT, COMES IN OFF OF A TRAIL FROM THE NORTH. STARTING AT THE TRAIL, LINE OF SIGHT TO THE LARGE PLATEAU AREA AND THE ALLOY DOME, THE ROAD, IN THE MIDDLE OF NOWHERE ON THE JICARILLA RESERVATION, IS PRECISELY 12,888 FT. LONG AIRLINE DISTANCE. THE TOTAL ALIEN BASING AREA, WHICH APPARENTLY CONTAINS SEVERAL CULTURES, (NOW ALL UNDER THE DESIGNATION "UNITY" IN THE COMPUTER LANGUAGE) IS APPROXIMATELY THREE (3) KM WIDE BY EIGHT (8)

KM LONG. A CONSERVATIVE GUESS BASED ON THE NUMBER OF SHIPS PRESENTLY OVER THIS AREA AND THE NUMBER ON THE GROUND IN THE CIR AND THE PHOTOGRAPHS; THE TOTAL ALIEN POPULATION IS ESTIMATED TO BE AT LEAST TWO THOUSAND (2,000) AND MOST LIKELY MORE. THE ALIEN INDICATES MORE ARE COMING OR ARE ON THE WAY.

I WON'T ATTEMPT TO SPECULATE IN THIS RE-PORT HOW THE INITIAL US CONTACT WAS MADE——WHAT TRANSPIRED, NOR HOW MANY WERE ABLE TO ESCAPE. THE ALIEN HAS COMMU-NICATED HIS ACCOUNT, AND IF TOTALLY TRUE, IS CERTAINLY IS NOT PALATABLE.

MUCH DETAIL HAS BEEN OMITTED FOR FU-TURE DISCUSSION IF DESIRED——HOWEVER THE IMPORT IS THIS. CONSTANT COMPUTER COM-MUNICATION—-FULL ON LINE IN FEBRUARY OF THIS YEAR——MANUAL PRIOR TO THAT—HAS AL-LOWED A CONSTANT ACCOUNTING OF WHAT IS AND HAS BEEN GOING ON——CONDITIONS OF MORALE AND TOTAL INSIGHT INTO "WHAT MAKES THE ALIEN RUN". THIS IS <u>VERY</u> VALUABLE DATA.

1) MOST IMPORTANTLY, THE ALIEN WILL ALLOW NO ONE TO GO WITHOUT AN IMPLANT AND AFTER KNOWLEDGE OF IT IS WIPED OUT. THEY SIMPLY WILL NOT ALLOW IT. ALL INDICA-TIONS ARE THAT COMMUNICATION OR LAN-GUAGE CANNOT RESULT WITHOUT THE IMPLANT. (WITH THE EXCEPTION OF THE BINARY AND THE COMPUTER). THIS WOULD INDICATE A POSSIBLE

IMMEDIATE THREAT OR DANGER FOR ANYONE—
MILITARY, AIR FORCE, OR OTHERWISE THAT HAS
BEEN AT THE BASE. THEY <u>WILL</u> <u>NOT</u> REMEMBER
THE IMPLANT IN ANY CASE (THE CONTACTEE
HERE INCLUDED).

THE REASON FOR THE IMPLANT IS MULTIPLE
FOR BOTH LANGUAGE OR COMMUNICATION BY
THOUGHT (THERE IS APPARENTLY NO LANGUAGE
BARRIER WITH THOUGHT) AND ALSO FOR <u>COM-</u>
<u>PLETE</u> <u>ABSOLUTE</u> CONTROL BY THE ALIEN
THROUGH PROGRAM—BY THEIR BEAM OR DI-
RECT CONTACT.

I HAVE TESTED THIS AND FOUND THAT DUR-
ING THIS PROGRAMMING THE PERSON IS TO-
TALLY ALIEN; ONCE ONE LEARNS TO RECOGNIZE
THE SIGNS AND THE PERSON THEN HAS NO MEM-
ORY OF THE ACT/ CONVERSATION AFTERWARD. IF
THIS HAS HAPPENED TO THE MILITARY, I NEED
NOT ELABORATE AS TO THE POSSIBLE CONSE-
QUENCES. THE VICTIM'S "SWITCH" CAN BE
PULLED AT ANY TIME AND AT THE SAME TIME
THEY ARE "WALKING CAMERAS AND MICRO-
PHONES" IF THE ALIEN CHOOSES TO LISTEN IN
WITH THE USE OF THEIR BEAMS. NO CLASSIFIED
AREA OF ENDEAVOR IN THE US IS INVIOLATE
UNDER THESE CONDITIONS. HOWEVER—REAL-
IZE—THE SCARS, BARELY VISIBLE—<u>CAN</u> BE
SEEN—<u>ALL</u> ARE EXACTLY LOCATED AND <u>ALL</u> ARE
ACCESSIBLE BY X-RAY.

2) ALSO NOTE THAT ALL OF THE ALIENS—
HUMAN, HUMANOID ALIKE—ALL MUST HAVE IM-

PLANTS—WITHOUT THEM, NO DIRECT COMMU-
NICATION IS APPARENTLY POSSIBLE. SO ONE CAN
MOST GENERALLY ARBITRARILY SAY THAT IF A
PERSON STATES HE/SHE HAS COMMUNICATED BY
THOUGHT WITH AN ALIEN—HE/SHE MOST LIKELY
HAS BEEN IMPLANTED. THEY MAY ALSO CLAIM TO
BE OVERLY PSYCHIC AND BE ABLE TO PROVE
THIS—AGAIN THROUGH THE LINK TRANSPLANT,
HE/SHE IS GIVEN THE INFORAMTION BY THE
ALIEN AND DOES NOT REALIZE.

3) MOST IMPORTANTLY, THE ALIEN, EITHER
THROUGH EVOLVEMENT OR BECAUSE THE HU-
MANOID IS MADE—WILL EXHIBIT TENDENCIES
FOR BAD LOGIC (BAD BY EARTH LOGIC COMPARI-
SON) SO THEY <u>ARE</u> <u>NOT</u> INFALLIBLE—IN POINT
OF FACT THEY APPEAR TO HAVE MANY MORE
FRAILTIES AND WEAKNESSES THAN THE NORMAL
HOMO SAPIEN. TO THE ALIEN, THE MIND IS THE
KEY AND THEREIN LIES A GREAT WEAKNESS
WHICH WILL BE DISCUSSED LATER.

4) THEY ARE NOT TO BE TRUSTED. IT IS SUS-
PECTED IF ONE WAS CONSIDERED A "FRIEND"
AND IF ONE WERE TO CALL UPON THAT "FRIEND"
IN TIME OF DIRE PHYSICAL THREAT, THE
"FRIEND" WOULD QUICKLY SIDE WITH THE
OTHER SIDE.

THE COMPUTER INDICATES THAT IN COMPARI-
SON, THAT NO KNOWN EARTH PROTAGONIST—
RUSSIAN OR OTHERWISE EXHIBIT THESE
TENDENCIES TO ANY MAJOR DEGREE INDICAT-
ING THE DANGER INVOLVED IN MAKING ANY

KIND OF AGREEMENT WITH THESE ALIENS—AT LEAST OF THIS SPECIES.

5) THE ALIEN DOES KILL WITH THE BEAM GENERALLY. RESULTS ON A HUMAN WILL EXHIBIT A THREE TO FOUR CM PURPLE CIRCLE. IF DONE FROM THE REAR, ON ONE OR BOTH SHOULDERS. THE RESULTS ON CATTLE ARE THE SAME, ESSENTIALLY EXHIBITING PURPLE BENEATH THE HIDE, WITH BURNED CIRCLES ON THE OUTSIDE.

6) CATTLE MUTILATIONS ARE THE OTHER SIDE OF THE COIN AND WILL NOT BE DELVED INTO HERE THOUGH THEY ARE PART OF THE OVERALL. IT APPEARS THAT THE HUMANOIDS ARE FED BY A FORMULA MADE FROM HUMAN OR CATTLE MATERIAL OR BOTH AND THEY ARE MADE FROM THE SAME MATERIAL BY GENE SPLICING AND USE OF FEMALE ENCOUNTER VICTIM'S OVUM. THE RESULTANT EMBRYOS ARE REFERRED TO BY THE ALIEN AS AN ORGAN. TIME OF GESTATION TO FULL USE AS A UTILITY, READY TO WORK APPEARS TO BE ABOUT ONE YEAR. A YEAR IN ALIEN TIME— I DO NOT KNOW.

SOLUTION: I DOUBT THERE IS AN IMMEDIATE OR TOTAL "CURE" PER SE—HOWEVER, THEY MUST BE STOPPED AND WE HAVE TO GET OFF DEAD CENTER BEFORE WE FIND TIME HAS RUN OUT. THEY ARE PICKING UP AND "CUTTING" (AS THE ALIEN CALLS IT) MANY PEOPLE EVERY NIGHT. EACH IMPLANTED INDIVIDUAL IS APPARENTLY READY FOR THE PULL OF THEIR "SWITCH". WHETHER ALL IMPLANTS ARE TOTALLY EFFEC-

TIVE I CANNOT PREDICT, BUT CONSERVATIVELY I WOULD ESTIMATE AT LEAST 300,000 OR MORE IN THE US AND AT LEAST 2,000,000 IF NOT MORE WORLDWIDE.

WEAPONRY AND INHERENT WEAKNESSES

WEAPONRY IS OF THE KEYS AND IN THE ALIENS PRESENT STATE WE <u>CAN</u> PREPARE AN EFFECTIVE OFFENSE.

ONE TENDS AT THE OUTSET (I DID) TO LOOK AT THEIR MACHINES AND SAY—THAT THERE IS NO DEFENSE OR OFFENSE. ONE IS OVERWHELMED BY THEIR SPEED, APPARENT CAPABILITY OF INVISIBILITY AND "CLOAKING", AND OTHER COVERT CAPABILITIES NOT DISCUSSED AT THIS TIME. IN PARTICULAR—THE BEAM WEAPONS ARE THEMSELVES A DIRECT THREAT AND ONE THAT OBVIOUSLY ONE THAT MUST BE SERIOUSLY CONSIDERED BUT NOT OVERLY SO.

LET US FIRST LOOK AT JUST WHAT THIS WEAPON IS. IT IS AN ELECTROSTATIC WEAPON WITH PLASMA GENERATING VOLTAGES—AND AN INTERNAL STORAGE DEVICE—IT IS PULSE POWERED. THE BEAM, TOTALLY EFFECTIVE <u>IN</u> <u>ATMOSPHERE</u> CAN BE LOADED WITH HYDROGEN OR OXYGEN. AVERAGE, GROUND WEAPONS—MAXIMUM TWO (2) KM IF IT IS DRY, CAPABLE OF SUSTAINING JUST SO MANY FULL POWER DISCHARGES—SLOW LEAKAGE OCCURS CONTINUOUSLY, THEREFORE THEY MUST BE RECHARGED

PERIODICALLY. IF IT IS RAINING THE WEAPON BE-
COMES INEFFECTIVE AND IS SWAMPED THUS
DISCHARGED. THE RANGE IS NEAR TOTALLY LOST
AT THAT POINT.

ON THE DISKS AND SAUCERS, THE WEAPON IS
GENERALLY ON THE LEFT SIDE OR TOP CENTER
AND HAS A MAXIMUM RANGE OF TWO HUNDRED
(200) METERS AT WHICH POINT IT WILL PLOW A
TRENCH IN DESERT SOIL. WHEN FIRED—IT FIRES
BOTH TO THE FRONT AND TO THE BACK
EQUALLY. REASON? BECAUSE OF THEIR MODE
AND METHODS OF FLIGHT. IF EQUILIBRIIUM IS
NOT MAINTAINED, THE SAUCER WILL SPIN OUT.

HAND WEAPONS? ESTIMATE BASED UPON VISI-
BLE DAMAGE OBSERVED, NOT TOO MUCH VELOC-
ITY OR STAYING POWER BUT AT SHORT
RANGE—DEADLY (LESS THAN A .45 CAL AUTO-
MATIC). AT ONE METER RANGE, ESTIMATE OF
1600° F OR HIGHER; IT CAN VAPORIZE METAL.

APPARENTLY THE DISKS AND WEAPONS OP-
ERATE FROM A STORAGE SOURCE. IN TIME,
WITHOUT PERIODIC RECHARGE, THIS STORAGE
IS DEPLETED. THE DESIGN THEY TRADED TO
US WAS AT LEAST THIRTY YEARS OLD—EMPLOY-
ING AN ATOMIC SOURCE. POSSIBLY THEY MAY
STILL HAVE SOME—IT WOULD APPEAR SO——
THEIR STAYING POWER IS OBVIOUSLY MUCH
LONGER.

AIRCRAFT HELICOPTER VULNERABILITY

ANY OF OUR AIRCRAFT, HELICOPTERS, MISSLES, OR ANY AIR FLIGHT VEHICLE CAN BE TAKEN DOWN INSTANTLY WITH NO USE OF WEAPONRY. THE ALIEN SIMPLY NEED DO NO MORE THAN MAKE ONE INVISIBLE PASS AND THEIR BOW WAVE OR SCREEN OR BOTH WILL TAKE THE AIR LIFT VEHICLE DOWN. THE PILOT OBVIOUSLY WILL NOT EVEN KNOW WHAT HIT HIM.

FOR THE HUMAN ON THE GROUND, THE ALIEN CAN USE WEAPONRY OR BOW WAVE. THE PARTIAL PRESSURE ENVELOP CAN HIT WITH THE POWER OF A TORNADO—SHOCK RISE TIME AND G FORCE IS INSTANTANEOUS.

HOWEVER, THEY DARE NOT HIT THE CRAFT PHYSICALLY BECAUSE THEY ARE PRAGILE AND IN FACT, UNDER SLOW FLYING CONDITIONS WITHIN OUR ATMOSPHERE, HOLD A VERY TENUOUS POSITION. WITHOUT POWER, BALANCE OR EQUILIBRIUM, THEY LOOSE IT.

IN BRIEF—THESE ARE APPARENT CAPABILITIES OBSERVED AND GLEANED THROUGH THE COMPUTER COMMUNICATION AND OBSERVATION. YOU MAY KNOW OF THESE, HOWEVER, THAY ARE DIRECTLY RELATED TO THE LAST AND FINAL PORTION OF THIS REPORT. WHAT CAN BE DONE?

1) BECAUSE OF THE ALIEN'S APPARENT LOGIC SYSTEM (THEY APPEAR TO BE LOGIC CONTROLLED) A KEY DECISION CANNOT BE MADE

WITHOUT HIGHER CLEARANCE. ALL ARE UNDER THE CONTROL OF WHAT THEY CALL "THE KEEPER"; YET IT WOULD APPEAR THAT THIS IS NOT THE FINAL SAY. THEREFORE, DEPENDENT UPON URGENCY, DELAYS OF AS LONG AS TWELVE TO FIFTTEN HOURS CAN OCCUR FOR A DECISION. HOW SHORT/LONG THIS TIME FRAME UNDER BATTLE CONDITIONS MAY BE, I DO NOT KNOW.

BECAUSE OF THIS APPARENT CONTROL, INDI-VIDUAL INSTANTANEOUS DECISION MAKING BY THE ALIEN IS LIMITED. IF THE "PLAN" GOES EVEN SLIGHTLY OUT OF BALANCE OR CONTEXT, THEY BECOME CONFUSED. FACED WITH THIS, POSSIBLY, THE HUMANOIDS WOULD BE THE FIRST TO BREAK AND RUN.

THE SAME APPLIES TO THE MISSION MASTER PLAN, IF ONE CAN CALL IT THAT. IF PUSHED OUT OF CONTEXT, IT WILL COME APART—THEY WILL BE EXPOSED TO THE WORLD SO THEY WILL POS-SIBLY RUN BEFORE THEY FIGHT IN THE OPEN. THEY DEFINITELY <u>DO</u> <u>NOT</u> WANT THAT TO HAP-PEN.

PSYCHOLOGICALLY, AT PRESENT, THEIR MORALE IS DOWN—NEAR DISINTEGRATION. THERE IS PRONOUNCED DISCENSION IN THE RANKS; EVEN WITH THE HUMANOIDS. COMMUNI-CATION CAN ENCOURAGE THIS (NO NECESSITY TO EXPOUND UPON THIS OTHER THAN TO SAY BE-CAUSE OF THEIR OWN INTERNAL VULNERABIL-ITY MIND-WISE TO EACH OTHER, THERIN LIES A PRIME WEAKNESS). INTER-ECHELON OR INDIVID-

UAL "TRUST" APPEARS TO BE TOTALLY LACKING, SO SUSPICION OF EACH OTHER IS RAMPANT. THEY ARE HIGHLY SEGREGATED AS TO LEVELS—A "LOW" DARE NOT CONFLICT WITH A "MEDIUM" OR "HIGH" OR IT LITERALLY MEANS DEATH. DEATH BEING, TO THE HUMANOID, DEPROGRAM-MING OR, IN THE END PERHAPS TOTAL PHYSICAL DEATH. THEY APPEAR TO BE TOTALLY DEATH-ORIENTED, AND BECAUSE OF THIS, ABSOLUTELY DEATH-FEAR ORIENTED. THIS IS A PSYCHOLOGI-CAL ADVANTAGE. THE COMPUTER ALSO GIVES IN-DICATIONS OF A REAL POSSIBILTY OF ADVERSE "GROUND PROGRAMMING".

2) CONSIDER THEIR SHIPS—MOST IF NOT NEAR ALL RUN ON A CHARGE. THAT SOURCE DEPLETES AND SO DEPENDENT ON SIZE—DEPLETION CAN OCCUR FOR SOME WITHIN A WEEK OR LESS. SHIPS CAN REPLENISH EACH OTHER, BUT ONLY UP TO CHARGE BALANCE. THIS IS DONE WITH AN-TENNAE-LIKE EXTENSIONS AND THE CHARGE IS DISTRIBUTED OBSERVING CONSERVATION OF EN-ERGY LAWS. THEY CAN REPLENISH FROM POWER LINES——BUT AGAIN ONLY TO A POINT——SO THEIR FLIGHT TIME IS LIMITED. DEPRIVED OF THEIR BASE AND RECHARGE CAPABILITY, IT IS IN-DICATED THAT ALL SHIPS WILL COME DOWN WITHIN 6 MONTHS TO A YEAR UNLESS THEY CAN GET TRANSPORTED OUT—THAT IS BACK TO THE PRIME LAUNCH SHIP.

THE DISKS AND SAUCERS IN GENERAL CAN-NOT FLY IN SPACE BECAUSE OF THEIR MODE OF

FLIGHT. THEREFORE, DEPRIVED OF HOME BASE, IT IS NOT LIKELY THEY CAN SURVIVE. THEIR CAPABILITY IN POWER SURVIVAL OUTLASTS THEIR CAPABILITY IN FOOD OR FORMULA SURVIVAL. FI THEY DO NOT GET FORMULA/FOOD WITHIN A CERTAIN PERIOD OF TIME THEY WILL WEAKEN AND DIE.

IN THE CASE OF MT. ARCHELETA AND SOUTH PEAK, THEY ARE DEPENDENT UPON THE NAVAJO RIVER FOR WATER SUPPLY AND WATER TO THEM IS TOTALLY LIFE. WITHOUT WATER THEY HAVE NO POWER; WITHOUT POWER, NO OXYGEN OR HYDROGEN TO SERVICE THE SHIPS AND WEAPONS. WATER TO SUSTAIN THE ORGANS AND FEEDING FORMULA.

SIMPLE? NOT REALLY. HOWEVER, THERE IS A WATER INTAKE AND THERE IS A DAM UPSTREAM THAT CAN BE TOTALLY CUT OFF AND THE WATER REROUTED TO CHAMA, NEW MEXICO. SHOULD THIS OCCUR, AT LEAST THREE OF THE INTERNAL BASES WILL GO DOWN. THEY COULD POSSIBLY GO TO ATOMIC POWER PERIODICALLY BUT OBVIOUSLY PROBLEMS WITHOUT COOLING. ONCE THE BASES ARE PRESSED ON A LARGE SCALE, ALL DISKS AND SAUCERS WILL GO AIRBORN IMMEDIATELY. TROOPS ON THE GROUND CAN GAIN TERRAIN COVER TO QUITE A DEGREE——IT IS ROUGH TERRAIN.

OUR NEED IS FOR A WEAPON, WORKABLE AND PREFERABLY NOT LIKE THE ALIEN'S. I BELIEVE UNLESS THE ALIEN IS CAUGHT UNAWARES (WITH

THEIR SCEEN UP THEIR ARE EQUAL SO THEY ARE LIKE CHILDREN PILLOW BOXING) THERE CAN BE NO RESULT; THE WEAPON MUST PENETRATE THEIR SCREEN AND IT ALSO MUST PENETRATE THE GROUND. I BELIEVE I HAVE THAT WEAPON. TWO SMALL PROTOTYPES HAVE BEEN FUNDED AND CONSTRUCTED BY MY COMPANY. TESTS CONDUCTED TO DATE INDICATE THAT THEY WORK AND WORK RATHER WELL CONSIDERING THEIR SMALL SIZE. BECAUSE OF THIS WEAPON'S PRESENT STATUS AND PROPRIETARY NATURE (A BASIC PATENT IS IN PROCESS), THE THE THEORY WILL NOT BE EXPLAINED HERE. HOWEVER, THE WEAPON APPEARS TO DO TWO THINGS AT VERY LOW POWER. 1) THE DISKS WITHIN IT'S RANGE BEGIN TO DISCHARGE WHEN EXPOSED TO THE WEAPON BEAM. TO COUNTERACT, THEY MUST APPLY MORE POWER AND SO DOING CONSUME MORE POWER. AGAIN CONSERVATION OF ENERGY LAWS STRICTLY APPLY.

THIS EFFECT CAN BE OBSERVED ON THE DETECTION INSTRUMENTS AS THEY BACK AWAY IN RESPONSE TO SLOW DISCHARGE. DISCHARGE, AT LOW POWER IS SLOW BUT AT HIGHT POWER IN THE FINAL SOPHISTICATED WEAPON, THE RATE CAN BE INCREASED BY MANY ORDERS OF MAGNITUDE. 2) MOST IMPORTANTLY, THIS WEAPON CAN PENETRATE THE SCREEN—HULL, ALLOY, EVERYTHING. THEY CANNOT SHIELD IT IN ANY WAY. LASTLY, BECAUSE OF THE IMPLANTS, THE WEAPON GETS TO THEM MENTALLY; THEY

LOOSE JUDGEMENT AND INDICATE ALMOST IM-
MEDIATE CONFUSION, PARTICULARLY THE HU-
MANOIDS.

IT IS BELIEVED AT THIS EARLY STAGE—BASED
ON PRESENT TESTING THAT THE WEAPON WHEN
FULL ON AND FULL SIZE WILL KILL OR BRING
DOWN DISKS AT SUBSTANTIAL RANGE THE ALIEN
WEAPONS OPERATE SUBSTANTIALLY THE SAME AS
TEHIR DISKS USING A CHARGE SOURCE AND
CHARGE DISTRIBUTION. SO, IN THE SAME SENSE
IT IS INDICATED THAT THIS WEPAON DESIGN
WILL PULL THEIR CHARGE WEAPONS DOWN
VERY RAPIDLY.

THE RANGE OF MY WEAPON EXCEEDS THAT OF
THEIR PRESENT WEAPONS AND IN ITS MOST SO-
PHISTICATED FORM CAN BE READILY COMPUTER
CONTROLLED TO ALLOW EXTREMELY RAPID
TRACKING AND LOCK-ON REGARDLESS OF SPEED
ALONG WITH ELECTRONIC WOBBULATION OF
THE BEAM. IT IS A BEAM WEAPON AND EVEN AT
THIS EARLY STAGE OF MINIATURE PROTOTYPE
TESTING AND DEVELOPMENT, IT INDICATES
EVENTUAL SUPERIORITY TO THEIR WEAPONS.

4) INITIAL LOGISTICS WOULD INDICATE A PLAN
SEQUENTIALLY IMPLEMENTED AS FOLLOWS:

THIS PLAN DOES NOT INCLUDE ALL REQUIRE-
MENTS AND PREPARATORY SAFETY MEASURES TO
BE EMPLOYED BY THE GROUND FORCE; HOW-
EVER, IF AIR FORCE INTELLIGENCE DESIRES TO
PURSUE THE APPROACHES SUGGESTED IN THIS

REPORT, EACH SIGNIFICANT REQUIREMENT WILL
BE DISCUSSED IN DEPTH.

THE ATTACK MUST BE DIRECTED ALMOST EN-
TIRELY ON THE GROUND FOR THE OBVIOUS REA-
SON. ONE WOULD, IF FAMILIAR WITH THE ALIEN
CAPABILITY, INDICATE THAT VEHICLE INGNITION
PROBLEMS WILL BE ENCOUNTERED. THIS IS PRE-
CISELY TRUE; HOWEVER, THE REASON FOR IS
NOT MYSTERIOUS BUT IS BASED ON GOOD SOLID
LAWS OF PHYSICS AND ARE KNOWN. EXPERIENCE
GAINED THROUGH MY STUDY, IT IS NOW KNOWN
HOW TO PREVENT THIS FROM HAPPENING AND
WILL BE DISCUSSED IN DETAIL AT SOME LATER
DATE. ALL ELECTRICAL AND SINCE VEHICLE IG-
NITION PROBLEMS WILL BE ENCOCUNTERED.
ALL ELECTRONIC EQUIPMENT MUST BE "HARD-
ENED" USING SPECIFIC TECHNIQUES PRIOR TO
IMPLEMENTATION. BECAUSE OF THE KNOWN CA-
PABILITY OF THE ALIEN (BY USE OF SCANNING
BEAMS TO KNOW IN ADVANCE ALL DETAILS OF
PLANNING) ONLY THE INITIAL OUTLINE IS PRE-
SENTED IN THIS REPORT.

AGAIN THROUGH THE COMMUNICATIVE IN-
TERACTION WITH THE ALIEN, TESTING HAS SI-
MULTANEOUSLY BEEN DONE UPON THIS FACET,
I.E. EAVESDROPPING AND WAYS TO ABORT THIS
CAPABILITY HAVE BEEN TESTED AND PROVEN.

THE PROGRAM WOULD BE INSTIGATED IN
PHASES. THE FIRST PHASE—PLANNING AND LO-
GISTICS—.WOULD INCLUDE CONTINUED IMPLE-
MENTATION AND TESTING OF THE FINAL

WEAPON PROTOTYPE THRU THE PRE-PRODUC-
TION STAGE. PRODUCTION OF AT LEAST 50 MINI-
MUM QUANTITY SHOULD BE PLANNED.

ON A FULL-TIME SHIFT BASIS, IT IS ESTIMATED
THAT AT LEAST ONE YEAR OR LESS WOULD BE RE-
QUIRED TO ARRIVE AT THE PRE-PRODUCTION
STAGE. A TEAM WOULD BE ORGANIZED BY THUN-
DER SCIENTIFIC TO ACCOMPLISH THIS. THE KEY
WORK IS NOW AND WOULD BE DONE BY AN ASSO-
CIATED COMPANY, BENNEWITZ LABS, LTD.

SPECFIC ATTACK PHASES WOULD BE INCORPO-
RATED.

1) THE FIRST PROCEDURE WOULD BE TO
CLOSE THE GATES OF THE DAM ABOVE THE
NAVAJO RIVER. THIS DAM WOULD BE HELD
CLOSED FOR THE DURATION. INTERNAL TO THE
ONE CAVE, THERE IS A SMALL DAM FOR WATER
STORAGE. ITS CAPACITY IS SMALL. THERE IS ALSO
A DISCHARGE OUTLET DOWNSTREAM THAT
COULD BE CLOSED, CAUSING WASTE WATER TO
BACK UP INTO THE CAVES. THE WATER IS VACUUM
PUMPED APPARENTLY BY SOME ELECTROSTATIC
MEANS FROM THE RIVER. AT CLOSE RANGE, THE
WEAPON WILL TAKE OUT THIS CAPABILITY.

2) ONCE DEPRIVED TOTALLY OF WATER FOR A
MINIMUM OF FOUR WEEKS, CONDITIONS IN THE
ALIEN BASES UNDER DISCUSSION WILL HAVE
BADLY DETERIORATED. PSYCHOLOGICAL SHOCK
IS EXTREMELY EFFECTIVE WITH THE ALIEN;
TOTAL ADVANTAGE CAN BE TAKEN BY INSTANTA-

NEOUS ACTION OR PLANNED OBSERVABLE DEVI-
ATION FROM THE NORM. AT LEAST THREE BASES
WILL GO DOWN.

3) IF THEY FOLLOW THEIR NORMAL PATTERNS
AS WHEN PRESSED PREVIOUSLY, THEY WILL
LAUNCH MOST, IF NOT ALL SHIPS.

4) PRIOR TO THE IMPLEMENTATION OF WATER
DEPREVATION, THE WEAPONS SHOULD BE DE-
PLOYED AT STRATEGIC HARDENED LOCATIONS
AND ACTIVATED IN A CERTAIN PRE-PLANNED
MANNER DETERMINED BY FINAL WEAPON COOR-
DINATE LOCATIONS.

5) THIS WILL PUT AN IMMEDIATE POWER
DRAIN UPON THOSE AIRBORNE AND THE ALIEN
WEAPONS RINGING THEIR BASES.

6) BECAUSE OF THE INHERENT PSYCHOLOGI-
CAL ASPECT OF THES ALIEN, MUCH CAN BE DONE
IN THE OPEN WITH NO ATTEMPT TO PRESERVE
SECRECY. MUCH OF WHAT IS DONE CAN BE OF A
DIVERSIONARY NATURE. UNDER MOST CONDI-
TIONS THEY WILL ATTEMPT TO HARASS BUT WILL
NOT OPENLY ATTACK.

7) THROUGHOUT AND PRIOR TO THIS, THE
OPEN COMPUTER COMMUNICATIONS LINK WILL
BE OPERATIONAL FOR CONTINUED PSYCHOLOGI-
CAL INTERROGATION.

8) AT SOME POINT IN TIME—AGAIN RESTING
UPON BATTLE STATUS, THE DEPLOYMENT OF OF-
FENSIVE FORCES WILL BEGIN. THIS DEPLOY-

MENT SHOULD BE DONE IN A NEAR INSTANTA-
NEOUS MANNER UNDER CERTAIN SPECIAL CON-
DITIONS THAT CAN BE DISCUSSED.

9) THE WEAPON SYSTEM SHOULD BE KEPT
POWERED UP THROUGHOUT. IN THIS MANNER,
THE DISKS WILL BE MADE TO STAY AIRBORNE.
THEY CANNOT LAND DURING THE INTERVAL
THAT THE SYSTEM IS POWERED.

10) WHEN THE WEAPON IS USED IN ONE SPE-
CIFIC POWER MODE, IN ADDITION TO CONTINU-
OUS DISCHARGE ON THE DISKS THAT ARE
AIRBORNE AND THE GROUND BASED WEAPONS,
THE MIND CONFUSION AND DISORIENTATION
WILL BUILD IN THOSE PERSONNEL AT THE BASE
AND UNDERGROUND. AT THE END OF FOUR OR
FIVE WEEKS OR LESS, ALL WEAPONS SHOULD BE
TOTALLY DISCHARGED AND THE POWER OUT ON
THE BASES. MOST PERSONNEL, IF NOT ALL, WILL
BE TOTALLY INCAPACITATED. THE FEEDING FOR-
MULA WILL BE DOWN AND IT'S CRITICAL PRO-
CESSING RUINED. ALL EMBRYOS SHOULD BE
DEAD AND ALL HYDROGEN AND OXYGEN CON-
SUMABLES DEPLETED.

11) BASED UPON DATA GATHERED ON THE
MINIATURE PROTOTYPE WEAPONS, THE FULL
POWER WEAPONS SHOULD HAVE NO PROBLEM
HOLDING OFF THE DISKS. IN MANY CASES SOME
WILL BREAK WITHIN THE FIRST FORTY-EIGHT
HOURS WITHOUT BEING DIRECTLY HIT.

12) AT THAT POINT, STANDARD WEAPON TECH-

NOLOGY AND LOGISTICS CAN COME INTO PLAY AND USED TO THE EXTENT OF DESTRUCTION DESIRED AT THE DIRECTION OF THOSE IN CHARGE.

13) THE COMMUNICATIONS CAN BE USED THROUGHOUT TO DETERMINE STATUS AND NEAR THE END TO ATTEMPT TO INSTIGATE SURRENDER. IF NO RESPONSE RESULTS, THEN THEY SHOULD SIMPLY BE CLOSED IN AND WAITED OUT.

SUMMARY

IT IS IMPORTANT TO NOTE THAT THE INITIAL IMPLEMENTATION OF THE COMPUTER COMMUNICATIONS WAS NOT INSTIGATED FOR THE PURPOSE OF TALKING TO ONE OF THE ALIENS FOR "THE FUN OF IT"; BUT WAS DELIBERATELY INSTIGATED TO USE AS A TOOL TO STUDY, IN DEPTH, LONG TERM WITHOUT THE NEED FOR PHYSICAL CONFRONTATION THE STRENGTHS AND WEAKNESSES OF THE ALIEN.

THE WEAPON THEORY AND PROTOTYPES WERE BUILT TO CAPITALIZE UPON AND TEST THE TWO KEY AND PROMINENT WEAKNESSES DISCOVERED. THIS IN-HOUSE FUNDED PROGRAM HAS BEEN EXPENSIVE, IN EXCESS OF $200,000; ON BEHALF OF OUR NATION AND HANDLED IN THE BEST REPRESENTATIVE MANNER HUMANLY POSSIBLE.

(1) THE PRIME AND WEAKEST AREA THAT WAS DISCOVERED, PROBED AND TESTED IS EXACTLY

WHAT THEY HAVE USED THINKING IT WAS THEIR KEY STRENGTH—THAT BEING THE MANIPULA-TION OF AND CONTROL OF THE MIND; NOT ONLY OF COMMAND BUT ALSO HUMANOID. MANIPU-LATED IN REVERSE PSYCHOLOGICALLY AND BY THE LANGUAGE (COMPUTER) AND DUE TO THE EXTREME MENTAL DISTORTION AND INCAPACITY CAUSED BY THE WEAPON, IT HAS BEEN FOUND THAT THIS FACET IS FOR THEM A DISASTER AND A DIRECTLY VULNERABLE INTEGRATED WEAK-NESS.

(2) THOUGH THEIR SHIPS ARE MAGNIFICENT THEY ARE ALSO WEAK—SOLELY BECAUSE OF THEIR METHOD AND UNIQUE MODE OF FLIGHT. THEY DO NOT HAVE A STABLE FIGHTING PLAT-FORM. CHARGE DISTRIBUTION CAN ALSO BE DIS-CHARGED. THE WEAPON DOES THIS—EVEN IN IT'S PRESENT MINIATURE PROTOTYPE STAGE.

IT IS NOT THE PURPOSE OF THIS REPORT TO IMPLY THAT THE OVERALL PROBLEM WILL BE SOLVED WITH THE CAPTURE OF THESE BASES. OBVIOUSLY IT WILL NOT, BUT IT IS A FIRMLY BASED BEGINNING WITH A HIGH DEGREE OF RATED PROJECTED SUCCESS RATIO. IT IS NOT IN-TENDED TO IMPLY THAT THE ALIEN WILL NOT FIGHT; THEY MAY—THOUGH THEIR INCLINATION IS GENERALLY THE OPPOSITE—THIS BASING AREA IS KEY. WITHOUT IT, THEIR MISSION IS IN VERY DEEP TROUBLE. IT IS NOTED THAT THESE ARE NOT THE ONLY BASES ON EARTH THERE ARE OTHERS. WITH A CONSERVATIVE ESTIMATE USING

TYPICAL LOGICAL SUPPORT NUMBERS, IT IS NOT UNREALISTIC TO SAY THAT THERE ARE 50,000 ALIENS WITHIN THE ECOSPHERE OF EARTH AND NEAR SPACE.

SOME OF US WILL BE LOST IN THE ENDEAVOR THAT IS OBVIOUS—HOWEVER, DONE <u>NOW</u> THE ADVANTAGE IS GAINED ALONG WITH NEW ADDITIONAL TECHNOLOGY TO PREPARE FOR THE NEXT STAGE.

THE KEY TO OVERALL SUCCESS IS THEY <u>TOTALLY</u> RESPECT <u>FORCE</u>. AND WITH THEM, THE MOST EFFECTIVE METHOD IS TO STUBBORNLY CONTINUE TO PICK AND PULL AT THEIR DEFENSE WITH <u>NO</u> LETUP. FACED WITH THE TOTAL LOSS OF A BASE THAT IT HAS TAKEN <u>YEARS</u> TO CONSTRUCT, IT IS BELIEVED THAT THEIR MISSION <u>WILL</u> <u>BE</u> GROSSLY WEAKENED AND BADLY SLOWED.

AS AMERICANS IN THIS PARTICULAR INSTANCE, WE <u>MUST</u> REALIZE THAT WE CANNOT REPLY UPON OUR INHERENT MORAL PRINCIPLES TO PROVIDE THE ANSWER. NEGOTIATION <u>IS OUT.</u> THIS PARTICULAR GROUP CAN ONLY BE DEALT WITH—NO DIFFERENTLY THAN ONE MUST DEAL WITH A MAD DOG. <u>THAT</u> METHOD THEY UNDERSTAND. THEY <u>HAVE</u> INVADED <u>OUR</u> COUNTRY AND OUR AIR AND THEY ARE FREELY VIOLATING THE PERSONAL AND MENTAL INTEGRITY OF OUR PEOPLE. THERFORE, IN ELIMINATING THIS THREAT MOST CERTAINLY WE CANNOT BE CALLED THE "AGRESSOR", BECAUSE WE <u>HAVE</u> LITERALLY BEEN INVADED.

IN FINAL CONCLUSION A) THEY CANNOT UNDER ANY CIRCUMSTANCES BE TRUSTED. B) THEY ARE TOTALLY DECEPTIVE AND DEATH-ORIENTED AND HAVE NO RESPECT FOR HUMAN OR HUMAN LIFE. C) NO NEGOTIATION, AGREE-MENT NOR PEACEFUL COMPROMISE CAN BE SET-TLED UPON IN ANY WAY. D) NO AGREEMENT SIGNED BY BOTH PARTIES WILL EVER BE AD-HERED TO NOR RECOGNIZED AND RESPECTED BY THE ALIEN, THOUGH THEY MIGHT MAKE US ATTEMPT TO BELIEVE OTHERWISE. E) AB-SOLUTELY NO QUARTER CAN BE ALLOWED UNDER ANY CIRCUMSTANCES. ONCE THE OF-FENSE IS INSTIGATED, IT CANNOT BE ABAN-DONED. IF IT IS, RECIPROCAL REPRISAL WILL IMMEDIATELY RESULT. THEY MUST BE MADE TO COME DOWN—DESTRUCT THEMSELVES WHICH IS A STANDING ORDER IF THE SHIP IS FAILING OR TO LEAVE EARTH IMMEDIATELY—NO LEEWAY OF ANY KIND CAN BE ALLOWED NOR TOLERATED.

WE IN OUR INNOCENT HUMAN WAY, NEGOTI-ATED THE FIRST TIME BY COMPROMISE—TOOK TOO LITTLE WITH NO MAJOR SAFEGUARDS AND ALLOWED TOO MUCH. WE MUST NOT ALLOW THAT TO HAPPEN AGAIN.

BIBLIOGRAPHY

BOOKS

Andrus, Walter H. (Ed). *MUFON 1989 International UFO Symposium Proceedings.* Seguin, TX: MUFON, Inc., 1989.

Berlitz, Charles, and William L. Moore. *The Roswell Incident.* New York: Grosset and Dunlap, 1979.

Berlitz, Charles, and William L. Moore. *The Philadelphia Experiment: Project Invisibility.* London: Souvenir Press, 1979.

Bishop, Gregory (Ed). *Wake Up Down There! The Excluded Middle Collection.* Kempton, IL: Adventures Unlimited Press, 2000.

Blum, Howard. *Out There: The Government's Secret Quest*

for Extraterrestrials. New York: Simon & Schuster, 1990.

Brown, Anthony Cave. *Bodyguard of Lies.* New York: Harper Collins, 1975.

Burrows, William E. *Deep Black: The Startling Truth Behind America's Top-Secret Spy Satellites.* New York: Berkley Books, 1988.

Cannon, Martin. *The Controllers: A New Hypothesis of Alien Abductions.* Self-published monograph, 1989.

Clark, Jerome. *The UFO Encyclopedia: The Phenomenon From the Beginning. Second Edition. Detroit:* Omnigraphics Inc, 1998.

Defense Intelligence Agency. *DIA Organization Mission and Key Personnel: March 1981.* Washington, D. C.: Defense Intelligence Agency, 1981.

Gomez, Raymond E. *Report on the Evidence of U.S. Government Involvement in the Cattle Mutilations in Dulce, New Mexico Presented to the Honorable Pete V. Domenici, United States Senator.* Washington, D.C.: U.S. Senate, 1990.

Gravity Research Group. *Electrogravitics Systems: An examination of electrostatic motion, dynamic counterbary, and barycentric control.* (Report GRG 013/56). London: Aviation Studies (International) Limited, 1956.

Howe, Linda M. *An Alien Harvest: Further Evidence Linking Animal Mutilations and Human Abductions to Alien Life Forms.* Jamison, PA: Linda Moulton Howe Productions, 1997.

Moore, William L. and Jaime H. Shandera. *The MJ-12 Documents: An Analytical Report.* Burbank, CA: Fair Witness Project, Inc., 1990.

Moore, William L. *UFOs and the U. S. Government, Part 1: Complete Text of William L. Moore's MUFON Sympo-*

sium Speech Delivered at the Aladdin Hotel, Las Vegas, Nevada, July 1, 1989. Burbank, CA: Fair Witness Project, Inc., 1989.

Reich, Wilhelm. *Contact With Space: Oranur Report #7*. Rangeley, ME: Core Pilot Press, 1957.

Richelson, Jeffrey T. *America's Space Sentinels: DSP Satellites and National Security*. Lawrence, KS: The University Press of Kansas, 1999.

Sauder, Richard. *Underground Bases and Tunnels: What Is the Government Trying to Hide?* Kempton. IL: Adventures Unlimited Press, 1995.

Schnabel, Jim. *Remote Viewers: The Secret History of America's Psychic Spies*. New York: Dell Publishing, 1997.

Sun Tzu. *The Art of War.* (Tr. By Samuel B. Griffith). London: Oxford University Press, 1963.

Targ, Russell, and Harold Puthoff. *Mind Reach: Scientists Look at Psychic Ability*. New York: Dell Publishing, 1977.

Thomas, Gordon. *Journey Into Madness: The True Story of Secret CIA Mind Control and Medical Abuse*. New York: Bantam Books, 1989.

Tilton, Christa. *The Bennewitz Papers*. Crux Publications, 1991.

Valdez, William (n.d.). *Sociology 412-001 (Report) Presented to Peter Di Vasto*. Dulce, NM.

Vallee, Jacques. *Messengers of Deception*. Berkeley, CA: And/Or Press, 1979.

Valone, Thomas. (Ed.) *Electrogravitics Systems: Reports on a New Propulsion Methodology*. Washington, D.C.: Integrity Research Institute, 1994.

Vesco, Renato. *Intercept, but Don't Shoot*. New York: Grove Press, 1971.

Warren, Larry and Peter Robbins. *Left at East Gate.* London: Michael O'Mara Books, Ltd., 1997.

Williamson, George Hunt, and Alfred C Bailey. *The Saucers Speak! A Documentary Report of Interstellar Communication by Radiotelegraphy.* Glendale, CA: New Age Publishing, 1954.

INTERVIEWS

Deuley, Thomas. April 15, 2003.

Doty, Richard. October 8, 2003.

Emenegger, Robert. September 10, 2003.

Massey, Gary. September 30, 2003.

Miles, Lewis. June 29, 2003.

Moore, William L. Various from January 2003 to December 2003.

Sprinkle, R. Leo. May 23, 2003.

Stefula, Joseph. December 10, 2003.

Valdez, Gabriel. June 30, 2003; October 9, 2003.

ARTICLES

Gran, Susie. "UFOs: U.S. reports tell of five sightings in 1980 over Kirtland; city man claims alien contact." *Albuquerque Tribune,* April 8, 1983, pp. A1/ A6.

Moseley, James. "The Paul Bennewitz Case Revisited." *Saucer Smear* 47.5. June 15, 2000, pp.1-3.

AP/UPI WIRE SERVICE REPORTS

"'Principal' Field of Special Weapons Now at Sandia Base." *Albuquerque Journal*, 23 July, 1947, p. 1.

"Army 'Secret' in Plain View of Travelers." *The Denver Post*, 24 August, 1947, p. 6A.

"Army, Navy Weapon Research Centers in Empire Area States." *The Denver Post*, 24 August, 1947, p. 6A.

"Mountain Caverns Dug for 'Super Defenses.'" *Portland Oregonian*, 25 August, 1947, p. 5.

"Caverns Data Super-Secret: Army, Navy Mum on Defense Project." *Portland Oregonian*, 27 August, 1947, p. 4.

"Government Reports Describe UFO Sightings at KAFB in '80." *Albuquerque Journal*, 9 April, 1983, p. A1.

VIDEO

High Strange New Mexico. Dir. James Lujan. Zia Films, 2003.

INTERNET RESOURCES

Anonymous, Computer UFO Network.
http://www.cufon.org/

Anonymous, "Eyeballing the Kirtland Underground Munitions Storage Complex and Sandia National Laboratory."
http://cryptome.org/kumsc-eyeball.htm

Anonymous, "Ground-Based Laser Energy Projection: Development and operation of a state-of-the-art test bed for ground-based laser beam control technology is highly successful."
http://www.afrlhorizons.com/Briefs/Sept01/DE0108.html

Anonymous, Kirtland Air Force Base.
    http://www.kirtland.af.mil/index.htm
Anonymous, NSA UFO-related documents site.
    http://www.nsa.gov/docs/efoia/released/ufo.html
Anonymous, *"Project Sigma."*
    http://yawp.com/3rd-i/rsrc/gloss/p/proj_sigma.html
Anonymous, "Suspected Officially Classified Government
    Disinformation on UFOs?: The Hill Top Memo."
    http://www.v-j-enterprises.com/hillmemo.html
Allen, Brian. "Liar Liar Pants on Fire."
    http://www.thelosthaven.co.uk/LiarLiarPants.htm
Branton. "THE SECRETS OF THE MOJAVE *(Or, The
    Conspiracy Against Reality)."*
    http://www.think-aboutit.com/branton/secrets_of_the_
    mojave13.htm
Carpenter, Joel. "The Kirtland UFO Incident-1957 Albu-
    querque, New Mexico November 4, 1957."
    http://www.nicap.dabsol.co.uk/kirtland57jc.htm
Collins, Robert. "UFO Frauds and Deceptions." (Originally
    on usenet: alt.alien.research,alt.alien.visitors,alt.fan.art-
    bell,alt.paranet.ufo,alt.paranormal.)
    http://www.conspiracy-net.com/archives/articles/alien-
    ufo/coverups/CNAe0015.txt
Ecker, Don. "Freedom of Disinformation." *Fortean Times
    #122.* April 1999.
    http://www.forteantimes.com/articles/122_disin2.shtml
Ibid. "This was written by Don Ecker in the summer of 1990
    for *UFO* magazine, in which it appeared."
    http://www.skepticfiles.org/ufo2/cooperex.htm
Ibid. From: "Don Ecker/ To: ALL/ Subject: EXPOSE."
    (Originally on usenet:
    alt.alien.visitors,alt.conspiracy,sci.skeptic.)

http://paul.rutgers.edu/~mcgrew/ufo/don.allen/bill.cooper

Federation of American Scientists. "Mystery Aircraft." http://www.fas.org/irp/mystery/resource.htm

Fenstermacher, Dan. "Arms race: The next generation." *Bulletin of the Atomic Scientists*, 47,2. March 1991. http://www.thebulletin.org/issues/1991/m91/m91fenstermacher.html

Fugate, Robert. "Using Lasers to Create Artificial Stars." http://www.ieee.org/organizations/pubs/newsletters/leos/oct96/html/fugate.htm

Lambright, Chris. "Intrusions on Sandia." http://www.cufon.org/contributors/chrisl/PB/bennewit.htm

Lear, John, et al. "John Lear Interview." Internet interview February 14, 1988. http://www.holysmoke.org/wb/wb0168.htm

Ibid. "The UFO Cover-up." http://ufos.about.com/gi/dynamic/offsite.htm?site=http://www.all%2Dnatural.com/lear.html

Military Research and Development Subcommitee—Committee on Armed Services Hearings. "Threat Posed by Electromagnetic Pulse (EMP) to U.S. Military Systems and Civil Infrastructure." http://commdocs.house.gov/committees/security/has197010.000/has197010_1T.htm

National Maritime Museum. "VLT telescope produces images as sharp as Hubble." http://www.nmm.ac.uk/site/request/setTemplate:singlecontent/contentTypeA/conWebDoc/contentId/431/navId/00500300f003

V. Chuck. "Subject: Re: EMP (Electro-Magnetic-Pulse) luggage scanning." (Originally on usenet: misc.security.) http://yarchive.net/security/luggage_scanning.html

Rogers, Keith. "Historian documents seven Stealth fighters that crashed." *Las Vegas Review Journal* (online edition) March 25, 2001.
http://www.reviewjournal.com/lvrj_home/2001/Mar-25-Sun-2001/news/14372366.html

Wood, Ryan. "A chronological listing of who received the Majestic, MAJIC, MJ-12 documents."
http://www.majesticdocuments.com/sources.html

ACKNOWLEDGMENTS

When writing about the weird world of UFO studies and its relationship to the National Security State, problems inevitably arise. Who do we believe: government agents sworn to protect sensitive information and abide by their security oaths, or UFO researchers who are the recipients and victims of roundabout statements and disinformation dropped on them? The nature of disinformation is that it contains a small bit of truth buried under a heap of lies and half-truths. The only option left to a writer trying to sort out this mess is to talk to as many witnesses and participants as possible and try to see which stories stand the test of time and specific questioning, and qualify things that don't fit or are unsupported. Another method is to try to piece history together with previously released government records. Due to time constraints, the huge task of peppering the U.S. Air Force and other organizations with new Freedom of Information Act (FOIA) requests had to be left to others who had already done this hard, and for the most part, very frustrating work. In time, other documents and accounts might come to light. Others are also encouraged to pick up where I have left off.

In 2001, James Moseley published *Shockingly Close to the Truth,* an amusing autobiography (cowritten by Karl Pflock) of his fifty years in the UFO business. Of his many keen observations, one in particular sticks in my mind. Moseley said that he (and many others) have periodically become exasperated with the lack of answers and inevitable frustrations in attempting to get to the bottom of the UFO mystery. Whatever is behind it ultimately doesn't want the human race to know what's really going on, and because of this, we may never know the whole story, or if we can even comprehend it on its own terms. Countless researchers and crusaders are constantly dropping out of the scene, only to take it up months or years later in a quixotic effort to find answers, which most know will never come.

Those who stick with it eventually come to the realization that, as with any journey in life, the goal is not the goal—the journey is where the gold lies. Most of the people I contacted to talk to about Paul Bennewitz and his harrowing journey realize this, and are still stabbing away at the UFO enigma, enjoying it for the lifelong mental exercise that it ultimately becomes.

There were many people who didn't want to talk to me, or gave enigmatic answers. Some have requested the comfort of pseudonyms. The fallout from the Bennewitz affair still has the ability to silence, over a decade later. Some of the individuals who did agree to talk were still somewhat emotionally involved with the story, which made for some dramatic encounters. For these reasons, some names have been changed.

Researchers and writers who provided valuable assistance, leads, and advice include (but are not limited to) psychologist Dr. Leo Sprinkle, Gabe Valdez, Karl Pflock, James Moseley, Robert Emenegger, Kenn Thomas, Robert Sterling, Nick Redfern, Grant Cameron, Richard Sarradet, Lewis Miles, Robert Wood, Dennis Stacy, Vicki and Don Ecker, Linda Howe, Thomas Dueley, Dr. Bruce Maccabee, Ann Druffel, Dr. James Harder, Adam Gorightly, Camille James, Gary Massey, Joe Stefula, Paul Krassner, Robert Anton Wilson, John Keel, Paul Davids, Laura Hauther, Skylaire Alfvegren, Internet radio station killradio.org, my editor Patrick Huyghe, and, of course, my parents for encouraging my path.

"Evil government people" who generously lent a little or a lot of their time, opinions, and recollections include Richard Doty, Walter Bosley, and physicist Eric Davis. One former Air Force Weapons Lab scientist who did not want his name used was particularly helpful and patient and has my deep gratitude as well.

According to many UFO researchers, I should include Bill Moore on this list of government employees, but I'll just leave him in the "excluded middle" and thank him for his support, assistance, and longtime friendship. This book would have been impossible without his generous cooperation and incredible patience with my annoying questions and thinly veiled accusations.

INDEX

273

Printed in the United States
By Bookmasters